The Communist Parties
of Western Europe

Contributions in Political Science
Series Editor: Bernard K. Johnpoll

The Communist Parties of Western Europe

A COMPARATIVE STUDY

R. NEAL TANNAHILL

Contributions in Political Science, Number 10
GREENWOOD PRESS
WESTPORT, CONNECTICUT · LONDON, ENGLAND

335.43
T 166 c

Library of Congress Cataloging in Publication Data

Tannahill, R. Neal.
  The Communist parties of Western Europe.

  (Contributions in political science; no. 10
ISSN 0147-1066)
  Bibliography: p.
  Includes index.
  1. Communism—Europe. 2. Europe—Politics and
government—1945- 3. Communist parties. I. Title.
II. Series.
HX239.Z7T36   335.43'094   77-94750
ISBN 0-313-20318-0

Library of Congress Catalog Card Number: 77-94750
ISBN: 0-313-20318-0
ISSN: 0147-1066

First published in 1978

Greenwood Press, Inc.
51 Riverside Avenue, Westport, Connecticut 06880

Printed in the United States of America

10 9 8 7 6 5 4 3 2 1

79-8577

To my parents and my friends

CONTENTS

TABLES

ABBREVIATIONS OF COMMUNIST PARTY ORGANIZATIONS

CPGB   Communist Party of Great Britain

CPI   Communist Party of Ireland

CPN   Communistische Partij van Nederland, Dutch Communist Party

CPSU   Communist Party of the Soviet Union

DKP   Danmarks Kommunistiske Parti, Danish Communist Party

DKP   Deutsche Kommunistische Partei, West German Communist Party (after 1968)

KKE   Kommounistikon Komma Ellados, Communist Party of Greece

KPD   Kommunistische Partei Deutschlands, German Communist Party (before 1968)

KPÖ   Kommunistische Partei Österreichs, Austrian Communist Party

NKP   Norges Kommunistiske Parti, Norwegian Communist Party

PA   People's Alliance (Altýdubandalagid), Communist Party of Iceland

PCB   Parti Communiste de Belgique, Belgian Communist Party

PCE   Partido Comunista de España, Communist Party of
      Spain
PCF   Parti Communiste Français, French Communist Party
PCI   Partito Comunista Italiano, Italian Communist Party
PCL   Parti Communiste de Luxembourg, Communist Party of
      Luxembourg
PCP   Partido Comunista Português, Communist Party of Por-
      tugal
PdA   Partei der Arbeit, Swiss Communist Party
SKDL Suomen Kansan Demokraatinen Liito, Finnish People's
      Democratic League, Electoral Front of the Finnish Com-
      munist Party
SKP   Suomen Kommunistien Puolue, Finnish Communist
      Party
VPK   Vänsterpartiet Kommunisterna, Swedish Communist
      Party (Left Party—Communist)

INTRODUCTION

The phenomenon of the emergence, persistence, and growth of Communist parties in the non-Communist nations of Western Europe has long fascinated Western diplomats, statesmen, and scholars. Moreover, in recent years, the political ascent of Communist parties in Italy, Portugal, France, and elsewhere on the continent has quickened this interest and has made Communism in Western Europe a particularly important topic for investigation.

This study of the Communist parties of Western Europe has four general goals. The first is to examine the emergence and historical development of Western Europe's Communist parties, focusing on positions and policies, both in a domestic and an international context. Although there are a number of excellent case studies of Western European Communist parties,[1] most of them deal with the larger parties, particularly the Italian and the French, and there is a scarcity of works that consider Communism in Western Europe from a comparative perspective.[2] There are even fewer studies that employ a historical perspective.

The second goal is to go beyond description to explanation. Ostensibly, the Communist parties of Western Europe have many similarities in background, objectives, and world view; yet they have developed in different ways in their various domestic environments. Through the comparative method, this study tries to identify those factors that have shaped the development of the Western parties and the evolution of their interaction with their domestic and international environments.

A third goal of this study is to contribute to the comparative study of political parties. Although Communist parties are different from non-Communist parties in many ways, there are also similarities. Many of the factors affecting Communist parties also affect non-Communist parties. Consequently, the study can shed light on political parties in general.

Finally, it is the aim of this study to add to the understanding of the relationships among Communist parties. An important part of a Communist party's environment is the international Communist movement. Therefore, this study examines each party's relations and relationship to the movement as a whole and to other non-ruling and ruling Communist parties around the world.

To accomplish these goals, a comparative analysis of the Communist parties of Western Europe is made,[3] focusing on their founding, evolution, and positions vis-à-vis their domestic environments and the international Communist movement. The disadvantage of this approach is that the sheer size of the undertaking makes it impossible to examine any one party in depth as in a case study, but the approach makes up in breadth what it lacks in depth. By examining small as well as large Communist parties, illegal as well as legal, and relatively pro-Soviet as well as relatively independent parties, the study is better able to identify and understand the factors shaping the policies and postures of the Communist parties in Western Europe. After all, comparison is one of the foundations of the scientific method. Through quantitative comparisons when the data are available and qualitative comparisons when they are not (as is often the case with this subject), we can best achieve the goals we have outlined.

Part One is descriptive. Its purpose is to introduce the reader to the Communist parties of Western Europe, giving an overview of their domestic and international postures and positions. It outlines the remarkable diversity of Western European Communism, examining the evolution of each party.

Part Two is basically analytical. Each chapter focuses on one set of factors that has shaped Communism in Western Europe. It explores the effects of each set of factors on the Western parties and examines the manner in which these factors interact to mold the policies and postures of Western Europe's Communist parties.

No political party exists in a vacuum. Each party functions in an environment that poses contingencies and offers opportunities. The environment makes demands on a party, supplies it with resources, and establishes "rules of the game" under which it must compete. Chapters 3, 4, 5, and 6 consider, in turn, the international, social, political, and constitutional aspects of the Western European Communist parties' environment, exploring how these aspects differ for each party, thus producing different effects.

Although a party is the product of its external environment, it is not a passive reactor. Rather, its reactions to environmental stimuli are shaped by internal factors. The most important internal factors are a party's membership and electorate, and its history. Chapters 8 and 9 examine these factors and explore how they affect party responses to the stimuli of the external environment.

The key factor, however, through which other factors are mediated, is leadership. A political party is not a biological entity that responds reflexively to external stimuli. Rather, it acts because of the conscious or unconscious actions or inactions (in the sense that failing to act is also seen as a response) of flesh and blood individuals to stimuli that come from the external environment.

Because of the rigid, hierarchical nature of most Communist parties, leaders are particularly important in shaping party policies and affecting party positions, but they do not act with perfect freedom in any existential sense. First, they are constrained by their own experiences and backgrounds. This is explored in Chapter 7. Second, they must respond to contingencies posed by an external environment over which they and their party may have minimal control. This is considered in chapters 3 through 6. Finally, the nature of the leaders' responses is constrained by the peculiar characteristics of their parties' membership and electorate and history. Again, chapters 8 and 9 focus on these characteristics.

Part Three brings things together. Chapter 10 aims for synthesis by considering how the evolution of each party's postures and policies has been affected by the factors considered in Part Two. Finally, Chapter 11 explores the future of Communism in Western Europe.

Notes

1. Ronald Tiersky, *French Communism, 1920-1972* (New York: Columbia, 1974); Donald L. M. Blackmer, *Unity in Diversity: Italian Communism and the Communist World* (Cambridge: MIT, 1968); Donald L. M. Blackmer and Sidney Tarrow, eds., *Communism in Italy and France* (Princeton: Princeton University, 1975); and Sidney Tarrow, *Peasant Communism in Southern Italy* (New Haven: Yale, 1967), are among the better recent examples. For others, see the Bibliography.

2. These include Neil McInnes, *The Communist Parties of Western Europe* (London: Oxford, 1975); William E. Griffith, ed., *Communism in Europe,* 2 vols. (Cambridge: MIT, 1964); and A. F. Upton, *The Communist Parties of Scandinavia and Finland* (London: Weidenfeld and Nicolson, 1973).

3. The universe includes the Communist parties of Austria, Belgium, Denmark, Finland, France, Great Britain, Greece, Iceland, Ireland, Italy, Luxembourg, Netherlands, Norway, Portugal, Spain, Sweden, Switzerland, and West Germany.

PART ONE

DIVERSITY IN WESTERN EUROPEAN COMMUNISM

The Communist movement in Western Europe has never been monolithic if by that we mean massive uniformity. In the beginning, although Western European Communist parties may have been designed from the same pattern, they were not cut from the same cloth. The fledgling parties born in the wake of the Great War may have shared a similar revolutionary élan and a vague image of the coming Socialist order, but they differed in strength, origin, leadership, ideological heritage, organization, and position vis-à-vis the social, political, and constitutional order in their respective countries. Their unity, which in the decade following the founding of the Third International in 1919 became monotonous if not perfect, was based largely on the prestige, leadership, and support, both financial and psychological, of the Soviet Union.

In the half century since the early days of the Comintern, the unity if not uniformity of the Communist movement in Western Europe has passed into diversity and even division. Centrifugal forces have triumphed over centripetal ones, and one can no more speak of a single Western European Communist movement than

*one can speak of a single world move-
ment. Today, in both their domestic and
international positions, the Communist
parties of Western Europe are characterized by a growing diversity.*

*The development and dimensions of
this diversity are the subject of Part One.
Chapter 1 focuses on the historical place
of each of the parties in its domestic environment; specifically, its strength, alliance strategies, domestic position, and
organizational pattern. Chapter 2 com-
pares each party's historic posture vis-
à-vis the Soviet Union and international
Communism.*

DIVERSITY IN THE DOMESTIC ARENA

Despite a similar Marxist-Leninist heritage, the Communist parties of Western Europe differ significantly in their domestic positions and postures. First, they vary in size and strength. Some are major parties; others are little more than impotent sects. Second, different parties have adopted different political strategies. Some seek a united front with forces of the non-Communist Left; others pursue a broad alliance strategy with Centrist as well as Leftist elements; at times others have chosen to go it alone and refuse all possible alliances. Third, the Communist parties of Western Europe present different conceptions of the "Road to Socialism." Some have come to see it in reformist terms, although for others the road is still paved with Stalinist verities.[1] Finally, the parties diverge organizationally. Some cling to the norms of democratic centralism; but others have introduced subtle and not-so-subtle innovations.

Size and Strength of the Parties

The Communist parties of Western Europe vary in size and strength from great mass parties to miniscule sects with virtually no political influence.

Italy

The largest and most advantageously placed Communist party in Western Europe today is the Italian Communist Party (PCI). The PCI was comparatively weak at its founding in 1921 and suffered a long period of illegality under the Fascists, but since World War II it has grown into the most powerful party of the Italian Left. Its membership is estimated at more than one and three-quarters million. Unlike other Communist parties in Western Europe, it has increased its percentage of the vote at each legislative election since 1945, winning 34.4 percent of the votes and 227 of 630 seats in the last Chamber of Deputies election in June 1976, finishing a close second behind the perennial party of government, the Christian Democrats (DC), who gathered 38.7 percent of the ballots. (For membership and election statistics, see the tables in the Appendix.)

The PCI has transformed its electoral success into a considerable measure of political power at the local and regional levels. Alone or in alliance with the Socialists and other parties of the Left, the PCI has for decades controlled about 20 percent of the nation's smaller cities and towns, and about 30 percent of the larger cities and provinces, primarily in Northern and Central Italy, including the major city of Bologna since 1945.

In the regional elections of June 1975, the PCI made substantial gains, winning 32.4 percent of the vote compared with the Christian Democrats' 35.6 percent, and to these gains, it added success in local elections coinciding with the June 1976 parliamentary election. As of the spring 1978, the Communists and their allies control every major city in the country and participate in the government of fourteen of Italy's twenty regions and forty-eight of its ninety-four provinces. In all, some 55 percent of the Italian population lives under local or regional Left-wing administrations, and the PCI is the largest single political employer in the country for all those posts below the level of the national government.

The PCI has long controlled a large bloc of seats in the Chamber of Deputies and has participated with varying degrees of influence in the legislative process through its position on legislative committees. Since the 1976 election, however, the Communists have assumed formal positions of power. A Communist, Pietro Ingrao, now presides over the Chamber of Deputies, and the PCI controls seven parliamentary commissions: finance, constitutional affairs, public works, and transport in the Chamber; budget, agriculture, and health in the Senate.

Not only does the PCI exert strong electoral and political influence, but it also makes its presence felt in other areas of Italian life. The Party maintains or dominates a large number of mass organizations, including a peasant group, women's organizations, peace associations, friendship associations (the Italian-USSR Friendship Association, for example), and Italy's largest trade union federation, the CGIL. Finally, the PCI operates a number of industrial, commercial, and cooperative enterprises, including a large garment concern that maintains retail stores in most Italian towns.

France

Although it has not enjoyed the steady increase in electoral support of the PCI, since World War II, the French Communist Party (PCF) has regularly won one-fifth to one-fourth of the French electorate and has earned a major place in the French political milieu. In the beginning, the PCF was staked with a large portion of the old Socialist Party's electorate and organization, a base that steadily declined throughout the 1920s. With the Popular Front in the mid-1930s, however, the Party came into its own electorally and in membership terms. Ever since, it has been one of the major parties of France. In the most recent National Assembly elections held in March 1978, the PCF took 20.6 percent of the vote on the first ballot and claimed 73 of the 490 assembly seats at stake. (See the Appendix.) Also, in the presidential election of May 1974, Socialist François Mitterrand, the candidate of the Union of the Left (the Communists, Socialists, and Left Radicals), came within two percentage points of defeating Valery Giscard d'Estaing and capturing the presidency.

In local elections, too, the PCF has registered some significant successes. Before the municipal elections held in March 1977, the Communists controlled fifty cities with a population of 30,000 or more, and the Socialists forty-six. The Union of the Left won more than half of the popular vote in the election with the Communists gaining control of twelve more cities and the Socialists adding twenty-seven more. Consequently, the Left now controls more than three-fourths of France's largest cities, including Le Mans, Bourges, Montepellier, Nantes, Rheims, and Rennes.

Like the Italian Communist Party, the PCF maintains an extensive network of closely knit auxiliary organizations—part of what has been called a "countersociety."[2] It maintains or dominates student, youth, women's, and peasant groups, as well as the CGT, France's largest trade union federation. Like the PCI, the French Communist Party owns a number of businesses and industries, and controls some producer and consumer cooperatives.

Finland

The third major Communist party of Western Europe is the Finnish Communist Party (SKP). Founded in Moscow in 1918 after the Finnish Civil War, the SKP was an illegal party in Finland, but succeeded in laying a base for itself among Finland's working class and in the labor movement. The SKP was legalized after the signing of the armistice ending the Continuation War with the Soviet Union in 1944. Since then, the SKDL, the electoral front dominated by the SKP, has consistently won about one-fifth of the popular vote and one-fifth of the seats in legislative elections. In Finland's most recent election in September 1975, the SKDL won 19 percent of the popular vote and forty (of two hundred) parliamentary seats.

In 1966 the SKP parlayed its parliamentary strength into a place in the Finnish government by entering a coalition with the Social Democrats and Agrarians. Although the SKP left the government in 1971, in late 1975, negotiations were begun directed at the formation of a multi-party government including the Communists to deal with the nation's worsening economic situation. On November 30, 1975, the negotiations culminated in the formation of a national emergency government including the Communists, Social Democrats, Centrists, Liberals, and the Swedish People's Party. The weight of Finland's economic miseries proved too great for the coalition, however, and the government fell on September 17, 1976, with the Communists returning to the opposition. Then in May

1977, the Communists again joined the government in coalition with the Centrists, Social Democrats, Liberals, and Swedish People's Party, with SKDL members heading three out of fifteen cabinet posts (labor, transport, and education).

Like its French and Italian counterparts, the Finnish Communist Party has a firmly established place in the economic, social, and political life of its country. It runs a number of commercial enterprises and maintains an accompaniment of auxiliary organizations. Also, the SKP exercises considerable influence in the trade union movement, although it must take a back seat to the Social Democrats in Finland's major trade union federation, the SAK, whose directorage is currently composed of fourteen Social Democrats and eight Communists.

Portugal

After the overthrow of the Salazar-Caetano dictatorship in Portugal in April 1974, by the Armed Forces Movement (AMF), the rise of the Portuguese Communist Party (PCP) was meteoric. For most of its existence, however, the PCP suffered the onus of illegality. Begun in 1921 as a splinter group of the Portuguese Socialist Party, the PCP was barely established when it was declared illegal in 1926. During its period of illegality, the Party carefully developed an efficient clandestine organization despite rather persistent persecution by the Salazar regime. Consequently, the Communists were well prepared to take advantage of the political freedom offered them after the 1974 coup. Relying on support in the unions, in the mass media, among university students, and in the AMF in particular, the PCP pressured its way into the government and, for much of 1975, the Communists seemed to be moving toward a position of political dominance.

Although the Communists in Portugal were well organized, events proved they were very much in the minority, both in the country at large and in the military. The first test came in April 1975. In the election for the largely powerless constituent assembly, the PCP won only 12.5 percent of the vote and 30 of 248 seats. Even though PCP influence continued to be strong in the AMF, moderates soon gained the upper hand. Since November 1975, the Council of the Revolution has been dominated by officers who want to leave politics to the politicians and return to civilian rule. Parliamentary elections in 1976 found the PCP winning only 14.6 percent of the vote and 40 seats, and in June 1976, the Communist candidate for the presidency, Octavio Pato, won only 7.6 percent of the vote. In July 1976, when Socialist Mario Soares formed Portugal's first freely elected government in more than fifty years, the PCP found itself in opposition, where it has remained.

The strength of the Communist Party in Portugal has long been incorrectly estimated. During its period of illegality, observers conceded that the Party was tightly organized and enjoyed some influence among urban workers in Lisbon and Oporto and among farm laborers in the upper Alentejo region, but estimated its membership at a mere two thousand.[3] The PCP's rapid ascent in 1974 and 1975, however, proved these estimates too conservative as the Communists demonstrated considerable influence in the Armed Forces Movement, the broadcast media, the labor movement, and the population at large. This time the Communists' true strength was overestimated as observers feared that Portugal was "going Communist."

Subsequent events have demonstrated, however, that the PCP is neither as weak as many assumed it was in 1973 nor as strong as it appeared in its halcyon days of 1974 and 1975. The Party's forte lies in its organization of perhaps 100,000 to 120,000 members. It has a number of strongholds among workers in Southern Portugal and the Party still has some residual influence in the military and in the unions. Electorally, the Communists apparently can command from 10 to 15 percent of the popular vote.[4]

Spain

Like its Portuguese counterpart, the Spanish Communist Party (PCE) has just emerged from a long period of illegality and persecution. In 1921 the Party came into being as the result of a split in the social democratic movement, itself a relatively minor movement in Spain. (The Anarchists were the strongest group on the Left.) The PCE was so weak that when Primo de Rivera came to power, he did not bother to ban the Communist press (he did ban the Party). The Communists' weakness continued into the Republican period. In 1931 the legalized PCE received only 4.4 percent of the

vote, winning no seats, and in 1936 the Communists were only
allotted 16 of the Popular Front's 267 seats. During the Popular
Front, however, the PCE enhanced its position considerably. Membership soared and the Communists gained considerable influence
within the military and the government, particularly in the last
years of the Civil War.

After the Civil War, the PCE was declared illegal and Franco
conducted a brutal campaign of repression against the Communists, who retreated to exile and the underground. After World War
II, the PCE built up its organization abroad and at home, where it
became one of Spain's larger and better organized opposition
groups, its strength being greatest among urban intellectuals, farm
workers, and industrial workers organized around the then illegal
trade union movement known as *Comisiones Obreras* (workers'
commissions).

After the death of Franco in 1975, the Spanish government
embarked on a policy of gradual evolution to political democracy.
The PCE was allowed more freedom of operation, and in April
1977, the Party was granted legality. Subsequently, the Communists
participated in the June 1977 parliamentary election, winning 9.4
percent of the vote and nineteen (of three hundred and fifty) seats.
In the trade union movement, the PCE has a strong base because of
its influence in the *Comisiones Obreras,* but most Spanish workers
are not unionized. Currently, the Communists and the Socialists are
competing to enlist workers in their respective unions.

Iceland

The Icelandic Communist Party has achieved significant electoral
successes since World War II. Established as an independent party
in 1930, the People's Alliance (PA), once the Communists' electoral
front and now the Party itself, began rather slowly. Since 1940,
however, it has won between 13.9 and 19.5 percent of the votes in
every parliamentary election. In the last parliamentary election in
June 1974, the Party won 18.3 percent of the vote. On two occasions
since 1950, the PA has participated in a government, from 1956 to
1958, and from 1971 through August 1974.

The Icelandic Communists have also made their mark below the
national level. The Party wins its share of the vote in local elections,

holding seats in several municipal councils, including Reykjavík council and, along with the Progressives, the PA controls the Icelandic Federation of Labor. Despite its impressive domestic posture, the PA remains a small party in absolute terms (about twenty-five hundred members) in a small country.

Greece

Although the Greek Communist Party (KKE) is now divided and politically weak, its past successes and resilience indicate it may again become a major political force in Greece. In November 1918, several small Socialist groups merged to form the Socialist Workers' Party of Greece, which in 1924 became the Communist Party of Greece. The new party was small and lacked influence, winning only 10 of 286 seats in parliament in 1926, and even in the midst of the depression in 1932, the KKE won only 58,000 votes out of 1,170,000 ballots cast. In 1936 the Party was further weakened by persecution under the Metaxas dictatorship.

Not until World War II did the Greek Communist Party finally begin to come into its own politically. During the German occupation, the Communists took the lead in the resistance movement, using their forces to fight the Germans and domestic opponents alike. In 1943 the KKE launched a civil war that ended with the Lebanon agreement of April 1944, which saw the formation of a coalition government with strong Communist participation. On December 3, 1944, the Communists attempted a coup and the civil war resumed until the British intervened with a peace agreement, giving the KKE leadership amnesty. The Communists reorganized their forces, however, and launched a guerrilla war in early 1946, which lasted until the defeated Communists were driven underground or into exile in 1949.

Although the Communist Party was illegal in Greece from 1947 until 1974, the KKE participated in electoral politics primarily through the United Democratic Left (EDA), a legal party founded in 1951. The EDA won as much as 24.4 percent of the vote in 1958 and as little as 11.8 percent in 1964, but it, too, was outlawed in 1967 after the colonel's coup.

Meanwhile, a division between the party in exile and the domestic party widened into a party split, so that now one must speak of a

KKE Interior and a KKE Exterior.[5] In September 1974, the Karamanlis government lifted the ban on the Communist Party and the
two factions managed to form an electoral coalition along with the
EDA to contest the November 1974 parliamentary election, winning 9.5 percent and eight of three hundred seats. The coalition
broke up after the election, however. In the 1977 election, the
Exterior faction campaigned alone, winning eleven seats on 9.4
percent of the vote. The KKE Interior combined with the EDA and
three small Leftist groups to form a joint ticket, but finished far
behind the KKE Exterior, gathering only 2.7 percent of the vote
and two seats in parliament.

Although the KKE has lost ground in the last decade because of
persecution by the military dictatorship and deepening internal
divisions, it historically has held an important place in postwar
Greek politics, particularly among tobacco workers in Xanthi,
factory workers, stevedores, and intellectuals. Now that the Communists can once again operate openly, Communism may reemerge
as a major political force in Greece. Indeed, it appears to be making
some gains at the local level, in the unions, and in the universities.

Luxembourg

The only other Western European Communist party with a rea-
sonable claim to major party status is the Communist Party of
Luxembourg (PCL). After its founding in January 1921, the Luxembourg Party struggled to gain an electoral footing and did not
win its first parliamentary seat until 1937. Currently, however, the
PCL enjoys a firm if modest electoral position. In the most recent
parliamentary election in May 1974, the PCL won 10.4 percent of
the popular vote and elected five of the Legislative Assembly's fifty-
nine deputies. Although the PCL's strength has varied considerably
since World War II (from a low of 2.5 percent in a partial legislative
election in 1948 to a high of 16.9 percent in another partial election
in 1951), it has averaged about 10 to 11 percent of the vote and
about 10 percent of the seats in the legislature.

The PCL has also won a place below the national level of government. The Party has registered some successes in local politics,
particularly in urban areas. Together with the Socialists, the PCL
controls the municipal government of the country's second largest

city, Esch-zur-Alzette, whose mayor is a Party member. The PCL also enjoys a measure of influence in Luxembourg's largest trade union federation, the United Federation of Free Trade Unions. Nevertheless, as with the Icelandic Communist Party, the small absolute size of the PCL (about six hundred members) and the relative insignificance of Luxembourg as a nation relegate the Party to the role of little more than a medium-sized fish in a small pond.

Sweden

Although no other Communist party in Western Europe can seriously pretend to major party status, a number have on occasion exercised a modicum of political influence as minor parties in multi-party systems by finding themselves in the position of holding the swing votes in an evenly balanced parliament. The recent history of the Swedish Communist Party (VPK) illustrates both the prospects and the problems of such a position.

The VPK held the balance of power between the Social Democratic forces of Prime Minister Olof Palme and the bourgeois opposition following both the 1970 and 1973 elections. Although it was able to exercise some indirect influence, the VPK found itself in a dilemma. On the one hand, the Social Democratic government refused to consult or negotiate with the Communists. On the other, if the VPK chose to vote against the government on a crucial issue, the Party would be opting, in effect, to throw out a Socialist government and replace it with a conservative one. This the Communists did not want to do. Consequently, the Social Democrats controlled the situation. As one Western diplomat put it, "It's a case of the dog wagging the tail, to uncoin a phrase." Unfortunately for the VPK, its leverage, such as it was, came to an end in 1974 when the Social Democrats reached an alliance of sorts with the Liberal Party, thus freeing themselves from reliance on the Communists. If the VPK had any remaining hopes of returning to a position of influence, they were dashed in September 1976, when a conservative coalition was voted into office, ending the long period of Social Democratic government.

Despite recent fortuitous circumstances, the VPK has seldom found itself well-placed electorally. Only in the highly favorable atmosphere of the last months of World War II did the Swedish

Communist Party receive as much as 10 percent of the vote. In no other election before or since has it registered more than 7 percent, with its usual total more often approaching 3 or 4 percent. In Sweden's last parliamentary election (September 1976), the VPK gathered 4.7 percent of the popular vote, winning only 17 of the Riksdag's 349 seats.

The VPK's national role has generally been minimal. Organized labor is the stronghold of the rival Social Democrats, with the Communists controlling no national unions and only a tiny minority of local unions (about eighty of nine thousand, with many of these concentrated in the remote North). Ironically, the Party has even had trouble maintaining control of its own youth affiliate, which has been shaken by defections to ultra-Leftist groups.

Norway

Another party that, despite its small size, has recently enjoyed some political influence because of opportune circumstances is the Norwegian Communist Party (NKP). From 1961 to 1973, the NKP did not hold a single seat in the Storting, and it has not won more than 6 percent of the popular vote since 1945. Indeed, since its emergence as an independent party in 1923, the NKP has won more than three parliamentary seats only twice, in 1945 (eleven) and in 1924 (six). In the September 1973 elections, however, the NKP and two other Left-wing groups together won sixteen seats, one of which was held by Axel Larsen, who at that time was the NKP's chairman. With the Storting closely divided, the NKP found itself in the propitious position of holding the balance of power. In late 1975, however, Larsen resigned from the Party over the issue of turning the electoral alliance into a new Left-wing party, and the NKP was again without parliamentary representation. Subsequently, in the September 1977 election the NKP found itself reduced to a mere 0.4 percent of the popular vote, winning no parliamentary representation. (The Left-wing alliance was nearly wiped out as well, falling to only 4.1 percent of the vote and two seats.)

The small Norwegian Communist Party has little influence in domestic politics. Not only has it failed to record many electoral successes, but it has been unable to stake out a place for itself in the

Norwegian Federation of Trade Unions or, like the Swedish Party, to be sure of the allegiance of its youth affiliate.

Denmark

The Danish Communist Party (DKP) has experienced a recent electoral revival. In December 1973, the DKP won 3.6 percent of the vote and elected six deputies to the Folketing in an election marked by heavy protest voting against the established parties. In January 1975, the Party continued its resurgence, increasing its representation to seven seats, and maintained that number in the February 1977 elections. Despite recent gains, the DKP's electoral record has been far from glorious. Until 1932 the DKP had never won representation in parliament. Then after a high point in 1945, when the Communists won 12.5 percent of the vote, the Party went into a steady decline, and it was unable to elect a single deputy or to win more than 1.4 percent of the vote from November 1960 until the end of 1973.[6] In spite of the DKP's recent electoral gains, the Party has failed to establish a strong position in the trade union movement.

Switzerland

Although it is relatively small (seven thousand members) and is unrepresented on the forty-four-member Council of States (the upper house), the Swiss Communist Party (the Partei der Arbeit, or PdA) has consistently won representation in the lower house of the Swiss legislature. Since 1922 the Party has won between two and seven seats in the legislature, except for the 1943 election, when the Party was illegal. In the last election in October 1975, the PdA won four seats, approximately maintaining the relative position it has held in the two hundred-member legislature for the last twenty-five years. Also, the Party holds a smattering of municipal and cantonal offices. Despite its steady electoral performance, the PdA has little influence in Switzerland.

Netherlands

Like the PdA, the Dutch Communist Party (CPN) has consistently won representation in the legislature while failing to make a significant impact on national politics. From 1918 to 1937, the CPN won from 1.2 to 3.4 percent of the vote. Since the end of World War II, the Party has generally done better at the polls, but in the May 1977 election, the CPN hit a postwar low, receiving only 1.7 percent of the vote and winning but two seats. The CPN's efforts at achieving political influence outside the electoral arena have been disappointing. Its front organizations are declining in significance and it has made few inroads into organized labor.

Belgium

The Belgium Communist Party (PCB), like its Dutch and Swiss counterparts, has maintained a small but steady electoral base. Since 1925 the PCB has won at least one seat in parliament every election, with a high of 23 in 1946. More typically, however, the Party's parliamentary delegation has been between two and nine members. At the last election in April 1977, the PCB elected two representatives and won 2.7 percent of the vote. Also, like the Swiss and Dutch parties, the PCB's influence in national affairs is peripheral at best. The Party has won only a small number of seats in municipal and provincial politics, and in the major trade unions its influence is slight.

Ireland

The other Communist parties of Western Europe are miniscule, with little hope of winning national parliamentary representation. With a declining membership of barely three hundred, the Communist Party of Ireland (CPI) is hardly worthy of the name. Initially created in 1921, the Party vanished and had to be reformed in 1933. Throughout its history, the CPI has been a political failure. Its electoral organization is practically nonexistent, and except for some residual influence in the "official" IRA and the Northern Ireland Civil Rights Association, it is politically sterile.

West Germany

The German Communist Party (KPD) was once the pride of Western European Communism, but under the Bonn Republic, it is only a shadow of its former self. During the Weimar Republic, the KPD held as many as one hundred seats (in 1932) and was regarded as Western Europe's strongest Communist party. In 1933, however,

Hitler outlawed the KPD, dismantled its organization, and liquidated its leaders and militants. After the war, the Party demonstrated a residue of strength in the first election under the Bonn Republic in 1949, but then declined, losing Reichstag representation entirely in 1953. Another blow fell on the Party in 1956 when it was declared unconstitutional. During this period of illegality, the Communists tried to continue electoral politics through two front parties, the League of Germans (BdD) and the German Peace Union (DFU), but with very little success. Since the KPD was refounded in 1968 as the legal DKP, the West German Communist Party has participated in Reichstag, land, and municipal elections, but with a notable lack of success, electing only a smattering of representatives in local legislatures. In the last national parliamentary election in September 1976, the Communists won a mere 0.3 percent of the vote. Not everything, however, is dark for the DKP. It has rapidly increased its membership and is currently gaining in influence among the young, among trade unionists, and among Left-wing members of the Social Democratic Party.

Great Britain

Another party with negligible electoral strength, but some influence in other areas, is the Communist Party of Great Britain (CPGB). The Party has never been a success electorally. Not since 1950 has the CPGB even held a seat in parliament, and never has it won more than 0.5 percent of the popular vote. Nevertheless, the Party has gained influence disproportionate to its size in the trade unions, particularly in the Amalgamated Union of Engineering Workers and the Transport and General Workers Union.[7]

Austria

In the last twenty years, the Austrian Communist Party (KPÖ) has declined from minor party status to that of a dwarf party. Before 1945 the Party failed to win representation. Then from 1945 to 1959, the KPÖ held from three to five seats in the Nationalrat. Not since 1959, however, has it held a seat in the Austrian parliament, and at the last election in October 1975, the Party was able to gather only 1.2 percent of the popular vote. What is more, the Party has proved its weakness in recent local elections and is isolated from the Austrian working class.

Alliance Strategies

The Communist parties of Western Europe also differ in the alliance strategies they employ vis-à-vis other political parties.

Italy

One of the broadest and most innovative of the alliance strategies is that developed by the Italian Communist Party. In early 1921, the PCI was born out of a split in the Socialist Party at Livorno. While the Socialists and Communists were jockeying for position, the Fascists won power and outlawed opposition parties. Still, on Comintern orders, the PCI refrained from participating in anti-Fascist groups until 1934 when the Socialists and Communists signed a Unity of Action Pact. The unity was temporarily broken in 1939 when the Soviets and Nazis signed their nonaggression pact, but it was renewed in 1941 after the German invasion of Russia.

After the war, the PCI continued emphasizing cooperation with anti-Fascist forces, entering the government with the Socialists, Christian Democrats, and other parties of the anti-Fascist resistance. In May 1947, however, the PCI was excluded from De Gasperi's government, and the long era of Christian Democrat (DC) rule began. Despite this and the shadow of the Cold War, the PCI was never isolated and never sought isolation. In the 1948 election, the Communists and Socialists stood on a popular front basis, and although Christian Democrats and Social Democrats pulled out of the CGIL, the major Italian labor federation, the Socialists and Communists continued their union cooperation. Additionally, although Socialists and Communists refrained from future electoral alliances, the two parties continued to collaborate in local and regional governments, together running several Italian cities including Bologna.[8]

In 1956 the Hungarian crisis and the events of the Twentieth Congress of the Communist Party of the Soviet Union (CPSU) placed a severe strain on the relations between the PCI and its electoral allies. Thereafter, Pietro Nenni, the Socialist Party chief, began to disengage his party from the Communist sphere, and the threat of a Christian Democrat-Socialist government that might isolate the PCI became more and more plausible. In 1959 the Socialist Party Congress abrogated the Unity of Action Pact with the PCI, and by 1963 the threatened "opening to the Left" became a reality as the Socialists opted to join Aldo Moro's Christian Democratic government (a move that split the Socialist Party). Then in 1966 the unification of the Socialist and Social Democratic Parties again threatened to isolate the PCI. At the local level and in the CGIL, however, Socialist-Communist cooperation was still too beneficial to both parties for either to break it off.

By 1969 it was apparent that the PCI would not be isolated. The Socialist Party split again into its original components, and the "opening to the Left" had not harmed the Communists as much as some had anticipated. Since then cooperation between the Italian Communists and other Left-wing parties in the CGIL has continued, and an alliance has been reached with the CISL (formerly Christian Democratic), and the UIL (formerly Social Democratic). In local and regional politics, recent electoral gains by the Left, particularly the PCI, have increased the number of cities and regions in which Left-wing administrations are in power.

In recent years, the Italian Communist Party has offered a proposal for a broad alliance of "democratic forces" in Italy that goes beyond standard Left-wing political alliances. Following the September 1973 military coup against Chile's Socialist President Salvador Allende, Enrico Berlinguer, the secretary-general of the PCI, proposed a *"compromesso storico"* (historic compromise).

The lesson to be drawn from Chile, Berlinguer argued, was that even if the Left were to win 51 percent of the electorate, effective government would be impossible without the support of substantial segments of the middle class—in Italy, Catholics and Christian Democrats. Therefore, it would be necessary for the PCI and Socialist Party to reach an understanding, a *"compromesso storico,"* with those forces in support of a common "democratic" program.

Since the election of 1976, the Communists and the Christian Democrat Party have agreed to a great deal of cooperation on all levels of government. To a large extent, the historic compromise is being achieved through the back door. First, in the labor movement, all of Italy's major union federations have formed a cooperative alliance. In April 1977 the DC government successfully concluded a pact with the unions in which they agreed to allow changes in the cost-of-living index in order to aid the government's efforts to control inflation. Moreover, in early 1978, the unions publicly accepted the necessity of an austerity program to deal with Italy's economic and political crises.

Second, the DC, the PCI, and other parties have openly cooperated at the local and regional levels of government. Before the 1976 elections, cooperation was sporadic, but it has subsequently broadened, frequently at the Communists' initiative. In many regions where the PCI and its Leftist allies already enjoy a majority, the Communists have sought support from the DC as well. In Emilia-Romana, for example, the DC has agreed to support the PCI-Socialist administration, and in the regional administration covering Rome and other central provinces, the DC and PCI have reached a power-sharing agreement.

Finally, at the national level, Communist and Christian Democrat cooperation has increased to the point where the PCI is now in the antechambers of the government. Before the spring election of 1976, the DC and PCI hinted at cooperation and the DC government formally consulted the PCI at least once (in March, on the lira). After the June balloting, however, cooperation between the Communists and Christian Democrats was extensive. In the parliament, the two parties openly cooperated, agreeing to elect a Communist to preside over the Chamber and a Christian Democrat to preside over the Senate. Moreover, the PCI was given control of seven parliamentary commissions. In return, the PCI abstained on a vote of confidence, allowing Giulio Andreotti's government to take office.

Throughout the remainder of 1976, the Communist Party kept the DC government in office by abstaining on key votes, exchanging its passive support for influence in governmental policy making. Then, in the spring of 1977, Italy's six "constitutional parties"—the DC, PCI, Republicans, Liberals, Socialists, and Social Democrats—began formal negotiations to find agreement on a governmental program to deal with Italy's economic crisis. By July the parties had reached an accord on a limited legislative program, an accord that Berlinguer praised as a step toward entry into a coalition. In mid-July the program was presented to parliament, and the Communists found themselves backing the government for the first time in thirty years.

By the end of 1977, however, this arrangement was no longer acceptable to all of the parties involved. The Socialists, the Republicans, and the Communists called on the Christian Democrats to form a broad-based coalition government including the Communists. When the DC rejected this demand, the PCI and the two smaller parties withdrew their support from Andreotti's government, and in January 1978 Andreotti resigned. There followed a long period of negotiations, culminating in March in the formation of another Christian Democrat government led by Andreotti. This time, however, the Communists were explicitly part of the government's majority in parliament, although no Communists actually sit in the cabinet.

France

In France, the PCF has had an ambivalent relationship with the Socialists and a consistently hostile posture toward the Right. Although the Italian Communist Party after the 1920s pursued a collaborative policy with other anti-Fascist parties, the French Party, like many other parties in Western Europe, closely followed the fluctuations of the Comintern line.

By the end of 1921, it was apparent that the Bolshevik Revolution was not going beyond the borders of Russia, and to consolidate their position and end their isolation, the Soviet leaders adopted a united front policy. Consequently, after its birth in 1924, the PCF followed, somewhat reluctantly (and unsuccessfully), a united front policy with the Socialist rump. At the Fifth Comintern Congress in June-July 1924, the line on alliances was changed. United front *from above,* that is, alliances with Socialist parties, was condemned and a policy of united front *from below,* alliances with individual Socialists and groups of Socialists over the heads of their leaders, was endorsed.

By 1928 Comintern policy was modified again to include a "class-against-class" program. Socialists became "Social-Fascists" for the Communists, and in the 1928 election, the PCF refused to withdraw any of its candidates on the second ballot to help better-placed parties of the Left against Right-wing opponents. In short order, the PCF became isolated in both the political and labor union arenas.

The rise of Fascism in Europe in the 1930s placed considerable pressure on the French Left to unite against the common enemy, but the Communist leadership refused to end its class-against-class tactics. Instructions from Moscow, however, brought a reversal in policy, and in 1934 the Central Committee of the PCF made a direct offer to the Socialists to organize a common action against Fascism. After a number of polemical exchanges and more Comintern intervention, the PCF agreed to all major Socialist demands. The two signed a Unity of Action Pact in July 1934 and agreed on electoral cooperation in the 1934 election.

Proclaiming the slogan of *la main tendue* (the extended hand), the Communists expressed a willingness to cooperate with Radicals as well as Socialists. Following the 1936 election, a popular front government was formed by the Socialists and Radicals and supported by the PCF. In the early days of the Popular Front, the PCF fully cooperated with the Blum government in parliament and moved on the industrial front to calm labor unrest.

Despite occasional disagreements and sporadic labor unrest, the French Communists continued their support of the Front through the first half of 1937, and pledged loyal support for the Chautemps government after the Blum cabinet fell on June 21, 1937. Later, however, the PCF opposed Chautemps' program of economic and political stability and in 1938 Communist-supported strikes led to the fall of a second Blum government. For a time, the PCF backed the new Daladier government, but conservative economic policies and then the Munich Agreement[9] saw the Popular Front formally dissolved on November 10, 1938. Although no longer supporting the government, the Communists in 1938 were not isolated. Communists and Socialists were still cooperating on the union front and the continuance of an electoral agreement was likely.

Again, however, events outside of France set the tone for Communist alliance strategies. In August 1939, the Soviet Union and Nazi Germany, to the consternation of the West, signed a non-aggression pact. The Communists' support for the agreement was regarded as a treasonous action and a campaign of repression was begun against the PCF, including the banning of *L'Humanité*, the Party's national newspaper. After the Soviet attack on Poland on September 17, 1939, the PCF took a defeatist approach to the war.

Subsequently it was declared illegal and its elected officials were suspended.

In June 1941, Nazi Germany invaded the Soviet Union and the French Communists were again able to pursue a united front policy, which they did with great success during the Resistance and into the post-Liberation period. After the war, the Communists entered the government for the first time in a broad popular front that included the Socialists and the MRP (*Mouvement Républicain Populaire*).

In May 1947, the PCF broke with the government, ostensibly over the issue of wage increases, but, in reality, because of the international situation. Then, following the founding of the Cominform in October 1947, the Party rejected the idea of collaboration with the Socialists. With a new trades union split in late 1947 and an undisguised Socialist hostility toward the PCF, the Communists were once again beginning a long winter of political and union isolation.

With the ending of the Cold War and the birth of the Fifth Republic, the isolation of the Communists began to come to an end and the PCF again made overtures to the Socialists for cooperation. In 1962 the PCF unilaterally ordered a number of its candidates to stand down on the second ballot in favor of better-placed Socialists. The Socialists responded in kind, and in 1966 the Socialists and Left Radicals (FGDS), and the Communists reached a formal agreement for second ballot withdrawals in the 1967 elections. After the election, cooperation was extended to the National Assembly, where the FGDS and PCF voted together on all major issues. Negotiations were begun on a possible common program.[10] The events of May-June 1968 and the Soviet intervention in Czechoslovakia in August 1968 interrupted the march toward unity. Relations between the Socialists and Communists cooled, and they could agree on no common candidate for the 1969 presidential elections. Subsequently, however, relations improved and negotiations for a common program moved ahead. In June 1972, these negotiations were climaxed with the signing by the PCF, the Socialists, and a group of Left Radicals of a 60,000-word common program.[11] Moreover, in both 1966 and 1974, the Communists agreed to support the Socialists' candidate for president, François Mitterrand, on the first ballot.[12]

Since the near success of the Union of the Left in the 1974 presidential election, relations between the Communists and Socialists have waxed and waned.[13] Beginning in late 1974, the PCF launched a polemical campaign against the Socialists and Mitterrand, accusing them of undermining Left unity by failing enthusiastically to support Communist candidates on the second ballot in by-elections and by yearning to join a coalition under Giscard. For their part, the Socialists have defended themselves and assailed the PCF for supporting Portugal's Communist Party. After mid-1976 relations between the Communists and the Socialists improved significantly. Polemics between the two virtually disappeared, and in most cases the parties of the Left were able to agree on common lists for the 1977 municipal elections.[14]

With polls showing the Union of the Left holding a clear lead over the divided Right and Center-Right, the Leftist partners opened negotiations in May 1977 to update the Common Program. The negotiations did not go well, however, and the Union of the Left came to disunion. Throughout the summer, the PCF stubbornly insisted upon extensive nationalizations, wage and salary reform, and a more independent defense posture for France, all of which neither the Socialists nor the Left Radicals would accept. The rhetoric of the debate became quite heated, and in mid-September the leader of the Left Radicals, Robert Fabre, walked out of a Leftist summit meeting, saying his party could not accept the Communists' demands. Subsequently, the negotiations resumed, but only to collapse again. The Socialists offered some concessions to the Communists' demands, but the PCF refused to budge. Negotiations broke off in acrimony with each side blaming the other.

Not surprisingly, there was no common list of Left candidates for the first ballot in the March 1978 parliamentary elections. During the campaign, the Communists abused the Socialists as lackeys of the Right, while the Socialists tried to ignore their former partners. After the first round of voting, the Leftist parties set aside their differences, agreeing to support the Left candidate in each constituency with the best chance of winning, regardless of party. Unity came too late, however, to bring victory to the Left. Both the Communists and Socialists gained a few seats, but the Center-Right coalition retained a comfortable majority.

Spain

At its first Congress in 1922, the Spanish Communist Party called for a united labor front, but the comparatively weak party found little support for the idea from the Socialists and Anarchists until Primo de Rivera established his dictatorship in 1923. Nevertheless, the Party's strength declined under the repression of the dictatorship, and the Party's adoption of the Comintern's "Social-Fascist" line in the late 1920s left the PCE largely isolated and ineffectual.

In 1932, however, the Party broke with the Comintern line, adopted a united front policy, and a front was established for the 1933 election. In 1936 the Popular Front won a majority in the Spanish parliament, and the PCE became a part of the government with two party members in the cabinet. During the early period of the Popular Front government, the PCE cooperated with Socialists and bourgeois Republicans to save the Republic. Both the youth organizations and union federations of the Popular Front parties were merged.

As the civil war continued, the Communists began to assume a position of dominance. First, the PCE moved against the Anarchists and Trotskyists who wanted to turn the Popular Front into an instrument of social revolution. The Communists resorted to coercion and terror to eliminate opponents on the Left. Then, in the latter days of the Civil War, the PCE lost most of its moderate allies, who accused it of being too closely tied to Moscow and of seeking hegemony. After Franco's victory, the PCE called for a united opposition, but its former allies no longer trusted the Communists, a distrust that was reenforced as the PCE line switched repeatedly in 1939-41, reflecting Soviet policy.

After World War II, distrust of the Communists persisted, but the PCE found some acceptance of its calls for a unified anti-Franco effort. In 1945 the PCE joined the *Alianza Nacional de Fuerzas democráticas* set up by Socialists and Republicans, and in 1946 the Party announced it would support the Republican government in exile.

Increasingly, the PCE policy became one of *rapprochement* with all opposition forces, including Catholics and the middle strata[15] and increasingly the Party has won cooperation, particularly since the early 1960s. The Party made headway in the union movement, winning cooperation with Catholics and other Leftists through the workers' commissions. In July 1974, the PCE and various other opposition groups formed the *Junta Democrática*. It did not, however, include the Socialists.

Since the death of Franco, the alliance strategy of the PCE has borne more fruit. In March 1976, the Communists, Socialists, and others agreed to form a united opposition front. Then, in June 1976, thirteen parties of the Center and Left banded together in a coalition known as Democratic Coordination, stating they would not even apply for legalization unless legal status was also available to the PCE, one of the partners. Moreover, in September 1976, the three principal syndicates, the Communists workers, the workers union, and the General Union Workers (Socialist influenced), announced they had reached an accord of principle for the coordination of syndical organizations and agreed on a common program of demands.

Since the legalization of the PCE and the June 1977 elections, the Spanish Communist Party has campaigned for the creation of a broad coalition government (1) to strengthen democracy; (2) to enhance the PCE's political leverage; and (3) to limit the maneuverability of the larger Socialist Party, whom the Communists regard as their chief competitor. In pursuance of the strategy, the PCE has voted on a number of occasions to support the government of Adolfo Suárez and against the position of the Socialist opposition. In October 1977, there were indications that the Communists' strategy was bearing fruit when Prime Minister Suárez asked the leaders of the major opposition parties (including PCE leader Santiago Carrillo) to begin negotiations in hopes of drawing up an emergency plan for solving Spain's growing economic and political difficulties. So far some significant agreements have been reached and Carrillo is delighted that his party has a consultative role in the government of Spain in what some are calling the beginning of a Spanish "historic compromise."

Norway

In Norway, throughout the 1920s and 1930s, the NKP mirrored the Comintern shifts in alliance strategies. With the beginning of

World War II, however, the NKP supported the democracies against Germany, but corrected the policy by September 15, 1939. Although the Party was initially confused over the line to take on the German invasion of Norway, the Party soon called for an end to resistance, a move that general opinion regarded as treasonous.

As in France, after June 1941, the Communists turned again to a popular front strategy in the Resistance, and after the Liberation entered the first postwar coalition government. The Norwegian Labor Party and the NKP even initiated talks toward unification, but the Communists soon retreated.

Again, as in France, the coming of the Cold War led to the political isolation of the Norwegian Communists. They were excluded from the government and the strong Labor Party rebuffed the NKP at every turn.

In the 1950s, the alliance policy of the NKP took a zigzag course, first moving in a united front direction and then taking an anti-Labor posture. By the 1960s, the Party was trying to break out of its isolation by making popular front bids both to Labor and to the Socialist People's Party (SF), but all offers were rejected. Communist suggestions for an electoral alliance in the 1965 elections were ignored, but the NKP opted unilaterally to field candidate lists only in certain areas. Within the NKP, however, there was deep division over these popular front tactics and the leadership, in essence, allowed each provincial organization to make up its own mind. Nevertheless, both the SF and the Labor Party refused cooperation, and the NKP remained isolated.

In the late 1960s and early 1970s, the Party fluctuated between calls for Left-wing unity and allegations against the other Leftist parties, particularly Labor. Talks were begun in 1971 with the SF toward cooperation on an electoral basis, but the SF rejected any alliance.

In 1973, however, the NKP ended its long political isolation by joining the Socialist Electoral Alliance along with the SF and a splinter faction of the Labor Party. Although the coalition was founded primarily on the basis of opposition to Norwegian entry into the Common Market, merger talks were begun with the aim of forming a new Left-wing party. There followed a heated debate in the NKP, climaxing with the ouster of Reidar Larsen, the NKP's pro-merger chairman, and the exodus of many of his supporters. In the 1977 election, the NKP stood alone.

Iceland

In Iceland, although a Communist faction was formed in the Social Democratic Party in 1921, it did not secede until 1930. Then in 1937, when Communists pushed for a popular front, the Social Democrats refused, but their Left wing split to join the Communists in an electoral front. After Iceland won its independence in 1944, the Communists participated in a coalition government. Although an election defeat in 1947 and Cold War tensions sent the Communists into opposition, they were not isolated. They gained influence in the labor unions and, after the 1956 election, again entered the government, where they stayed until December 1958.

In the 1960s, the Icelandic Party continued its alliance policies. In 1963 it entered the elections allied with the small National Defense Party that later merged with the Communists as the Party converted its electoral front into the party organization. The ending of the front in 1968 split the Marxist Left into three segments: the PA, the pro-Moscow party, and a Socialist people's party. Following the 1971 election, however, the Communists along with the larger Progressive Party and the small Socialist people's party, the Organization of Liberals and Leftists (OLL), joined to form a Left-wing government. Since July 1974, however, the Progressives have formed a government with the Independence Party, the OLL has shrunk to a miniature, and the PA is back in opposition.

Ireland

In Ireland the CPI, refounded in 1933 after an abortive start in 1921, has modeled its alliance strategies on the International line. During the 1930s it called for a popular front, but without success. The Cold War found the Party retreating to a more isolationist line, but subsequently, the CPI has attempted futilely to organize a broad popular front.

Switzerland

Similarly, Communist alliance strategies in Switzerland closely followed Comintern policies before World War II, but the PdA was unable to win united front cooperation with the Socialists. After the war, the Communists again campaigned unsuccessfully for unity of action, but became more standoffish during the Cold War. Since the late 1950s, the Swiss Communists have endorsed an alliance policy, but with only marginal success at the cantonal and local levels.

Portugal

Like many of its Western European counterparts, the PCP's alliance policies generally followed the International line through the 1920s and 1930s. After 1941, however, the Party consistently promoted the idea of an anti-Fascist popular front and continued this line throughout the remainder of its long period of illegality. Moreover, the Communists were not without success in finding allies among the opposition. On a number of occasions, the PCP entered into electoral agreements for participation in Salazar's limited democracy. In 1962 the PCP joined with other opposition groups in the Patriotic Front of National Liberation, but was expelled from the front in 1970 over a disagreement about tactics and ideology. (The Front had come to be dominated by ultra-Left groups who both advocated armed struggle to overthrow the regime and opposed the PCP's support of Moscow against Peking in the Sino-Soviet dispute.)

Since the overthrow of the dictatorship, the Portuguese Communists' policy on alliances has taken several turns. Initially, the PCP supported a popular front of "democratic and progressive" forces, winning a place on the Spinola cabinet as the Socialists and Popular Democrats, too, sought anti-Fascist unity. As the Communists reached out for more power, however, relations with their moderate allies worsened, and the Socialists and Popular Democrats left the government in July 1975, saying it was under Communist control. On their part, the Communists called Mario Soares, the Socialist leader, "fascist and reactionary."[16]

After the moderates in the military won the upper hand in late 1975, however, the PCP was again interested in good relations with the Socialists. They campaigned for an electoral alliance for the spring 1976 parliamentary election, but the Socialist would have no part of it. Then, after the election, the Communists called for a Socialist-Communist coalition government, but again their appeals found no takers. When the Socialists formed a minority government, the Communists attacked it for following a policy of reconciliation with the Right. The PCP would have rather seen the formation of a broad coalition of all Left and Center parties.[17]

Then, in December 1977, on a confidence vote, the PCP joined with the Right to bring down the Soares government. In January 1978 Soares was able to form a new government, including the conservative Center Democrats along with his own Socialist Party. The Communists have labeled this new arrangement reactionary and worse.

Luxembourg

In Luxembourg the PCL's alliance strategies have been quite similar to those of the French Communist Party. Like the PCF, before World War II, the position of the PCL fluctuated with that of the Comintern. Then, after the war, the Party entered the government only to leave in March 1947 with the beginning of the Cold War. Also, like the PCF, in recent years the PCL has campaigned hard for collaboration with the Socialists, but with little success. Although the two parties are in coalition in Esch-zur-Alzette, the Socialists have rejected offers for national cooperation.

Belgium

In Belgium the PCB followed the Comintern line in its early years. After the Liberation, it became part of a Socialist-Liberal-Communist coalition government until March 1947, when the Party began a long period of isolation. Although the Party adopted a unity of action policy in late 1954, the PCB has gained little cooperation from the Socialists outside of an occasional local issue and some infrequent union cooperation.

Netherlands

The history of the alliance tactics of the Communist Party of the Netherlands is quite similar to that of the PCB, with the exception that the Party's move toward collaboration with the Socialists in the latter 1950s was met with resistance on the part of a large number of the Party's union militants, who refused to merge their organization with that of the Socialists. Recently, the CPN has broadened its alliance appeals, calling in 1972 for collaboration with "all democrats and progressives,"[18] but, in any case, the CPN's repeated pleas for cooperation have fallen on deaf ears.

Sweden

In Sweden the early history of the Communist Party was marked by deviation as a series of leaders sought a *rapprochement* with the Social Democratic Party, rather than following the Comintern's class-against-class line. After intervention by Moscow, the Swedish Party eventually became more conformist, and in 1947-48 it adopted the new Cominform hard line against the Social Democrats. In the 1950s, the Party again returned to united front tactics, even withdrawing some candidates in favor of the Social Democrats in some districts in 1958. Nevertheless, the Social Democrats have adamantly and persistently rejected all offers for collaboration.

Great Britain

The British Communist Party has also failed in its many attempts at trades union and electoral collaboration with a larger Socialist party. In the 1920s, the CPGB's appeals for cooperation were rebuked unmercifully. Although the British Communists hesitated to adopt the class-against-class line, a Comintern-directed purge reduced the Party to subservience and conformity to the International's instructions. After World War II, the CPGB again followed alliance strategies parallel to those of Moscow. In recent decades (at least since 1956), the British Party has campaigned for cooperation with the Labour Party, especially in the union arena (except for periods following particularly stinging Labour rebukes), but with virtually no success. Although as individuals Communists have won positions in a number of unions, neither the Trades Union Council nor the Labour Party recognizes the CPGB in any official role.

Greece

Throughout the early years of its history, the KKE followed the Comintern policy on the question of alliances, but whether its line was class against class or popular front, the KKE found no support from other parties until World War II. Then, the Communists organized the National Liberation Front (EAM) to fight the Germans. In 1943, however, the Communists turned their attention to wiping out their Greek political opponents as well, until 1944 when an agreement was reached whereby they joined the Greek government in exile. Cooperation ended in November 1944, as the KKE resumed the Civil War, which lasted until the truce of January 1945. Although 1945 found the KKE calling for "popular unity," the Party was actually preparing for a new civil war.

After the Communists' defeat, the KKE split over the issue of united front tactics as the old leadership clung to isolationist positions. After a leadership purge and the Twentieth Congress of the CPSU, however, the KKE adopted a united front theme, encouraging the EDA to seek electoral alliances. The new policy found success in 1956 as many non-Communist leaders agreed to join with the EDA in a Democratic Alliance, which won 48 percent of the vote in the parliamentary election. Subsequently, however, the EDA won little cooperation with non-Communist parties, except for the occasion of isolated strikes and demonstrations.

Since the Party split in the late 1960s, one of the disagreements between the KKE Exterior and the KKE Interior has been that of alliance strategies. The KKE Exterior forsook alliances, but the Interior faction advocated broad cooperation of democratic forces against the military junta. In 1973, however, the KKE Exterior switched positions, calling for a popular front against the military regime. After the fall of the junta, both KKE factions temporarily joined in an electoral coalition to contest the November 1974 elections, but the coalition ended after the voting. Finally, in the 1977 election, the KKE Exterior campaigned alone, while the Interior faction allied with four other Leftist parties.

West Germany

Before it was crushed by the Nazis in 1933, the German Communist Party closely adhered to Comintern guidelines. After the war, the reborn KPD called for collaboration with the Social Democrats (SPD), but was taking a harder line in the years preceding its renewed illegality in 1956. In its clandestine period, the Party tried to promote unity of action with the SPD. After being reconstituted as the legal DKP, the West German Communist Party in 1969 achieved an electoral union with several Socialist splinter groups, although the Social Democrats refused cooperation. Subsequently, the DKP has fluctuated in its approach to the SPD, calling in its more recent pronouncements for "unity of action."

Finland

In Finland the SKP's position toward the Social Democratic Party (SDP) has been ambivalent. After its founding in exile in 1918, the SKP initially took a hard line toward the "collaborationist" SDP. Unable to field its own candidates legally and unable to compel its supporters to abstain, the SKP found itself having to support Social Democrats electorally in a number of elections while working to capture the SDP's youth organization and to win a position in the unions. Also, from 1925 on, although the Communists controlled the major union federation, the SAJ, they compromised with the Social Democrats on numerous occasions to maintain Leftist unity.

In 1928 the SKP adopted the Comintern's hard-line posture and ranted against the SDP. Subsequently, the SKP established its own union movement, but found itself ill placed to withstand growing Fascist influence in Finland. After the adoption of the popular front program by the International, the SKP followed suit and slowly began reestablishing its position.

After the war, the SKP, now legal, hoped the SDP would join it in a common electoral front, the SKDL. Only individual branches of the Social Democrats did, however, and the SKDL became an electoral and parliamentary organization for the Communists rather than a connecting link between the two Left-wing parties. In national politics, the SKP entered a broad coalition government of Communists, Social Democrats, and Agrarians, and before the 1945 election, the SDP narrowly rejected an offer for electoral cooperation. Then in April 1945, the SKP joined in the "Big Three Agreement" with its coalition partners. Finally, the SDP and SKP agreed to an electoral committee in local elections in late 1945.

In local elections in late 1947, however, the Social Democrats refused alliance. Then after heavy losses in the 1948 election, the SKP left the government. Although the Finnish Communists were now isolated politically and opposed the minority SDP government, they still supported the principle of a broad coalition of democratic forces. Throughout the Cold War period, the SKP continued to endorse the idea of a broad coalition government, including Communists, Social Democrats, and Agrarians, while struggling rather bitterly with the SDP in the union arena. On their part, the Social Democrats proved to be the party most adamantly opposed to SKP participation in government.

In 1966 the Communists finally succeeded in having the Big Three Coalition restored, as they entered the government along with Agrarians and Social Democrats. In the next year, the Communist-dominated union federation and the SDP union organization united under a single governing board.

Although this was what the SKP had been campaigning for, the Communists withdrew from the cabinet in March 1974, primarily because of an internal opposition, a large, organized "Stalinist" faction that opposed cooperation with the Social Democrats. Consequently, the Party's efforts toward *rapprochement* with the Social Democrats have been on-again, off-again, and the decision to enter a national emergency coalition in late 1975 was reached only with reluctance.[19] Once again, the SKP was torn between a majority who wanted to enter the government to defend the interests of the workers and a hard-line minority who wanted no part of the "bourgeois coalition." Following the collapse of the national emergency government in September 1976, the Communists returned to the opposition only to join another broad-based coalition in May 1977.

Austria

In its early years, the Austrian Communist Party closely adhered to the International line and participated in a postwar provisional government until 1949. As with other Communist parties in Western Europe, the KPÖ adopted a united front program in the late 1950s and 1960s, even opting unilaterally in 1966 to support Socialist candidates in twenty-four of the country's twenty-five electoral districts. In response, the Socialists took a vigorously anti-Communist line. After the disaster of the 1966 policy and the post-Czechoslovakia 1968 factional division in the Party, the KPÖ renounced the popular front, choosing instead a policy of unrelenting opposition to the Socialist Party. Recently, the Party has again called for Socialist-Communist cooperation.

Denmark

In Denmark the fledgling DKP pursued the Comintern's united front policy (unsuccessfully), but balked at adopting the class-against-class tactic. Only reluctantly did the Party accept the International's line on the Nazi-Soviet Pact and the early days of World War II. After the war, three Communists were in Denmark's coalition government, and the Party followed a policy of collaboration with the Social Democrats. Following an electoral setback in 1947, however, the DKP left the government and the Party was divided over the path it should take. Into the 1960s, the Party strove for a united political front and a united labor front. After its return to parliament in 1973, the DKP used its position to attack the Socialists. By 1976, however, the Communists were again calling for Leftist unity.

Domestic Programs

Despite a similar Marxist-Leninist background, the Communist parties of Western Europe present domestic programs that range in tone and substance from the reformist, almost social democratic, to the neo-Stalinist. The domestic programs, like the Western parties' alliance strategies, have tended to vary with the International line, being dogmatic during class-against-class periods and more conciliatory in popular front periods. As with alliance strategies, however, the domestic programs of the Western parties have been characterized by diversity.

Iceland

In Iceland the "Road to Socialism" for the PA has been far from revolutionary. During the economic crisis of the 1930s, the Party conducted some agitation, but, particularly since World War II, the Icelandic Party has made its mark through the skillful exploitation of peculiarly Icelandic issues, such as opposition to the United States base at Keflavik and support for Icelandic fishing rights. The Party explicitly accepts the peaceful road and, in its manifestos and actions, both in government and in opposition, has demonstrated a commitment to non-revolutionary reformist policies.

Britain

Similarly, the British Communist Party has come to accept the peaceful and democratic Road to Socialism. Never genuinely revolutionary, the CPGB in its early days concentrated on union organization and industrial militancy. Although Lenin himself once had to persuade the Party to accept a parliamentary approach, the CPGB has long since rejected violent revolution as unnecessary and unlikely.[20] The Party's cadres tend to be pragmatic, expecting a bread-and-butter approach in union affairs.[21] In general, the Party employs constitutional means to achieve its ends—writing letters, lobbying, petitioning, and so on—and most industrial unrest is not the direct responsibility of the Communist Party but rather ultra-Left groups. The latest version of the British Road to Socialism formally abandons the doctrine of the dictatorship of the proletariat, proclaims that Socialism can be installed without a civil war, promises that the Communists will allow themselves to be voted out of office, and admits that in the capture of power the role of Leftist workers could be more important than that of the Party.[22] Currently, the CPGB emphasizes economic issues, offering suggestions for curing Britain's economic ills, including price controls, higher wages, cuts in defense spending, increased public ownership, frozen rents, and a wealth tax.

Italy

Another party that has self-consciously proclaimed a non-revolutionary line is the Italian Communist Party. In its earliest days, the PCI was divided between a group led by Amadeo Bordiga, and another headed by Antonio Gramsci. The former recommended Communist abstention from parliament, while the latter urged the Party to adopt the united front policy and participate in parliament. Although the Comintern supported Gramsci, and Bordiga was ousted from leadership, the debate continued in the PCI in the early and middle 1920s.[23] Eventually, the position of Palmiro Togliatti, Ruggero Grieco, and Angelo Tasca, that the Party's policy be one of gradualist advocacy of democratic objectives designed to win mass support, carried the day. The PCI switched positions along with the changed Comintern line in the latter 1920s. Then when the Comintern adopted a popular front policy in 1935 (for which Togliatti campaigned at the Seventh Comintern Congress), the Italian Communists were quick to promote it by playing down revolutionary rhetoric and stressing anti-Fascist unity.

After the Liberation, the PCI emphasized moderation and cooperation rather than revolutionary action. "The goal that we will propose to the Italian people when the war is over," Togliatti declared, "will be that of the creation in Italy of a democratic and progressive regime. . . ."[24] Upon Togliatti's return to Italy in 1944, he accepted the King and Marshall Bordiga as commanders of the anti-Fascist forces, thus being more accommodating than even the Liberals. Opting to follow the constitutional road to power, the PCI decided that democracy must be parliamentary,[25] and announced for an Italian rather than a Russian Road to Socialism.[26]

In response to the Cold War, Togliatti redoubled his efforts to establish the Party's credentials as a democratic, reformist party, even going so far as to accept the inclusion of the Lateran Pacts in the new Republican constitution.

The failure of the Party to win power and the atmosphere of the Cold War led to its temporarily taking a harsher line. The PCI supported a number of strikes and demonstrations, but in general the Party adopted a policy of loud demands for reform with little action.

After the Twentieth CPSU Congress in 1956, the question of the Italian Road once again was moved to the front burner in the PCI, with some (not the top leadership) going so far as to make openly revisionist statements.[27] For his part, Togliatti wholeheartedly accepted the peace and détente theme of the Twentieth Congress, emphasizing the several roads to Communism line.[28] Crises in Poland and Hungary, however, compelled Togliatti to take a more conservative position, at least temporarily.[29] At the Eighth PCI Congress in December 1956, the leadership staked out a moderate policy that saw the purge of many conservatives[30] and the exodus of a sizable number of revisionists.[31]

In no sense, however, were the Italian Communists retreating from their own reformist themes. In 1957 Togliatti quarreled with the French Communists over the Italian Road theme[32] and Marxist dogma.[33] Later, at a Moscow conference, Togliatti declared sectarianism to be a greater danger than reformism.[34]

After the Twenty-Second Congress of the CPSU in 1961, a new burst of reformism occurred in the PCI as the Party reemphasized the peaceful road and launched appeals to broad groups in Italian society.[35] In a document published posthumously in late 1964, Togliatti detailed his Party's *Via Italiana al Socialismo.* The PCI seeks, he said, "a form of socialist society based upon . . . our traditions of a multi-party system, on full respect for constitutional guarantees, and for religious and cultural liberties."[36]

Since 1964 the PCI has continued to elaborate and broaden its reformist approach to Socialism in Italy. The Party's *Via Italiana* is marked by four main themes: (1) constructive participation in parliament and in elections and local government; (2) a strategy of alliances; (3) an ideology of "reform of structure" as the preferred means of constructing Socialism in Italy; and (4) activity in local government.[37] Speaking for the PCI, Enrico Berlinguer, the present head of the Party, has stated that a Communist Italy would be a democratic Italy with all but Fascist opposition parties allowed to function. Also, the new government would neither withdraw precipitiously from NATO and the EEC nor abolish all private enterprise.[38] In recent policy statements, the PCI has also strongly stressed honest and efficient administration, promoted tax reform, and called inflation Italy's greatest danger.[39]

Spain

In 1921 the Spanish labor movement was thoroughly revolutionary, but was embodied in Anarcho-Syndicalism. Even the relatively weaker Socialist Party often took maximalist positions; so the tiny Communist Party had to take positions to the Left of those advocated by the Comintern to establish its own identity.

During the Civil War, the PCE enjoyed an important and eventually dominant place in the government. In this position, it behaved as the most moderate, most trustworthy, and most effective of all working-class organizations, forming close ties with the bourgeois Republican parties. The PCE vigorously opposed the revolutionary ideas of the Anarchists and Socialists, developing a program that was very close to that of the middle-class parties on the loyalist side.

After Franco's victory in 1939, the PCE continued the struggle by supporting guerrilla activity in Spain, but also continued its relatively moderate program, calling for land reform and the nationalization of monopolies, credit institutions, big banks, mines, railways, and the like. In the early 1950s, the Communists ceased guerrilla activity and by 1956, had begun to stress the peaceful overthrow of Franco.[40] The PCE hoped that a nonviolent uprising by the mass of workers, students, peasants, and members of the petty bourgeoisie would force a change of regime. The catalyst for that change, the Party hoped, would be a general strike—an idea that was tried and failed in 1958, 1962, and 1965.

As the certainty of Franco's mortality became increasingly apparent, and with his eventual death, the PCE committed itself to parliamentary democracy and the peaceful, democratic Road to Socialism. The Party's current vision of a Socialist Spain includes respect for fundamental political liberties, plurality of parties, universal suffrage, freedom of information and criticism, freedom of artistic and intellectual creation, and the renunciation of any attempt at imposing an official philosophy.[41] Indeed, at the PCE's Ninth Congress in April 1978 the Party voted to drop their term "Leninist" from the Party's description of itself. On specific issues, the PCE says it will accept monarchy if the Spanish people want it,[42] and it favors Spanish entry into the Common Market.[43] In parliament the PCE has emphasized moderation, understanding, and national conciliation.

Netherlands

In the Netherlands, the CPN has moved from a position of orthodox Marxism to an acceptance of the peaceful road theme. In its early years, the Party was marked by a division between revolutionary-minded leaders and parliamentarians, but as in Britain, the parliamentarians gained ascendancy. Despite the CPN's attachment to parliamentarism, it remained wedded to orthodox Marxist verities through the 1950s, responding only half-heartedly to the détente theme of the Twentieth CPSU Congress. In 1964, however, despite internal dissensions, the Dutch Party adopted a more nationalistic program, including an acceptance of the peaceful road, a position that has been embellished in recent years as the CPN has gone so far as to back away from demands for Dutch withdrawal from NATO and the EEC.

Norway

In Norway, too, the Communist Party in its early years took a radical, albeit parliamentary, approach. Moreover, after the Twentieth Congress of the CPSU in 1956, the NKP was unwilling to come to terms with de-Stalinization. In 1963, however, the NKP adopted a new program, emphasizing the peaceful, parliamentary Road to Socialism. The issue upon which the NKP has campaigned the hardest in recent years has been opposition to Norwegian entry into the Common Market.

Belgium

Similarly, the Belgian Communist Party has long followed an orthodox, but in practice parliamentary, Road to Socialism. Like many of its sister parties in Western Europe, the PCB followed a hard-line policy during the 1928-34 period, relaxed its orthodoxy during the Popular Front era, flip-flopped repeatedly from 1939 to 1941, became conciliatory during the early postwar era, and returned to hard-line orthodoxy with the coming of the Cold War. Eventually, in the mid-1950s, the Belgian Communists began stressing the peaceful road to Communism theme. In recent decades, the PCB has increasingly cultivated an image of respectability anchored in parliamentary legality. The issues that the PCB has stressed have included opposition to defense spending and opposition to government measures designed to surmount the country's economic problems, which the Communists see as unfairly burdening the workers.[44]

Switzerland

In Switzerland the Communist Party began activity after 1922 that was designed to disrupt Swiss society, including an anti-religious movement and a united front from below campaign. In the 1930s, the Party continued its hard-line posture but generally deemphasized revolutionary actions. In 1966 the PdA revised its program in favor of a less rigid, more flexible approach, including acceptance of the peaceful road thesis and a multi-party system. Into the latter half of the 1970s, the PdA has increasingly withdrawn into staunch parliamentarism, rejecting extremism and violence. In recent election campaigns, the PdA has emphasized economic issues, calling for rent and price freezes coupled with salary increases.

Sweden

The first program of the Swedish Communist Party in 1917 was hardly revolutionary, but after Comintern affiliation in 1919, the Party's program was a revolutionary one, both in means and aims. By 1943, however, the Party was hinting that Socialism could be achieved by peaceful means, and in 1946 Party leader Linderot spoke of majority approval of Socialism. With the Cold War and electoral decline, however, the Party adapted its propaganda to the Cominform line. Then in 1956 the Swedish Communists accepted with pleasure the peaceful road thesis.

In recent years, the Swedish Communist Party has gone quite far in modernizing its program. Since 1967, when it symbolically changed its name from the Swedish Communist Party (SKP) to the Left Party—Communist (VPK), the Party has offered a unique brand of Communism in its domestic program. The program proposed by the VPK in 1967 called for a decentralized model of Socialism combined with broad guarantees for civil liberties. At the Party's congress in October 1972, the VPK pulled back from its "new Left" brand of Communism by adopting a revised, somewhat more militant program. In 1975, however, at the Party's Twenty-Fourth Congress, the VPK reemphasized its moderate stance. In terms of specific issues, the VPK calls for a shorter work day, more day-care space, tax reform, a price freeze on vital necessities, greater employee power in business, and the nationalization of private commercial banks, insurance, energy, the drug industry, and arms production.[45]

France

Although some Western European Communist parties have adopted the peaceful path to Socialism smoothly and even eagerly,

the French Communist Party has moved only cautiously and un-
evenly. It is not that the PCF has acted in a revolutionary manner.
Like most other Communist parties in Western Europe, it has not.
Time and again, in the turbulent days following the Liberation,
during the Algerian crisis, and in May-June 1968, the French Communists refused to capitalize on potentially revolutionary situations, acting instead as a stabilizing force. The PCF has been
accused of fulfilling a stabilizing and legitimizing function in the
French political system.[46] The French Communists, however, have
been reluctant to let go of the old verities of Marxism-Leninism, at
least on a permanent basis.

We can identify eight phases in the evolution of the PCF.[47] In the
beginning, from 1920 to 1923, the PCF was little more than a
detached branch of the Socialist Party. In its ideology and organization, the PCF was not what is usually considered a Communist
party.

In the second period from about 1923 to 1927, the PCF under-
went a process of Bolshevization, whereby the Party adopted the
organization and tenets of Russian Bolshevism.

The third period was the Social-Fascist period (1928-34) in which
the Communists attacked the Socialist Party as little different from
the Fascists. It was a time of dogmatism as well as isolation.

The Popular Front period from 1934 to 1939 was one of reinte-
gration. It was in this period that the French Communist Party
became a *national* party by clothing itself in the patriotic symbolism
of the French Revolution and defending *fonctionnaires,* the franc,
French culture, workers, peasants, and the middle class.[48]

In the fifth period, 1939 to 1941, the French Communists suffered
a time of isolation because of their identification with the Soviets'
war policy and their consequently "antipatriotic" defense posture.

From June 1941 to 1947, the sixth period, the PCF came back
into the patriotic fold. During this period of War Communism, and
subsequent Government Communism, the Party generally pursued
quite pragmatic, "national" policies.

During the Cold War era, from 1947 to the late 1950s, the Party
went through a period of hyperdogmatism and intellectual sterility.
On different occasions, the PCF sponsored strikes, riots, demonstrations, and parliamentary obstructionism.

In the final period, since the late 1950s, the PCF, although campaigning for and eventually constructing an alliance with the Socialists, has cautiously and hesitantly embarked on the path of revising some of its ideological positions that are the most offensive to possible allies. For years the Party agonized over the questions of whether there could be a multi-party system during and after the construction of Socialism, whether there could be an alternation of power, and whether a Socialist government would accept a negative electoral verdict.[49]

Although the PCF has moved slowly, in the last few years, the Party has come around to a clear acceptance of the democratic Road to Socialism. The Socialist-Communist Common Program is a relatively pragmatic document that compromises some of the differences between the two parties.[50] In it the Communists explicitly accepted such concepts as the multi-party system under Socialism and alternation in power, while putting their objections to NATO and the EEC in cold storage. For their part, the Socialists agreed to accept more nationalizations (armaments, aeronautics and space, the nuclear industry, pharmaceuticals, electronics, mineral resources, chemicals, computers, and the banking and financial sector), and implicitly agreed to refrain from seeking alliance with the Right.[51] Although the PCF momentarily retreated from its unaccustomed moderation by taking a harder line at the extraordinary Twenty-First Congress in October 1974, moderation was again the watchword as Party leader Georges Marchais explicitly abandoned the doctrine of the dictatorship of the proletariat at the Party's Twenty-Second Congress in February 1976.[52]

During negotiations to update the Common Program in 1977, however, the Communists stubbornly insisted on a number of demands that were unacceptable to their Left-wing allies. First, the PCF wanted to extend nationalizations to include the entire steel industry, oil companies, the Peugeot-Citroën auto plants, and all subsidiary companies owned by the nationalized industries. Second, the Communists wanted a higher minimum wage and a ceiling on executive salaries so the difference between the minimum and the highest wage would be a factor no greater than five. Finally, the Communists decided to accept France's nuclear force. French weapons should not be aimed at the Warsaw bloc alone, however, but also at the West.

Portugal

Throughout most of its history, the PCP has approached problems from an orthodox, Leninist perspective. During its long period of illegality, the Party was a leader of the opposition against Salazar, advocating strikes and self-determination for Portugal's colonies. As late as 1968, the PCP was still calling for "armed struggle," and the Party's 1965 program saw "national unity" through an "armed popular uprising" as the most likely agent of change.

By 1970, however, the Communists adopted a more moderate platform of advocating mass action by parliamentary means. With the fall of the dictatorship in 1974, the PCP presented a moderate image. It spoke of few nationalizations and discouraged strikes,[53] but as its influence increased and it became more confident, the PCP took a harder line. At the Communists' urging, the government extended nationalizations to the banking and insurance industries in particular and moved to control the communications media.

Since the precipitous decline of its influence over national politics, the PCP has settled into a restrained pattern of opposition. On the one hand, the Party firmly opposes the new government and clings to many traditional Communist dogmas. Although the phrase "dictatorship of the proletariat" has been dropped, Party leader Cunhal makes it clear that this is merely a change in terminology and not a change in policy.[54] On the other hand, the Communists seem committed to parliamentary opposition. They have vigorously attacked the ultra-Left extraparliamentary groups and have pledged their support to the constitutional regime.[55]

West Germany

In West Germany, the Communist Party has a long history of militancy. During the last years of Weimar, the KPD was uncompromisingly hostile in its attitudes toward the government and revolutionary actions were not out of the question. After the Party's rebirth in the wake of World War II, its position was one of relative moderation, but with the coming of the Cold War, the KPD preached a revolutionary line. During its clandestine period, however, the German Communists turned to a more moderate approach. After their party was reestablished as the legal DKP, they carefully ruled out violence and the dictatorship of the proletariat, stressing the peaceful road.[56] Since the West German *rapprochement* with the Soviet Union and Bonn's assurances of the continued legality of the DKP, the Party has taken a more hard-line approach. On specific issues, the Party has recently attacked defense spending and called for a price freeze and job recruiting.[57]

Denmark

The Danish Communist Party, too, has taken a hard-line approach in recent years. Much like other Western European Communist parties, the DKP moved from its Socialist heritage to a position of orthodoxy in the late 1920s, returned to moderation during the Popular Front era, the Resistance, and early postwar periods, and then returned to a hard-line position during the Cold War years. Then in 1965 the DKP spelled out a new domestic program, fully accepting the parliamentary Road to Socialism. "Socialism," Party leader Jespersen wrote, "is the continuation of the best traditions of the democratic struggle of our people. Socialist democracy will be inviolable, and [under it] the existence of the multiparty system [will be] guaranteed by the constitution."[58] In recent years, particularly since the Party's return to parliament, the DKP has taken a harder line, calling for a revolutionary transition to Socialism through parliamentary means, mass actions, and strikes.[59] In recent election campaigns, the Party has stressed tax reform and the withdrawal of Denmark from NATO and the EEC.[60]

Ireland

In Ireland the Communist Party's programmatic development has been similar to that in Denmark. Following a period of Cold War rigidity, in 1962 the CPI adopted a program accepting the peaceful Road to Socialism as well as Irish unification and independence from Britain's "imperialistic" control. Recently, however, the Irish Party has taken a harsher line, calling for the formation of a "National Liberation Front" in Ireland. Although the CPI favors a peaceful, political solution to the question of Socialism in Ireland, it does not eschew violence. Currently, the CPI concentrates on issues such as the reunification of Ireland, the end of British influence in Ireland, and withdrawal from the EEC.[61]

Greece

No Western European Communist party has a more revolutionary background than the KKE. After an early purge of moderates, the KKE took a very hard-line posture, declaring force to be the only path to power in 1923. Although the Party tried to make electoral hay with bread-and-butter appeals in the 1930s, it turned to a strategy of unrest in 1936, calling a general strike that only succeeded in precipitating the Metaxas dictatorship. During the Resistance and again in 1946, the KKE returned to violence, launching a civil war; but again the Party was crushed.

In the early 1950s, the EDA, the Communist-dominated electoral front, presented a minimalist program, attempting to exploit economic and social grievances. Then in 1956, after the CPSU's Twentieth Congress, the KKE began advocating the peaceful road, saying that the realization of democratic reforms is the first step to Socialism.[62]

In the last decade, the two factions of the Greek Communist Party have differed on policy. The KKE Exterior has deemphasized the peaceful road, arguing that the military junta could only be changed by force. On the other hand, the KKE Interior has continued to advocate the peaceful approach, pledging its respect for the democratic process and majority rule. On other issues, both factions oppose NATO, but they disagree on the EEC with the Exterior Party opposing it and the KKE Interior accepting it.[63]

Austria

In its early years, the Austrian Communist Party had a relatively radical program, even launching an unsuccessful revolt in 1919. From then until the KPÖ was outlawed in 1933, it continued its hard-line program but stopped short of violence. After the war, the Party hoped to duplicate the *Coup de Prague,* but its efforts were thwarted. During the 1960s, the KPÖ changed its domestic program to one of more moderation, including an acceptance of the peaceful Road to Socialism thesis. After 1968, however, with the liberal-conservative division in the Party, the KPÖ's domestic policy became a point of controversy. Subsequently, although the KPÖ has not retreated to Stalinist rigidity, its domestic position is far from reformist. As Party Chairman Franz Muhri has written, the KPÖ "is working for socialism without civil war, but the possibility of this will depend on how far the front of class struggle expands in Austria and the world."[64] In current issues, the KPÖ concentrates much of its effort on attacking the Socialist government and calling for a move to a transitional stage between capitalism and Socialism.

Luxembourg

Finally, the Luxembourg Communist Party has moved from a hard line to a more moderate posture domestically. After its founding in January 1921, the PCL launched a strike movement designed at disrupting Luxembourg society. Then, as with a number of other Western parties, the PCL took a moderate approach during the Popular Front period and during the period immediately after the war. During the Cold War, however, the PCL returned to a position of rigid orthodoxy. At the Party's Eighteenth Congress in 1965, the PCL adopted a program accepting the peaceful transition to Socialism, the multi-party system, and the feasibility of reform before the abolition of capitalism. Currently, the issues that the PCL more frequently stresses are opposition to Luxembourg's participation in the Common Market and the alleged exploitation of Luxembourg's workers by large companies and banks.[65]

Organization

Organizationally, the Leninist model calls for a small, disciplined, highly centralized cadre party based on the cell in which decision making is conducted by the norms of democratic centralism. Both in general and in specific instances, however, the non-ruling parties of Western Europe have deviated from this model.[66]

First, in theory and in practice, most of Western Europe's Communist parties have abandoned the ideal of a cadre party in favor of a mass party, a goal the Italians, French, and Finnish parties have achieved. Since World War II, most of the Communist parties of Western Europe have at least tried to build a mass membership party.

Second, despite a norm of party discipline and centralization, most Western parties have long histories of factionalism. As an extreme case of the effects of factionalism, in Finland the SKP has experienced a significant structural transformation in the wake of the emergence of a deep schism within the Party between "modernists" and Stalinists. In 1969 the division came to a head with the virtual establishment of an oppositionist organization within the Party itself as on both the Central Committee and the Politburo, a balance was established between the two groups at the February 1969 Party Congress. Although in May 1975 the two factions moved to patch the rift at the Seventeenth Party Congress, the result was more cosmetic than real. The Party continues to be characterized by an internal debate and a dual structure.

Listing all the major and minor divisions undergone by Western European Communist parties would be a monumental task, but in the last twenty years major schisms in the Western parties include the following: a split between progressives and conservatives in the Austrian Party following the Soviet intervention in Czechoslovakia in 1968; in the Belgian Party, the exodus of the *De Brug* group in the late 1950s and later desertion of Jacques Grippa and a group of followers to form a pro-Chinese party in the 1960s; the purge of Axel Larsen and subsequent departure of a large retinue of his supporters in the Danish Party; in France the Servin-Casanova *Affaire* that saw the expulsion of two Central Committee members for opposing Maurice Thorez's leadership; the rupture of the Greek Communist Party into Interior and Exterior factions; in Iceland the desertion of Stalinists from the PA in 1968 and the departure of Valdimarsson's group in 1969, each to form an opposition Leftist party; in the Italian Communist Party, the challenge from the *Il Manifesto* group in the late 1960s and early 1970s; in the Netherlands, the presence of factions that support both the Chinese and the Soviets in the international movement; in Britain a group of militants in Surrey that has broken with the CPGB over the Party's liberal program; in Norway the defection of the youth affiliate in 1967 to support a Muscovite minority, a purge of Maoists in 1970, and the recent party merger split; the split in the Spanish Party over the PCE's reaction to the Czechoslovakian invasion and the formation of a pro-Moscow splinter party; and in Sweden's VPK, a factional division over the Party's progressive policies that has seen a number of cells in Göteborg and Malmö leave the Party.

Third, in Belgium, Ireland, Spain, and Switzerland, Communist parties have introduced organizational variations corresponding to national conditions. In Belgium the Communist Party is divided into Flemish and Walloon branches, each of which applies the Party line in its own region and each of which has the right of veto over Party policies. The organization of the miniature Irish Communist Party also reflects national divisions with the Executive Committee divided into Northern and Southern branches. The Spanish Communist Party has regional branches in Catalonia, Galicia, and the Basque region. Finally, in Switzerland the structure of the PdA follows the federal structure of the Swiss confederation with cantonal sections and representation of the nation's three major linguistic groups on the Central Committee.

Fourth, a number of Communist parties have departed from the Leninist norm of democratic centralism. The Western European Communist party that has strayed the furthest is the Swedish Communist Party, which has been characterized as a "paradigm of revisionist development."[67] Since 1964 the VPK has undergone an internal democratization marked by freedom of debate and the toleration of a wide range of opinions. Along with the new program approved in 1967, the VPK, under C. H. Hermansson's leadership, also adopted new rules that virtually abrogated democratic centralism. Stressing individual members' freedoms and rights, the new rules guaranteed that delegate elections be by secret ballot and declared that the Party cannot order trades union or Diet representatives to vote in a prescribed way. Finally, all Party congresses were to be public.

Since its recent legalization, the Spanish Communist Party has undergone a remarkable democratization. At the Party's Ninth Congress held in April 1978, foreign observers were astonished to hear delegates openly criticize the Secretary-General's report and challenge the policies of the Party's leadership. On the important vote to drop the term "Leninist" from the Party's description of itself, 248 delegates voted "no" while 40 abstained. (The motion carried, however, with 968 delegates voting "yes.")

Although no other party has gone so far as the Spanish or Swedish parties in abandoning democratic centralism, others have gone through periods of debate and openness. In France the French Communist Party has long exemplified the orthodox model of democratic centralism. Following the 1974 presidential election, however, the Party leadership opened the Party press to grass-roots criticism and opinion. There was no hint of pluralism at the Party's Twenty-Second Congress in 1976, however, as all proposals were accepted without dissent. Since the March 1978 elections, however, the PCF has been shaken by a wide-ranging internal debate taking place within the Party. Apparently, a significant number of intellectuals have been joined by rank and file militants in questioning the leadership's conduct of the election campaign. In response, the Party's Central Committee has reasserted the correctness of its line and refused to open the door to a real debate.

On a number of occasions, the Italian Communist Party has experienced lively internal debate. Although sometimes the debate has been touched by bitterness, most of it has been calm and even constructive. The hallmark of the PCI's internal organizational posture is conciliation.[68]

Other notable exceptions to democratic centralism have included the early 1969 debate in Austria over the KPÖ's reaction to the Czechoslovakian crisis, a similar, long-running debate in Finland's SKP, and controversies in the Norwegian Party over Furubotn's purge and the ouster of the Vogt groups from leadership positions in 1967, as well as the recent party merger debate.

Fifth, a number of parties have seen a decline in the importance of the cell. In Italy, since World War II, the cell has declined in importance in the structure of the Italian Communist Party and is being replaced by the section. From 1950 to 1963, cells decreased from 54,000 to 33,000 and sections increased from 10,200 in 1951 to 11,000 in 1961.[69] In Sweden the VPK went so far as to openly devalue the cell in the 1960s in favor of the district. Moreover, in Spain Party leader Santiago Carrillo says that in the future his party will end the cellular structure.[70]

Finally, in Italy there are marked differences between the form the PCI takes in the North and the form it takes in the South. In the North, the Party is a mass party largely based on industrial workers and the factory cell. In the South, however, the Communist Party lacks a strong membership base and is composed mainly of poor peasants and agricultural workers.

The party at its best in the South is in fine a subtle set of ties among diverse and ill-defined social groups, working in various ways to promote unity and modernization. At its worst, unity appears in the shape of alliances with backward groups and modernization takes the form of appeals for mass patronage.[71]

Notes

1. In this study, the terms *reformist* and *progressive* are used to refer to policies that go beyond orthodox Communist analysis and prescription. For example, acceptance of private enterprise, the EEC, NATO, and individual rights and liberties are examples of reformist and progressive policies, as is the rejection of the doctrine of the dictatorship of the proletariat. On the other hand, *hard-line* and *conservative* policies are those reflecting traditional Communist analysis. Themes such as the pauperization of the proletariat and an emphasis on monopoly capitalism and imperialism as the cause of all of the West's problems are examples. Finally, the terms *revolutionary* and *non-revolutionary* refer to proclivities toward extralegal violence directed toward the overthrow of the established government.

2. Annie Kriegel, *The French Communists: Profile of a People,* trans. Elaine P. Halperin (Chicago: University of Chicago, 1972; first pub. 1968).

3. *Yearbook on International Communist Affairs* (Stanford: Hoover Institution, various years), hereafter YICA; Witold S. Sworakowski, *World Communism: A Handbook, 1918-1965* (Stanford: Hoover Institution, 1973).

4. The presidential election of June 1976 was a less reliable measure than the April 1976 parliamentary election, since in the latter balloting, the strength of the Left was divided by the candidacy of radical Major Otelo Saraiva de Carvalho.

5. The KKE Exterior now prefers to be known simply as the KKE. To avoid confusion we will continue calling it KKE Exterior, however.

6. From January 1970 until the September 1971 election, the Party did hold one seat in parliament because of the defection of Hanne Reintoft from the Socialist People's Party.

7. The London *Times,* 11 January 1974, reports that 10 percent of union posts are controlled by the Communist Party.

8. See Togliatti's call for continued collaboration of "democratic forces": *Rinascita,* January-February 1947.

9. Which the Communists vilified. *L'Humanité,* 2 October 1938.

10. "Déclaration commune de la FGDS et du PCF," 24 February 1968.

11. *Programme commun de gouvernement du Parti communiste et du Parti socialiste* (Paris: Editions sociales, 1972).

12. Alain Duhamel, "Le parti communiste et l'élection présidentielle," *Revue française de science politique* XVI, no. 3 (June 1966): 539-47. But not in the 1969 presidential election. Jean Ranger, "L'Electorat communiste dans l'élection présidentielle de 1969," *Revue française de science politique* XX, no. 2 (April 1970): 282-311.

13. See Ian Campbell, "The French Communists and the Union of the Left: 1974-76," *Parliamentary Affairs* XXIX, no. 3 (Summer 1976): 246-63.

14. Of 251 French cities with a population of 30,000 or more, the Left presented common lists in all but 15.

15. *Mundo Obrero,* 25 July 1956; Santiago Carrillo, *Después de Franco, ¿que?* (Paris, 1965); *Demain l'Espagne* (Paris, 1974); *L'Humanité,* 6 May 1970, 3 December 1970.

16. *New York Times,* 5 May 1976.

17. *O Diario,* 3 August 1976; *Le Monde,* 3 August 1977, 30 August 1977.

18. "Manifest van de CPN," *De Waarheid,* 1 September 1972.

19. For present position, see Aarne Saarinen, "The Strategic Aim of the Finnish Communists," *World Marxist Review* XVIII, no. 9 (September 1975): 93-95.

20. British Communist Party (BCP), *The British Road to Socialism* (London: BCP, 1951).

21. Kenneth Newton, *The Sociology of British Communism* (London: Penguin, 1969), p. 154.

22. *Le Monde,* 19 July 1977; *British Road to Socialism,* rev. ed. (1977).

23. Thomas R. Bates, "Antonio Gramsci and the Bolshevization of the PCI," *Journal of Contemporary History* XI, nos. 2-3 (July 1976): 115-31.

24. Quoted in Giorgio Galli, "Italian Communism," pp. 310-83, in William E. Griffith, ed., *Communism in Europe,* Vol. I (Cambridge: MIT, 1965), p. 305.

25. *Trent'anni di vita e lotta del PCI* (Rome: Rinascita, 1952), p. 203.

26. *Rinascita,* July 1947; *Due anni di lotta dei Communisti Italiani* (Rome: La Stampa Moderna, 1947), p. 3.

27. *Rinascita,* July 1956.

28. "Il XX Congresso de PCUS," pp. 27-72, in Palmiro Togliatti, *Problemi del movimento operaio internazionale 1956-1961* (Rome: Editori Riuniti, 1962), pp. 58-59.

29. Fabrizio Onofri, "Un inammissibile attacco alla politica del partito comunida italiani," *Rinascita,* July 1956, pp. 365-69; Palmiro Togliatti, "La realta dei fatti e della nostra azione rintuzza l'irresponsabile disfattismo," *Problemi del movimento,* pp. 369-72.

30. Togliatti pointed to sectarian challenge: "Togliatti's Report to the Congress," pp. 8-14, in *The Eighth Congress of the Italian Communist*

Party, Dec., 1956 (Rome: Foreign Section of the Italian Communist Party, 1957).

31. *L'Unità*, 27 September 1957.

32. "La via italiana al socialismo," in Togliatti, *Problemi del movimento*.

33. *L'Unità*, 20 January 1957; Maurice Thorez, *Cahiers du Communisme*, May 1957, pp. 657-86.

34. Palmiro Togliatti, "Sugli orienatamenti politici del nostro partito," *Rinascita*, November 1959.

35. Mario Gozzini, *Il dialogo alla prova: Cattolici e communisti italiana* (Florence: Vallecchi editore, 1964); "Report on the Debate of the Central Committee of the PCI on the Twenty-Second Congress of the CPSU," *New Left Review* XIII-XIV (April-June 1962): 152-92.

36. Palmiro Togliatti, *Promemoria* in *Rinascita*, September 1964, p. 1.

37. Sidney G. Tarrow, "Political Dualism and Italian Communism," *American Political Science Review* LXI, no. 1 (January 1967): 39-53.

38. Arrigo Levi, "Berlinguer's Communism," *Survey* XVIII, no 3 (Summer 1972): 1-15; *New York Times*, 12 January 1975, 28 February 1976.

39. *Le Monde*, 10-11 October 1976.

40. *Mundo Obrero*, 25 July 1956.

41. *Le Monde*, 23-24 April 1978.

42. *L'Humanité*, 6 August 1976.

43. *Le Monde*, 13 October 1976.

44. YICA, various years; Louis van Geyt, "Communal and Power Crisis in Belgium," *World Marxist Review* XVII, no. 9 (September 1974): 73-82; *Le Drapeau Rouge*, 9, 15, 25-26 January 1975, 6 March 1975, 10 April 1975.

45. YICA, 1976, 1977.

46. Georges Lavau, "Le parti communiste dans le systeme politique français," pp. 7-55, in Frédéric Bon, ed., *Le communisme en France*, Cahiers de la fondation nationale des sciences politiques, 175 (Paris: Armand Colin, 1969), pp. 75-77.

47. Jean Touchard, "Introduction a l'ideologie du Parti communiste français," pp. 83-106, in Bon, ibid. He uses six phases; we divide one of his phases in two and add an eighth to update the typology.

48. Daniel R. Brower, *The New Jacobins: The French Communist Party and the Popular Front* (Ithaca: Cornell, 1968).

49. See Roger Garaudy, ed., *Démocratie et liberté* (Paris, 1966): "Manifeste du Parti communiste français: Pour une démocratie avancée, pour une France socialiste" (Paris: Editions sociales, 1969). On the question of multi-partism: *Cahiers du communisme*, July-August 1959, p. 535; ibid., June 1961, pp. 67-68; ibid., June-July 1964, pp. 522-24. On the alternation

of power, see among others: *Le Monde,* 31 January-1 February 1971, 12 June 1971, 26 June 1971; and *Programme commun.*

50. *Programme commun.*

51. For an elaboration of the Party's new reformist positions, see Georges Marchais, *Le défi démocratique* (Paris: Grasset, 1973).

52. *Le Monde,* 5 February 1976.

53. YICA, 1975.

54. *New York Times,* 5 May 1976.

55. Ibid., 4 July 1976, 8 July 1976.

56. YICA, 1969, 1970.

57. YICA, 1976.

58. P. Erickson, "Congress of the Danish Communists," *World Marxist Review* IX, no. 1 (January 1966): 66-68.

59. YICA, 1975. See also Ib Nørlund, "The Search for New Ways and Fidelity to Principle," *World Marxist Review* XVII, no. 12 (December 1974): 52-59.

60. See *Land og Folk,* 13 February 1975.

61. YICA, 1975; *Morning Star,* 18 June 1975; Michael O'Riordan, "Inspiring Changes," *World Marxist Review* XXII, no. 5 (May 1974): 48-49.

62. YICA, 1968.

63. YICA, 1975, 1977.

64. Franz Muhri, "A Democratic and Socialist Alternative for Austria," *World Marxist Review* XXII, no. 5 (April 1974): 16-23.

65. YICA, 1975.

66. McInnes deals with the issue of organization in more detail. Neil McInnes, *The Communist Parties of Western Europe* (London: Oxford, 1975).

67. Kevin Devlin, "Prospects for Communism in Western Europe," pp. 16-69, in R. V. Burks, ed., *The Future of Communism in Western Europe,* Franklin Memorial Lectures, XVII (Detroit: Wayne State, 1968), p. 29.

68. John Barth Urban, "Italian Communism and the 'Opportunism of Conciliation,' 1927-1929," *Studies in Comparative Communism* VI, no. 4 (Winter 1973): 362-96.

69. Tarrow, "Political Dualism," p. 41.

70. *L'Humanité,* 6 August 1976.

71. Sidney J. Tarrow, *Peasant Communism in Southern Italy* (New Haven: Yale, 1967), p. 267.

chapter 2

DIVERSITY IN THE INTERNATIONAL ARENA

In March 1919, Lenin founded the Third International as an agency to bring about world revolution. With the failure of the revolution to spread beyond the borders of Russia, however, the Comintern was transformed into a vehicle for legitimizing Communist rule in Russia and a tool through which the world's Communist parties could be transformed into instruments of Soviet foreign policy. After the Fifth Comintern Congress in 1924, the Comintern ceased having any semblance to the relatively open discussion body that Lenin had envisaged. Rather, it became an agency of Soviet control and Stalin instructed all of the world's Communist parties to adopt the Russian Bolshevik model. Throughout most of the interwar period, Moscow insisted on complete control over member sections of the Comintern, down to minor details of policy.

In the early days, the Soviets won this control in many cases through direct intervention backed up by the enormous prestige of the Soviet Union as the world's first Socialist state. Moscow was not above giving orders or directing purges to win its will. With the dismantling of the Comintern in 1943 and the emergence of mass Communist parties in a number of Western European countries in the wake of World War II, Moscow's potential for direct interference was limited. Its capacity for indirect control based on the Soviet Union's prestige as the Socialist Fatherland remained great and, augmented by the Cominform after 1947, Moscow continued to exercise considerable direction during the early postwar and Cold War eras.

Since 1956, however, the international Communist movement has been shaken to its foundations by a series of crises and its unity has been shattered. First came Khrushchev's "secret speech" at the Twentieth Congress of the CPSU, revealing and condemning the crimes of Stalin. Then, in rapid succession, came Hungary, the shifts in the Soviet line toward Yugoslavia, the excommunication of Albania, the Sino-Soviet split, the ouster of Khrushchev, the Sinyavsky-Daniel trials, and, in 1968, the Soviet-led invasion of Czechoslovakia.

Before 1956 Communists (save for the Yugoslavs) and anti-Communists alike agreed on one point: Soviet Russia incarnated the cause of Communism. For many this ceased to be true after 1960. For others Czechoslovakia 1968 shattered the last illusions. No longer was there a single world movement with a center in Moscow, but several movements with centers in Peking, Belgrade, Havana, and, perhaps, Rome.

In the face of the crises of international Communism, the Communist parties of Western Europe have responded differently, ranging from traditional adherence to the Soviet Union to independent action.

Luxembourg

Although events of the last twenty years have gravely jarred international Communism, the faith of the Communist Party of Luxembourg has remained unshaken—by de-Stalinization, by Hungary, by the Sino-Soviet rift, or even by the events in Czechoslovakia.[1] Historically, the PCL has been an uncritical supporter of the Soviet Union and the Party has never wavered from that pattern. In 1968 the PCL was the only legal Western European Communist party to approve the Soviet intervention in Czechoslovakia.

Concerning the international Communist movement, the Luxembourg Party has unstintingly supported the leadership of the Communist Party of the Soviet Union (CPSU) against all possible rivals, even attacking C.H. Hermansson, the former leader of the Swedish Communist Party, for his independent attitude. On the Chinese issue, the PCL has been a persistent and harsh critic of Peking, loyally backing the efforts of the CPSU to isolate China within the movement and endorsed Moscow's call for a new world conference to excommunicate the Chinese.

West Germany

Another strong supporter of the Soviet Union in Western Europe is the West German Communist Party. After its birth in December 1918, the KPD was the object of Moscow's careful attention and the German Party became the model for Comintern policy in Western Europe.

Since World War II, the German Party has remained faithful to Moscow. During the early years of the Bonn Republic, during its fugitive period from 1956 to 1968 (after being declared illegal by the Federal Constitutional Court), and since its reconstitution as the legal DKP in September 1968, the Communist Party of West Germany has had very close ties with both the East German Communist Party and the CPSU. Unequivocally, the DKP has supported the Soviet intervention in Czechoslovakia and all other Soviet and East German positions concerning international affairs. Apropos the Sino-Soviet split, the West German Party has steadfastly adhered to the Soviet position, condemning the Chinese heresy in no uncertain terms, and the Party strongly supported the Soviet initiative for a world conference to condemn the Chinese.

Portugal

Throughout its history, the Portuguese Communist Party has loyally adhered to the leadership of the Soviet Union. On every issue of international importance—Hungary in 1956, Yugoslavia, de-Stalinization, the Sino-Soviet rift, the ouster of Khrushchev, the Czechoslovakian invasion, and many others—the PCP has taken Moscow's side. Frequently, the Party has attacked the Chinese and the PCP has been in the forefront of those calling for world conferences to isolate Peking. Moreover, Portuguese Communist leader

Cunhal has a personal relationship with Soviet Party Chairman Brezhnev,[2] and the Soviet Union, according to a CIA estimate, sends the PCP about $10 million a month.[3]

Ireland

Founded at the behest of Moscow in 1933, the Irish Communist Party has generally supported the Soviet Union's international positions. The CPI has endorsed Soviet initiatives toward détente and has stood behind Moscow in its dispute with the Chinese. At the world conference that took place in Moscow in June 1969, the CPI solidly endorsed CPSU positions. Then in 1974 Michael O'Riordan, the Party chairman, saluted the record of the 1969 conference and implied support for a new conference.[4]

The Irish Party's record of support for the Soviet Union has not, however, been unblemished. In 1968 the CPI stood among most other Western European Communist parties in deploring the Warsaw Pact invasion of Czechoslovakia. Subsequent actions, however, indicate that the CPI's break with Moscow in 1968 was an exception rather than the rule. Currently, the CPI does not hesitate to use phrases associated with Soviet hegemony of the Communist movement.

Denmark

For decades after its founding, the DKP was a loyal supporter of Moscow. In 1956, however, the Party was shaken by the twin shocks of de-Stalinization and Hungary, followed by the gyrations of Soviet policy toward Yugoslavia. For Axel Larsen, the leader of the DKP, the inconsistencies of the Moscow line were too much. After the Twentieth Congress of the CPSU, with its revelations about Stalin, the initiation of de-Stalinization, and the thaw toward Yugoslavia, Larsen, once a vocal admirer of Stalin, switched his position and adapted to the new line. When called upon to change positions again, however, Larsen in effect said that once was enough. He declared that the DKP should emancipate itself from Moscow and become a genuinely Danish Party. Subsequently, in October 1958, Larsen was deposed as Party leader and the less independently minded Knud Jespersen became his successor. In leaving the Party, however, Larsen took with him a considerable retinue of followers who soon founded the Socialist People's Party that subsequently outpolled the DKP.

The elimination of Larsen and his supporters did not lead to unquestioned support for the policies of the Soviet Union. The DKP criticized the Sinyavsky-Daniel trials and expressed misgivings over charges of Soviet anti-Semitism. Then in 1968 the Party stood in opposition to Soviet actions in Czechoslovakia.

Since the Czech invasion, however, the DKP has clung to the Kremlin line. Although it has not formally retracted its early criticisms, the Danish Party has apparently approved the current Husák regime in Czechoslovakia and supported the Moscow-directed "normalization" there. Also, the DKP has firmly backed the Soviet Union in its dispute with the Chinese, adhering since 1963 to a clear stand against the Peking line. Currently, the Party endorses Soviet efforts to isolate the Chinese within the world Communist movement.

Austria

Like the DKP, the Austrian Communist Party is now a strong supporter of the Soviet Union's positions. From its earliest days, the Austrian Party faithfully defended Moscow. Although its pro-Soviet orientation was somewhat marred by its criticisms of the Sinyavsky-Daniel trails, the KPÖ was among Moscow's earliest and firmest backers in the Sino-Soviet conflict.[5]

With Czechoslovakia, however, the Austrian Communist Party's generally consistent support of the Soviets wavered. Before August 1968, the KPÖ had expressed its approval of the Dubcek reforms, and when the Soviet invasion came, the Austrian Party quickly condemned it. Then at the 1969 World Conference of Communist Parties, the Austrians, along with the Italians, took the lead in asserting the independence and autonomy of each party, only signing the final document of the conference with reservations.

The KPÖ, however, was not united in its condemnation of Soviet actions in Czechoslovakia. Leading the criticism of the Soviet Union was a minority largely of intellectuals led by Franz Marek and Ernst Fischer. Opposing them was a more conservative group of veteran militants who strongly supported the Soviet Union. Between these two groups stood the Party's centrist leadership headed by Party Chairman Franz Muhri. In late 1968 and early 1969, a polemical debate between the main protagonists in the KPÖ raged in the Party press. At the Party's congress in January, the conservative group began to assert its strength and the Party began to modify its criticisms of the Soviets' actions in Czechoslovakia. By 1970 the conservatives had won a complete victory. The Marek-Fischer group was expelled from the KPÖ and the Party became a supporter of normalization in Czechoslovakia, praising the Husák regime. Currently, the international positions of the Austrian Communist Party closely reflect those of the Soviet Union.

Finland

The Finnish Communist Party has remained loyal to Moscow despite misgivings over Czechoslovakia and the complications of an intraparty split. Since the SKP was founded in August 1918, in exile near Moscow, the Finnish Communists have been closely tied to the Soviet Union, even supporting Moscow during Finland's wars with the Soviet Union. Following the armistice between Finland and the Soviet Union in 1944, the Finnish Communists continued to adhere to the Soviet line internationally. There was no real debate in the SKP over Khrushchev's "secret speech" and the Party weathered the Hungarian crisis well, endorsing Moscow's thesis. Nevertheless, the Czechoslovakian invasion of 1968 led to a public dispute between the SKP and the CPSU and to an intensification of divisions within the Finnish Party itself.

Even before the division over Czechoslovakia, there were three identifiable factions in the SKP: a group of anti-Stalinist progressives, a hard-line dogmatist faction, and, finally, a group of centrists. The Czech crisis and the SKP's reaction to it intensified and deepened the division within the Party.

Originally, the SKP endorsed the reforms initiated by the Dubcek regime in Czechoslovakia, but when it learned of the invasion, the Party cautiously withheld judgment. As events became clearer, however, the Finnish Party announced its disapproval of Soviet actions. A large section of the Party, nevertheless, remained loyal to the Soviet Union and the issue became another major bone of contention between the rival factions in the SKP.

Since 1968 the Finnish Party has not retracted its criticism of Soviet actions in Czechoslovakia, but it has minimized the original differences and returned to a generally pro-Soviet posture.[6] The SKP has been a strong ally of the Soviet Union in its disputes with China and an equally loyal proponent of Moscow's policy of international détente. Also, the Party strongly endorsed Moscow's call for a new world conference.

Switzerland

In Switzerland the PdA's traditional loyalty to the Soviet Union has been tempered by dissent over the Soviet-led invasion of Czechoslovakia. In its early history and later development, the PdA was strongly pro-Soviet. Although de-Stalinization became an object of internal contention, the Swiss Communist Party remained closely allied to Soviet positions. In 1968, however, the PdA blamed the Soviet Union for the invasion of Czechoslovakia and began a series of uninhibited criticisms that extended into 1969. At the June 1969 World Conference of Communist Parties, the PdA was among those who signed the final conference document only with reservations.

Since 1969 the Swiss Party has avoided references to the Czech invasion and has returned to alignment with general Soviet policies, including support of the Soviet Union in its dispute with the Chinese. Finally, the PdA has developed strong bilateral ties with the Italian Communist Party.

Belgium

In its earliest days, the Communist Party of Belgium was split between Trotskyist and Stalinist factions, but after the demise of the former in the late 1920s, the PCB closely followed the Soviet line. The Party zigzagged with the Soviet line from 1939 to 1941 and dutifully supported Moscow's Cold War positions.

Since the Czechoslovakian crisis, however, the Belgian Communist Party has moved from a position of loyal defense of the Soviet Union to one of cautious, even critical support of the views and policies of Moscow. Although the Hungarian invasion provoked defections and the Sinyavsky-Daniel trials led to some criticisms from the Belgian Party, the PCB was closely tied to the Soviets, particularly supporting Moscow's policy of peaceful coexistence and the Soviets' attacks on the Chinese. In August 1968, however, the PCB came down on the side of the Czech leaders and against the Soviets.

Following the height of the controversy over Czechoslovakia, the Belgian Communists moved both to reaffirm their ties with the Soviets and to assert their independence vis-à-vis Moscow. In 1971 Party President Marc Drumaux praised the CPSU but, at the same time, was careful verbally to maintain his own Party's autonomy. Currently, the PCB generally supports Soviet positions, but is not hesitant to offer criticisms. Although the Belgian Communists opposed the views of dissident Russian novelist Alexander Solzhenitsyn, they also opposed his expulsion from the Soviet Union.[7] In 1977 the Belgian Party expressed support for Spain's Santiago Carrillo whom Moscow had accused of "anti-Sovietism." Additionally, the PCB is somewhat more conciliatory toward the Chinese than the Soviets are.

Greece

Although the Greek Communist Party has a long history of alliance with the Soviet Union, the Party is now split and the issue of position vis-à-vis Moscow is one of the questions dividing the Party. In the early 1920s, the KKE was divided over acceptance of the Comintern's twenty-one conditions. After the 1923 parliamentary elections, however, moderates were purged and in 1924 the Party accepted the twenty-one conditions unanimously. Moreover, the KKE accepted the Soviet line on all important issues, even supporting Soviet calls for the establishment of an independent Macedonian and Thracian state, a position highly unpopular in Greece.

During the late 1920s and 1930s, the KKE was little more than an arm of the Comintern. Time and again, Moscow intervened to purge dissidents and install cadres loyal to itself. Obediently, the KKE adapted its domestic and international positions to conform with Soviet positions on Macedonia, on the Popular Front, on the Metaxas dictatorship, and on the Nazi-Soviet Pact.

Although the Greek Communists had given the Soviet Union unswerving support on all matters, they found in 1944 that they could not count on Moscow returning the favor. In November 1944, KKE leaders decided to launch a revolution. A truce ended the fighting in January 1945, but the Communists returned to the battlefield in 1946. Although the Soviets acquiesced, they made it clear that the KKE could expect no direct aid. Some supplies came from Eastern Europe, particularly Yugoslavia, but no troops were committed to the conflict and the Greek revolution was crushed.

Nevertheless, the KKE remained loyal to Moscow. It endorsed the Soviets' Cold War line and accepted the policy changes adopted at the Twentieth Congress of the CPSU. In the early 1960s, the Party joined the chorus condemning the Peking heresy.

By 1968, however, a division had developed in the KKE and the issue of the Czechoslovakian invasion widened the rift. The exiled KKE leadership firmly supported the Warsaw Pact intervention, but the clandestine EDA and many Communist leaders underground in Greece condemned the invasion. Subsequently, the Party split has deepened. The KKE Exterior clings to the Moscow line, while the Interior faction has begun copying the Italians' posture of international autonomy.

Norway

The Norwegian Communist Party has a long tradition as something of a maverick, but the NKP may now be losing touch with that tradition. In 1919 the Norwegian Labor Party joined the Third International virtually intact, but after four years of deviation, the Executive of the Comintern (ECCI) forced a split and only a minority remained to constitute the Norwegian Communist Party. The result of the massive purge was not, however, the totally compliant party that Moscow desired. Lacking ideological sophistication, the new NKP leaders frequently stumbled into error. At other times, the NKP's deviations were willful.

Although Khrushchev's secret speech denouncing Stalin precipitated something of a debate within the Norwegian Party, de-Stalinization had little immediate effect on the NKP. There was little sympathy for change among the leadership and no purges of domestic Stalinists followed.

Hungary was a greater shock for the Norwegian Communist Party, causing numerous defections. In general, the NKP assessment of the situation kept with the Soviet version of "counter-revolution," but not uncritically so.

Following the tumultuous Twenty-Second Congress of the CPSU in 1961, the Norwegians moved boldly to stake out an autonomous position for themselves in the international movement. Uncomfortable with the new emphasis on de-Stalinization, the NKP again refused to take any actions along those lines. More significantly, the Party refused to take any position on the Sino-Soviet split, but rather took a position of neutrality. Then in December 1962, the Party published an editorial declaring that each party is autonomous and independent.

Although on most major international issues (such as peaceful coexistence and the peaceful transition to Socialism) the Norwegians agreed with the Soviet Union rather than China, the NKP refused to support Moscow's tactics. The Norwegian Party called for a reconciliation, but not one that would subordinate one party to another, and sent no representative to the 1967 Karlovy Vary meeting preparatory to the world conference.

With the replacement of Khrushchev, the NKP again took the opportunity to disassociate itself from Moscow, even accusing the Soviet leadership of lying. Despite a good measure of internal dissension from Moscow loyalists within the Party, the NKP continued to stress "unity in diversity."

In 1968 the NKP vigorously attacked the Soviet-led intervention of Czechoslovakia. Then at the 1969 World Conference of Communist Parties, the Norwegian delegate, like his British counterpart, declared he had no authority to sign the final document.

Although the NKP continued its independent posture for several years after 1968, developments in 1975 may indicate a turning back toward Moscow. The Party split in 1975 over the issue of forming a single Left-wing party with its electoral alliance partners from the

last national election. Party Chairman Larsen was ousted and the
hard liners won, hard liners who lean more toward the Soviet camp
than the Larsen leadership.[8] Subsequently, the NKP has apparently
moved closer to the Soviet Union internationally.

France

The French Communist Party has long been one of Moscow's
most loyal and staunchest defenders in Western Europe, so loyal
and so staunch as to prompt Guy Mollet to declare "*le Parti
communiste n'est pas à gauche, il est à l'Est*" (The Communist Party
is not so much to the Left as it is to the East). Although before 1924
the PCF evinced considerable independence from Moscow, after
the Party's Bolshevization, it was barely independent, but rather a
section of the International, with French leaders making frequent
pilgrimages to Moscow where administrative problems and electoral tactics were discussed and often decided. Time and again, the
French Party changed its position to conform with somersaults in
Soviet policy toward class against class in 1928, the Popular Front
in 1934, the Nazi-Soviet Pact in 1939, the outbreak of war in 1939,
and the German invasion of the Soviet Union in 1941. But it was
not necessarily a process of the Comintern simply issuing orders
(although orders sometimes were issued). On many questions, Moscow gave no directions or the meaning of the instructions was
unclear. The Comintern's authority was thus somewhat akin to the
"law and the prophets," absolute, but hermetic.[9]

After World War II, the French Communist Party was less
directly under tutelage to the Soviet Communist Party.[10] Nevertheless, during the Cold War years, the PCF's support of Moscow
and opposition to the Western alliance was inflexible. In this setting, the PCF greeted the events of 1956 with uneasiness. The first
reaction of the PCF to Khrushchev's "secret speech" was careful,
even apologetic toward Stalin. Cautiously, the PCF called for a
"thorough Marxist analysis to determine all the circumstances under which Stalin was able to exercise his personal power. . . ."[11]
Later, the Party took a position critical of Stalin, but made a
distinction between the Soviet Union, which should head the movement, and its leaders, who were fallible. As for the rehabilitation of

Tito, the PCF accepted it only grudgingly. In sum, the French Party was very uncomfortable with the new course of de-Stalinization outlined at the Twentieth Congress of the CPSU. Although the PCF accepted the new Soviet line, its immediate effects on the operation of the Party were few.

The Hungarian invasion was an international crisis with which the PCF could more comfortably deal. Although the events in Hungary in the fall of 1956 visibly shook the Communist movement in many Western European countries, in France there was relatively little dissension within the Party. One deputy, Aimé Césaire from Martinique, resigned; and a number of critical intellectuals—Jacques-Francis Rolland, Claude Roy, Roger Vailland, and others—were expelled, but the bulk of the PCF remained loyal to the Party. The PCF was weakened, but not as seriously shaken as other parties in the West. Confident of the loyalty of the majority of its cadres and *apparat,* the PCF was in the forefront of those who encouraged the Soviets to handle events in Hungary with firmness.

For the next decade, the PCF continued its loyal support of the Soviet Union.[12] No Western party was more critical of the Chinese and no party more firmly backed the Soviets' call for an international conference of Communist parties to read the Chinese out of the international movement. On all principal questions, in the early 1960s, the PCF displayed a striking degree of solidarity with the CPSU.

Czechoslovakia was another matter. Initially, the reaction of the French Communist Party to Soviet intervention in Czechoslovakia was one of "surprise and reprobation."[13] The reaction of Party intellectual Roger Garaudy was more harsh. A "return to Stalinism both in theory and in practice," he declared.[14] Although Garaudy had supporters, particularly among intellectuals, a large group in the PCF remained loyal to the Soviet Union. Jeannett Thorez-Vermeersch, widow of Maurice Thorez, the long-time leader of the PCF, even resigned from the Politburo in protest over the Party's opposition to the Soviet actions in Czechoslovakia.

Although the PCF never retracted its criticisms of the invasion, it quickly moved to soften their impact and shore up its ties with the Soviet Union. After the initial shock lessened, the "reprobation" originally expressed by the Party became "regret." Finally, the PCF saluted "*l'accord*" between Moscow and the Czech government. Garaudy was censured by the Politburo for his remarks and, in 1970, expelled from the Party along with several other dissident intellectuals.[15] Subsequently, the Party supported the Soviets' efforts to reunite the international movement and endorsed the current Czech regime.

After 1968 the PCF maintained its traditional loyalty to the Soviet Union, but, at the same time, it affirmed a strong French nationalist orientation. Although the French Party endorsed Moscow's handling of the Solzhenitsyn affair, it objected to Soviet indications of support for Giscard in the 1974 French presidential election campaign.

In recent years, however, the French Communists have taken a series of steps that have moved them closer to the Italian Communists' position of international independence. In November 1975, the PCF and PCI joined in a commmon declaration insisting on the independence of each national party. At the same time, they demanded that the conference of European Communist parties proposed by Moscow be limited to questions of peace and détente in Europe rather than the expulsion of the Chinese—an action that could reunite world Communism under Soviet authority. Then at the Twenty-First Congress of the CPSU in February 1976, Enrico Berlinguer and Gaston Plissonnier, speaking for the Italian and French Communists respectively, defended their Parties' theses of Communist pluralism directly to the faces of their Soviet comrades. Notably, Georges Marchais boycotted the Congress, criticizing Soviet suppression of dissidents as "unjust" and "unjustifiable" acts of repression against Soviet citizens.[16] At the East Berlin Conference of European Communist Parties held in June 1976, the PCF took a stand with its Spanish, Yugoslav, Romanian, and Italian brethren, in particular, declaring the independence of each party from Soviet dominance. Moreover, Marchais used the forum of the conference to reprove the Soviets for failing to attack capitalism strongly enough.

The Netherlands

Although once closely tied to the CPSU, the Dutch Communist Party has moved first to a position of autonomy, then to a position of isolation in the international Communist movement, and now back toward a policy of participation. After an early factional period (into which the Comintern intervened), the CPN became a loyal follower of the Soviet Union and from its Bolshevization around 1925 until after World War II, the Dutch Party was little more than a noisy mimic of Moscow.

Khrushchev's secret speech at the Twentieth CPSU Congress, however, proved to be a bombshell for the Dutch Communists. Although the Party leadership only half-heartedly accepted de-Stalinization and enthusiastically acclaimed the Hungarian intervention, the events of 1956 kindled a brush fire of dissension within the Party ranks. Part of this dissension took the form of an oppositionist party that contested the 1959 elections against the CPN, but most of the opposition—Stalinist, revisionist, Maoist—stayed within the ranks of the Party.

In the face of the division within the CPN, the Party walked a tightrope on the Sino-Soviet dispute, criticizing first one side and then the other and resisting Soviet pressures for a showdown conference to deal with the Chinese heresy.

At the Twenty-First Congress of the Dutch Communist Party in 1964, the CPN adopted a more autonomous position. Under the leadership of Paul de Groot and his successors, this policy of independence increasingly became one of international isolation. In 1967 de Groot denounced Soviet interference into the internal affairs of the Dutch Party and the CPN refused to send representatives to the preparatory meeting to the proposed world conference held at Karlovy Vary, Czechoslovakia. The Dutch sent no one to the celebration of the Fiftieth Anniversary of the Revolution held in Moscow and even discouraged rank and file members from traveling in Communist countries. By the time of its own congress in December 1967, the CPN was virtually isolated as delegates from abroad were conspicuously absent.

Despite its near isolation and vigilance against outside interference, the CPN was not reticent about criticizing other Communist parties and Communist states. In 1968 the Dutch Party roundly condemned the Czechoslovakian invasion and, keeping with its policy, refused to attend the 1969 World Conference to reunite the movement. De Groot himself took the Soviets to task for the German-Soviet Pact of 1939 (which, of course, he supported at the time) and the treatment of Soviet Jews. In 1972 the Soviet and Dutch parties indulged in a bitter polemic over de Groot's positions, which, despite a long attack in *Pravda*, the CPN reaffirmed as its own. In 1974 the CPN vigorously condemned Moscow's handling of the Solzhenitsyn affair and adamantly opposed the call for a new world conference.

In the last few years, however, the CPN has been edging back toward active participation in the international movement. In 1975 the CPN backed the Portuguese Communist Party without reservation. Such an identification with another party was quite unusual for the diffident Dutch Communists. Also, a representative from the CPN showed up at the last minute in East Berlin in June 1976 for the European Conference of Communist Parties (where, incidentally, the CPN criticized Comrade Brezhnev for attacking Peking). In October 1976, the CPN was represented at a conference of Western European Communist parties organized to study agricultural problems. Then in April 1977, the CPN sent an official delegation to the Soviet Union for the first time in fourteen years. A communiqué published in Moscow said that the two parties have the same points of view on international problems.[17]

Italy

From its founding in 1921, the Italian Communist Party was closely tied to the Communist Party of the Soviet Union (despite a healthy measure of independent thinking on the part of the PCI). Indeed, were it not for Soviet assistance the PCI would likely not have survived the long period of Fascist-imposed illegality. Since 1956, however, the PCI has moved sometimes cautiously, sometimes resolutely, toward a position of autonomy and independence vis-à-vis the Soviet Union.

The shock of Khrushchev's rude destruction of the Stalin myth provided the political and psychological basis for a gradual restructuring of the Italian Communists' relations with the Soviet Union. In an interview in *Nuovi Argomenti*, Party leader Togliatti discussed the problems raised by the revelations of the Twentieth CPSU Congress, declaring that the sins of Stalin should not be regarded as the result of one man's weakness, but that the Soviet system itself must share the guilt.[18] Boldly continuing, Togliatti asserted the following:

The Soviet model should no longer be obligatory. . . . The complex of the system is becoming polycentric, and in the Communist movement itself one can no longer speak of a single guide.[19]

Later, in June at the PCI Central Committee meeting, Togliatti reemphasized polycentrism.[20] Although in the West, Togliatti's position on polycentrism was seen as something akin to a declaration of independence from the Soviet Union, more realistically, it was less a call for change than an assessment by Togliatti of what he saw as objective reality.

In any case, Moscow was not amused. On June 30, 1956, *Pravda* carried an editorial critical of Togliatti. In response, Togliatti took a hard line against the riots in Poland and moved to quiet criticism of the Soviet Union within his own Party.[21]

Hungary, too, was a shock for the PCI. In response, the Party adopted a pro-Soviet position, but not inflexibly so. Unlike the Soviets (and the French Communists), the PCI refrained from emphasizing the role of a counterrevolutionary underground, and within the ranks of the Party itself, there was considerable support for the insurgents. Despite these misgivings and the *Nuovi Argomenti* article, the PCI in the fall of 1956 remained a supporter of the Soviet Union.

After a period of relative calm, the renewed de-Stalinization push at the Twenty-Second Congress of the CPSU in October 1961 unleashed all of the forces of division within the PCI. The debate in the Party was harsh and bitter with criticisms of the institutions and practices of the Soviet Union being constantly reiterated. Reformers and moderates easily won the upper hand in the PCI and the concept of polycentrism was revived.

In the last years of his life, Togliatti led the PCI in open and active resistance to some aspects of Soviet policy. In September 1964, the Party attacked Soviet cultural policy.[22] The Italian Communists strongly defended cultural liberty in respect to the arts, literature, and religion,[23] and attacked the Soviets for their censorship of *Dr. Zhivago*[24] and repression of individuals. In the Sino-Soviet dispute, although the PCI condemned the hard-line positions of the Chinese,[25] the Party, rather than unreservedly backing the Soviets, called for a compromise and a toning down of rhetoric. In October 1963, the PCI explicity opposed the CPSU's call for a world conference to deal with the Chinese and reaffirmed that position in 1964.[26] Although the Italians opposed the ideological position of the Chinese,[27] they also opposed any effort by the Soviets to reestablish hegemony in the international movement—a hegemony that would reduce their own freedom of action.

Thus, the PCI clung stubbornly (and successfully) to its position of "unity in diversity." The success of the world movement, the Italians asserted, depended upon the development of qualitatively different relationships among component parts. Autonomy, the Italians argued, "means, and ought to mean, full respect for the principle of noninterference by any party in the internal affairs of other parties, but allowing for necessary debate and confrontation of opinion."[28]

One of the boldest efforts of Togliatti to establish the autonomy of his Party appeared posthumously when, in the face of Soviet opposition, the PCI published a document prepared by Togliatti before his death in the fall of 1964. Togliatti's "Testament," as it was called, was a manifesto of reformist Italian Communism. In it Togliatti, speaking for the PCI, refused to accept collective mobilization in regard to the Sino-Soviet dispute, rejected excommunication of the Chinese, and criticized the slowness of de-Stalinization in the Soviet Union.[29]

Togliatti's successors were no less independently minded than he, criticizing both the manner in which the ouster of Khrushchev was handled and the harsh verdicts handed down against Daniel and Sinyavsky.[30] Firmly, the PCI continued to stress each party's autonomy.

In 1968 the PCI deplored the Soviet-led invasion of Czechoslovakia as unjustified.[31] Long sympathetic to liberalization in Eastern Europe, the Italian Communists held firm to their condemnation despite official adverse Soviet reaction. The PCI unequivocally rejected the Brezhnev Doctrine, which the Soviets used to defend their intervention in Czechoslovakia:

We do not admit that the sovereignty of a socialist country can be in conflict with its "class and internationalist" character. Sovereignty is an unalienable right. For us, this is not an abstract interpretation, but a value which we cannot renounce.[32]

Then at the June 1969 World Conference of Communist Parties, which the Italians agreed to attend only on the stipulation that no party (i.e., the Chinese) would be read out of the movement, the PCI publicly criticized the Soviets for their handling of the Czech affair and refused to sign all but one noncontroversial section of the final document. Berlinguer, speaking for the PCI, denied that there "can be a single model for socialist society." Unity, he asserted, "can only be based on an appreciation of the original and creative capability of every national community and party."[33]

Since 1968 the PCI has maintained its autonomous position. Although on most international issues, the CPSU and PCI agree, on certain important questions the Italians have continued to express opinions at variance with the Soviets. On Czechoslovakia the PCI has reaffirmed its original dissent and augmented it with criticisms of normalization there. On the Sino-Soviet split, the PCI has refused to agree to an expulsion or isolation of the Chinese, even hinting at possible *rapprochement* between Peking and the Western European Communist parties.[34] On Soviet domestic policies, the Italians have criticized the treatment of Solzhenitsyn and Soviet Jews.[35] To the visible irritation of Moscow, the PCI has rapidly moved to disassociate itself from the activities of the Portuguese Communist Party.

In 1976 the PCI continued its independent line. First, at the Twenty-Fifth Congress of the CPSU in February, Berlinguer boldly outlined his Party's *Via Italiana* and strongly argued his Party's position of independence. At the very center of Soviet authority, Berlinguer spelled out his Party's views: membership in NATO, support for a "pluralist and democratic" system, cooperation with diverse ideologies at home, and support for individual liberties.[36] Then at the East Berlin Conference of European Communist Parties, Berlinguer again took the opportunity to declare his Party's independence. He reiterated the PCI's policy of international autonomy, criticizing Soviet actions in Czechoslovakia and reaffirming his Party's support of a pluralistic political structure.[37]

In 1977 the PCI continued its independent line, even recognizing Eastern European, particularly Czechoslovakian, dissidents. Moreover, the Italian Communists voiced support for Santiago Carrillo, the Spanish Communist leader, who was under criticism from the Soviets.

Great Britain

The international posture of the Communist Party of Great Britain has been marked by sharp contrasts. Although the British Communist Party is now independent of Moscow, its early years were marked by almost slavish submission to the Comintern, which had played a dominant role in its founding and organization. Moscow's supervision of the CPGB extended even to matters of detail, and in 1923 the whole of the Executive Committee was called to Moscow for instructions. When in 1929 some of the leaders of the British Party were reluctant to follow the Comintern line, they were replaced.

The ultraloyalty of the British Communist Party extended well beyond World War II, but in 1956 the twin shock of the Twentieth Congress and Hungary gravely shook the CPGB and severely strained its relations with Moscow. In the mid-fifties, there was a rising tide of discontent within the British Party, and the realization of the tyranny of the Stalinist system sank in. Against this background of rising unhappiness came the shattering events of 1956: the revelations of Stalin's "errors," the Poznan riots in Poland, and Hungary. Scores of militants in the CPGB voted with their feet and among those who remained, many unleashed severe criticisms against the Soviet Union.

The events of 1956 triggered the crystallization of an opposition within the British Communist Party against blind loyalty to the Soviet Union. Although the British Party remained pro-Soviet in orientation, it was no longer an uncritical loyalty. The CPGB was the first West European party to criticize the Daniel-Sinyavsky trials, and it also censured the Soviets for anti-Semitism.[38] Although the British were severely critical of the Chinese cultural revolution, they were also reserved toward the Soviet Union.

If Hungary had shaken the ties between the CPGB and the CPSU, Czechoslovakia shattered them. Immediately, the Party press called the Soviet-led invasion a "mistake"[39] and despite the presence of a sizable minority of Moscow supporters in the Party ranks, the British Communist Party extended and expanded its criticisms of the invasion. First, it opposed Moscow's call for a world conference of Communist parties to reunite the movement in the wake of the brouhaha over Czechoslovakia and the Sino-Soviet split. Then, when the conference was held in June 1969, the British Party refused to sign the final document and explicitly criticized the Soviet handling of Czechoslovakia. Finally, since the conference, the CPGB has not hesitated to condemn normalization in Czechoslovakia and has engaged in polemics with the Soviets over the issue.

Moreover, the British Party has continued moving away from the Moscow line. In January 1976 the CPGB published a statement in *Marxism Today* titled "Socialist Democracy—Some Problems." It is a firm attempt to disassociate the Party from the Soviet Union, and it attacks Soviet treatment of dissidents and Jews. In June-July at the East Berlin Conference, the British Communists joined with comrades from Western and Eastern Europe in asserting their parties' international autonomy. Finally, a new program, adopted by the Party Congress in November 1977, pronounced total independence from Moscow and supported the cause of Soviet dissidents.

Sweden

The Swedish Communist Party has seldom been an uncritical imitator of the Kremlin line, and since the early 1960s, it has attempted to break out of its domestic isolation by following a policy of independence from Moscow. From the time it joined the Third International in 1919 until 1929, the Swedish Party was characterized by splits, purges, and defiance of Comintern wishes. Even after 1930, when the Party became more submissive to Moscow, the Swedish Communists were not blind copycats of Soviet policy. Nevertheless, after World War II, the Party was essentially conformist to Soviet views.

As it was for other Western European Communist parties, 1956 proved to be a significant year for the Swedish Communist Party. Although it easily accepted the concept of peaceful coexistence,

Khrushchev's denunciation of Stalin was a blow for the Swedish Party, whose leadership and bureaucracy were compromised. Hungary added to the Party's woes and the two events, de-Stalinization and Hungary, spurred an internal debate.

By 1962 the long-simmering discussion of the Party's national role and its international ties became a debate, much of which was aired in the Party newspaper, *Ny Dag.* One faction called for a "nationalist" approach with concentration on Swedish issues and independence from Moscow, while another group in the Party held to Stalinist positions. At the Party's Twentieth Congress in early 1963, the dispute reached something of a climax. Although the old guard dominated the congress and elected a majority to the Central Committee, the "nationalist" elements won a major concession with the appointment of C.H. Hermansson, the moderate editor of *Ny Dag,* as Party chairman.

Despite his rather tenuous position, Hermansson moved quickly to give his Party a new image. Missing no opportunity to demonstrate his Party's independence, the new Party chairman lost no time in criticizing the foreign and internal policies of the Soviet Union, attacking the manner of Khrushchev's removal and softening the Swedish Party's support for Moscow in the Sino-Soviet split.

Buoyed by electoral gains and a bright personal image, Hermansson solidified his reformist position at the Party's Twenty-First Congress in 1967, which adopted a new program outlining a reformist domestic policy and an independent international posture. In spite of a hard core of oldtime Stalinists, the renamed "Left Party—Communist" moved to implement its autonomous international position by assuming a neutral position on the Sino-Soviet conflict and by dispatching only an observer to the Karlovy Vary preparatory meeting of West and East European Communist parties.

Since 1967, despite a growing Stalinist bloc, the VPK has barely hesitated to criticize the Socialist world. The Sinyavsky-Daniel trials, the Berlin Wall, the Warsaw Pact invasion of Czechoslovakia, the Soviet-directed normalization there, and the treatment accorded Alexander Solzhenitsyn have all come in for harsh criticism by the VPK.

Spain

From its early days, the Spanish Communist Party found itself under the wing of the Third International. In 1921 the acceptance of the twenty-one Conditions and subsequent formation of the PCE were accomplished under Comintern guidance. Subsequently, the Party split repeatedly over policy, but each time Moscow won its way. Then in the early 1930s, when the PCE was disorganized and divided, the Comintern sent advisors to reorganize the Party.

During the Spanish Civil War, the PCE continued under Comintern tutelage. In the face of rising German power, Moscow wanted to convince the West it would be a suitable ally; so the Spanish Communists behaved as the most moderate, most trustworthy, and most effective of all working-class organizations in Spain, building close ties with the bourgeois Republican parties. Because the Soviets wanted to prevent a Fascist regime from taking power in Spain, they sent a considerable amount of aid to the Republican regime until late 1937 or early 1938, funneling much of it through the PCE. Consequently, the Spanish Communists remained closely dependent on the Soviet Union during the Civil War, only occasionally showing signs of resistance.[40]

After Franco's victory, the PCE continued its close ties to Moscow. A number of the Spanish Communist leaders found exile in the Soviet Union and the PCE received some financial assistance from the Soviet Union. On all major policy issues the Spanish echoed the Soviet line, supporting the Russian position in the Cold War, following the changing line on Yugoslavia, and violently censuring the Chinese.

In the middle and latter 1960s, however, things began to change. Cautiously, the PCE praised the ousted Khrushchev in 1964.[41] In 1966 the Party criticized the Daniel-Sinyavsky trials. Further, the Spanish Communists began to strengthen their ties with the Italian and Romanian parties, two of Europe's more independent-minded Communist parties, and moved to disassociate themselves from what "was purely Russian in the Soviet Revolution."[42]

Then came Czechoslovakia. In the spring of 1968, several leaders of the PCE praised the liberalizing developments under the Dubcek regime. When the Soviet invasion occurred in August, both Santiago Carrillo and Dolores Ibárruri, the two highest officials in the PCE, were caught by surprise while vacationing in the Soviet Union. Immediately, they protested to the Kremlin, in reply to which Suslov purportedly told Carrillo, "When all is said and done, your's is only a small party."[43]

On August 23, the PCE made its criticism of the invasion public[44] and the Party's Executive Committee verified that position in September with the following statement: Spanish Communists can

neither conceive nor accept the hypothesis, which our enemies are today in a position to put forward, that once the Communist Party has come to power in Spain in partnership with the forces of labor and culture, another socialist power—no matter which—could dictate policies to us. Even less can we conceive or accept that such a Power could intervene militarily in our territory without the most energetic resistance on our part.[45]

Since 1968 the PCE has stuck to its position on Czechoslovakia and moved dramatically to a stance of autonomy in the international Communist movement. In 1969 it signed the final document of the World Conference of Communist Parties only with reservations and in 1969 and 1970 purged a number of pro-Soviet Central Committee members. In 1971 Carrillo visited Peking and the PCE became the first non-ruling Communist party to resume relations with the Chinese since the Sino-Soviet split. "There must be no guiding party or ruling center," Carrillo declared. "No party has the right to impose its views on another or to interfere. Each party has its own form and methods of action which are different from someone else's."[46]

The PCE has continued its autonomous line. In 1975 Carrillo denounced the devious tactics of the Portuguese Communist Party, criticizing Communist leader Cunhal as "narrow minded" and praising Socialist Mario Soares.[47] Further, he called for pluralist democracy in Socialist countries[48] and argued that the United States should leave Spanish bases "one day, just as the Soviets should leave Czechoslovakia."[49] At the Conference of European Communist Parties in East Berlin, Carrillo proved to be Moscow's most severe critic, declaring that Moscow is no longer the Rome of Communism. There is no longer a directing center, he declared.[50]

In 1977 the PCE and Carrillo in particular became the object of direct attack by the Soviets. *New Times,* a Moscow daily, lashed out against Carrillo in very strong terms, criticizing his new book, *Eurocommunism and the State,* as a "maneuver of imperialism" and accusing Carrillo of anti-Sovietism.[51] Then, in April 1978 after the PCE dropped the term "Leninist" from its self-description, Moscow launched a blistering attack against the Spanish Party without calling it by name. Eurocommunism, *Pravda* declared, weakens the workers' movement and puts it under the control of the bourgeoisie. It is impossible to renounce Lenin while declaring loyalty to Marx.[52]

Iceland

The Communist Party of Iceland has, throughout most of its history, maintained a position aloof from international affairs that do not directly affect Iceland. Organized from the Left opposition of the Social Democratic Party, the Icelandic Communists remained within that party (on the advice of the Comintern) until 1930 when they broke off and became an independent party. Always only loosely tied to the Soviet Union and never fully Bolshevized, the Party broke away from the Comintern in 1938 to reconstitute itself to include more Left-wing Social Democrats. By 1949, however, the Icelandic Communist Party came under the control of a pro-Soviet group who directed the Party along somewhat more orthodox lines. More "nationalist" elements once again assumed leadership in the Party in 1962, a leadership that was solidified when the bulk of the pro-Soviet militants seceded from the Party in 1968 following its condemnation of the Soviet invasion of Czechoslovakia.

The Icelandic Communist Party's present international position is one of critical aloofness from the international Communist movement. Rarely taking positions on issues not directly affecting Iceland, the Party has been generally isolationist in international Communist affairs and has adopted a neutral position on the Sino-Soviet split. The Icelandic Communists consider the rift as "idiotic and chaotic" and irrelevant to Icelandic concerns.[53] On Czechoslovakia, however, the Icelandic Party abandoned its usual reserve, condemning the invasion by the Soviet-led forces in the strongest possible terms. (The offended Soviets even refused to invite their Icelandic comrades to the 1969 World Conference of Communist Parties!) Since 1968, rather than softening its criticism, the PA has reiterated it and added new attacks on the Soviet-directed normalization in Czechoslovakia. In 1976 the PA continued its usual pattern by boycotting the East Berlin Conference. Then in 1977 the PA sent no representative to Moscow for the Twenty-Fifth Congress of the CPSU.

Notes

1. For example, the initial response of the PCL to the Twentieth Congress of the CPSU was to stress United States propaganda. *Zeitung,* 6 June 1956, cited in *The Anti-Stalin Campaign and International Communism,* ed. Russian Institute (New York: Columbia, 1956), p. 96.

2. *New York Times,* 5 May 1976.

3. Ibid., 10 June 1975.

4. Michael O'Riordan, "Inspiring Changes," *World Marxist Review* XVII, no. 5 (May 1974): 48-49.

5. "Resolution of the Central Committee of the Communist Party of Austria," *Volksstimme,* 20 February 1962.

6. Aarne Saarinen, "Leading Force of Democratic Development," *World Marxist Review* XVII, no. 11 (November 1974): 38-43.

7. *Le Drapeau Rouge,* 14 February 1974.

8. Moscow backed the hard-line faction. *Pravda,* 25 March 1975.

9. Annie Kriegel, *The French Communists: Profile of a People,* trans. Elaine P. Halperin (Chicago: University of Chicago, 1972; first pub. 1968), pp. 269-83.

10. Although, according to Schulman, on occasion the Soviets were not above giving instructions to the French Party, nor the PCF beyond accepting them. Marshall D. Shulman, *Stalin's Foreign Policy Reappraised* (Cambridge: Harvard, 1963), pp. 215-20.

11. *L'Humanité,* 19 June 1956.

12. Even attacking the Italian Party for its independent attitude. *France Nouvelle,* 10 January 1957; *L'Humanité,* 27 November 1961, 30 November 1961.

13. *L'Humanité,* 22 August 1968.

14. *Le Monde,* 28 August 1968.

15. For reasons broader than just the disagreement over Czechoslovakia.

16. *L'Humanité,* 5 February 1976.

17. *Le Monde*, 27 May 1977.

18. "L'intervista a *Nuovi Argomenti*," pp. 85-117, in Palmiro Togliatti, *Problemi del movimento;* originally in *Nuovi Argomenti* XX (May-June 1956).

19. Ibid., quoted in Giorgio Galli, "Italy," pp. 127-40, in Walter Laqueur and Leopold Labedz, eds., *Polycentrism* (New York: Praeger, 1962), p. 127.

20. "La via italiana al socialismo," pp. 121-69, in Togliatti, *Problemi del movimento;* originally in *L'Unità*, 26 June 1956.

21. Togliatti, *Problemi del movimento*, pp. 172-73; *L'Unità*, 3 July 1956; *Rinascita*, July 1956, pp. 369-72.

22. *Rinascita*, 5 September 1964.

23. Ibid., 4 July 1963.

24. *L'Unità*, 12 April 1962.

25. *Rinascita*, April 1961, pp. 353-63.

26. *L'Unità*, 26 October 1963, 23 April 1964.

27. See *Interventi della delegazione del PCI alle conferenza di Mosca degli 81 partiti comunisti ed operai* (Rome, 1962), pp. 40, 71.

28. "Per una nuova avanzate," *L'Unità*, 26 October 1963.

29. Palmiro Togliatti, *Prememoria*, in *Rinascita*, September 1964; William E. Griffith, "European Communism, 1965," pp. 1-38, in Griffith, ed., *Communism in Europe*, vol. II (Cambridge: MIT, 1966), pp. 33-34.

30. *L'Unità*, 16 February 1966.

31. "Comunicato dell'ufficio politico del PCI sull' intervento in Cecoslovacchia," *Il Partito comunista italiano e il movimento operaio internazionale, 1956-1968* (Rome: Editore Riuniti, 1968), pp. 310-11.

32. *L'Unità*, 15 January 1971.

33. Ibid., 12 June 1969.

34. *Le Monde*, 12-13 September 1976, 18 September 1976, 30 September 1976.

35. *Rinascita*, 23 February 1973; *L'Unità*, 3 March 1973.

36. *Le Monde*, 28 February 1976.

37. *New York Times*, 1 July 1976.

38. *Daily Worker*, 14 February 1965; *Morning Star*, 24 May 1965.

39. *Morning Star*, 22 August 1968.

40. See David T. Cattell, *Communism and the Spanish Civil War* (Berkeley: University of California, 1956).

41. *Mundo Obrero*, 15 October 1964.

42. See Santiago Carrillo, *Después de Franco, Qué?* (Paris: Ediciones Sociales, 1965) and *Nuevos Enfoques a Problemas de Hoy* (Paris: Ediciones Sociales, 1967).

43. *Le Monde*, 23 October 1970.

44. See *L'Humanité*, 7 September 1968.
45. *Mundo Obrero*, 15 September 1968.
46. Ibid., 10 December 1971.
47. *L'Unità*, 12 July 1975; *New York Times*, 23 July 1975.
48. *Frankfurter Allgemeine*, 19 November 1975.
49. *New York Times*, 28 July 1976.
50. Ibid., 30 June 1976.
51. *Le Monde*, 24 June 1977.
52. *London Times*, 25 April 1978.
53. YICA, 1975.

PART TWO

CAUSES OF
THE DIVERSITY

As we have seen in Part One, the Communist parties of Western Europe are neither replicas of the CPSU nor carbon copies of each other. Rather, each party has its own distinct character, both domestically and internationally, as the parties differ in size, organization, alliance strategies, domestic programs, and international postures.

What, then, are the causes of this diversity in the positions and postures of the Communist parties of Western Europe? By its very complexity, the diversity points to no easy explanation. Both the Icelandic Communist Party and the Communist Party of Luxembourg are moderate-sized parties in small countries. Yet Iceland's PA is internationally independent and domestically reformist, and Luxembourg's PCL is strongly pro-Soviet internationally and relatively conservative in domestic policies. The Danish and Swedish Communist parties are both small parties in Scandinavia, but the former is firmly aligned with Moscow and domestically conservative, and the latter is independent in its foreign policy and quite revisionist on domestic issues. A third contrast between parties in somewhat similar positions is that between France's PCF and Italy's PCI. Each is a major party in a large

*predominately Catholic country of South-
ern Europe. However, the Italian Communists have long been characterized as
conciliatory, opportunistic, independent
minded, and even pragmatic (or as pragmatic as a Communist party can be), and
the French PCF has been described as
Stalinist, dogmatic, sometimes sclerotic.
What accounts for this difference in parties ostensibly cut from the same political
mold, in apparently similar positions, in
somewhat similar political systems?*

*The explanation for the diversity of
Western European Communism lies in a
number of highly interrelated factors. But,
although everything may interact dynami-
cally, human language and thought force
us to delineate phenomena along spatial
and temporal lines if we are to describe
and explain the interaction. Having de-
fined the object of inquiry, the role of science is to cut through the rich complexity
of reality to focus on those discrete factors
accounting for the variations in that object
and then to define the nature of the causal
relationships. So a model must be constructed, a simplification of reality, to explain the diversity in policies and postures
of the Communist parties of Western Europe. That is the task of Part Two.*

*As outlined in the Introduction, a Com-
munist party finds itself affected by innumerable contingencies and possibilities
from its environment, an environment that
has been divided here into four broad
components: the international environment, the domestic social environment,
the domestic political environment, and
the domestic constitutional environment.*

It is from *the environment that the Communist party must draw its resources—its members, its voters, its finances. It is* within *the environment that the party must function and produce its outputs—programs, policies, actions. Finally, it is* upon *the environment that the party directs its efforts—to change or preserve policies, government personnel, public attitudes, the economic order.*

In the face of environmentally imposed demands and constraints, a Communist party responds (even the failure to act is a response in a broad sense), but a Communist party is not a biological organism that responds instinctively or by reflex action to external stimuli. Rather, it "chooses" a course of action or inaction. (Many responses do resemble reflexes in that the party seemingly turns to set patterns of response automatically. These set patterns, however, are the result of prior choices made in the party's past and preserved by the party.)

By definition, the party's choices are made by the leadership, but not by a leadership acting in a vacuum. First, the leaders' actions are greatly shaped by their personal backgrounds and experiences. Second, the environment sets certain parameters on the party, thereby constraining the leaders' actions. Finally, the leaders are constrained by internal factors, namely, the party's membership and electorate and its history. The result of this process is party behavior, which, in turn, feeds back onto the party directly and onto the party's environment. (See Figure 1.)

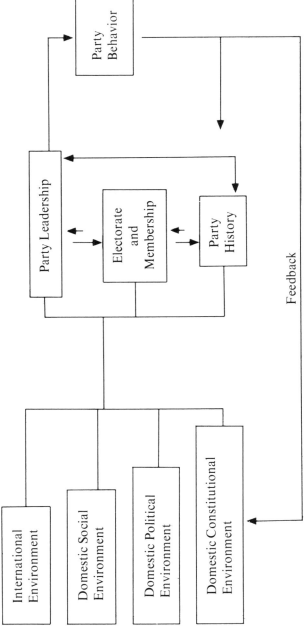

Figure 1. The Communist Party in Its Environment.

chapter 3

INTERNATIONAL ENVIRONMENT

Rather than being uniquely national political institutions, Communist parties, by their doctrine and their heritage, are members of an international movement. Consequently, developments in the international environment can have a significant effect on the fortunes and behavior of the Western European Communist parties. First, the events of the international environment affect the Western European Communist parties by influencing the receptivity of voters, potential militants, interest groups, and other political parties to the initiatives and appeals of the Communist parties. Second, the international environment has historically posed a number of direct and indirect constraints on Western European Communists, helping to shape the policies of the Western parties.

The International Environment and
Domestic Political Fortunes

The electoral fortunes of Western European Communist parties are strongly and directly tied to the status of the international Communist movement, which, for Western Europe, in large part still means the Soviet Union. When the prestige of Moscow and international Communism is high, the Western parties share in the glory; when it is low, they reap the misfortune.

At no time has the general prestige of the Soviet Union been

greater than at the conclusion of World War II during which the
Soviets were widely perceived in the West as fighting bravely and
sacrificing heavily for the common goal of defeating the Axis powers. Consequently, every legal Communist party in Western Europe
enjoyed relatively great electoral successes in the immediate postwar elections. In Britain, Switzerland, Sweden, Norway, the Netherlands, Iceland, France, Finland, Denmark, Belgium, and Austria,
the Communists won a larger percentage of the vote in late World
War II and early postwar parliamentary elections than they had
ever won before or have won since.[1] In two other cases, Luxembourg and Italy, the PCL and PCI each won larger shares of the
vote than they had ever won before, shares that have subsequently
been surpassed. Only in the highly unusual case of West Germany—a divided, defeated, and occupied country—was this not the
case.

Conversely, in times of international tension, the Western European parties fare less well electorally, particularly those parties
operating in nations tied formally or informally to the Western
political and military alliance. In Belgium, Denmark, France, West
Germany, the Netherlands, Norway, and Britain, countries all
firmly linked to the Western alliance, the electoral performance of
each country's Communist party declined during the Cold War
years (from about 1947 to about 1960). In Sweden and Switzerland,
nations with a Western orientation but no formal military ties to
the Western alliance, the electoral fortunes of the Swedish and
Swiss Communist parties showed a less definite decline. On the
other hand, in Finland and Austria, neutral countries with some
ties to both East and West, the Communist parties experienced no
electoral decline. The exceptions to this pattern are in two small
countries, Luxembourg and Iceland, and in Italy. In Iceland the PA
declined from its 1946 electoral zenith of 19.5 percent, but the
decline was not steady, and in Luxembourg, the pattern was unclear
because of the presence of both partial and general elections. Considering only the latter, there does appear to have been a downturn
in the PCL's electoral fortunes between 1945 and 1954 and then
something of a leveling off. In Italy, however, the PCI successfully
bucked the trend by increasing its parliamentary vote percentage
despite Cold War tensions.

Similarly, when the international prestige of the Soviet Union is low, the Western parties often pay an electoral price. Throughout much of Western Europe, Communist parties absorbed heavy losses in elections following on the heels of the Hungarian crisis of 1956. In parliamentary elections in Austria, Belgium, Denmark, France, Iceland, Holland, Norway, and Sweden in 1957, 1958, or 1959, Communist parties all lost ground. The only exceptions to the pattern occurred in Great Britain where the CPGB held its own in the 1959 election; in Luxembourg and Italy where Communist parties made very slight gains (up 0.2 percent and 0.1 percent respectively); and in two neutral nations, Finland (up 1.6 percent in 1958) and Switzerland (up 0.1 percent in 1959).

The Czechoslovakian crisis of 1968 also proved to be the electoral undoing of many of the Western parties. At the time of the invasion, many of the Western parties were engaged in Popular Front activities and dialogues with Christians and Socialists and they welcomed the reforms of the Dubcek regime in Czechoslovakia as an illustration of Socialism "with a human face." The Soviet invasion made a mockery of the electoral tactics of the Western parties. Not to have condemned it would have undermined the Western parties' program of appeals to the non-Communist Left in their own countries. Even so, many of the parties who did denounce the invasion suffered electoral setbacks. In Austria the KPÖ lost 50 percent of its vote in the April 1969 municipal election in Vienna. In Sweden, despite the VPK's vociferous disassociation from Soviet actions in Czechoslovakia, the Party fell to its lowest postwar share of the vote in the September 1968 parliamentary balloting. Similarly, in Belgium, Finland, Iceland, and Norway in late 1968, 1969, or early 1970, in parliamentary or municipal (in the case of Iceland) elections, the Communists suffered an electoral decline. Only in Luxembourg, where the PCL endorsed the Soviet-led invasion of Czechoslovakia, did a Western European Communist party record an electoral gain in a major election closely following the invasion.

International developments also profoundly affect Western parties' nonelectoral political fortunes. Whether non-Communist parties see Communist parties as potential alliance partners is largely determined by international factors. In the period of international good feelings at the end of World War II, Communist parties were admitted into postwar coalition governments in Austria, Belgium,

Denmark, Greece, Finland, France, Iceland, Italy, Luxembourg, and Norway. With the onset of the Cold War, however, the Communists were no longer considered as acceptable partners and in every case either left or were expelled from the government.

In 1956 the Hungarian invasion served to strain relations between Communist parties and other parties of the Left. In Italy, for example, the events of 1956 led to an increase in tension between the PCI and the Socialists, particularly in the CGIL, the Italian labor federation. In Iceland, following the June 1956 election, the Communists entered into a coalition government. The spectre of Hungary, however, served to isolate the Communists within the government and to compromise their effectiveness.

Currently, East-West détente has improved Western Communist parties' chances of forming electoral and governing alliances with non-Communist parties. As East and West find ground for *rapprochement* internationally, so have Communist and non-Communist parties reached understandings domestically. It has been no accident that Catholics and Socialists have been more receptive to Communist initiatives for "dialogue" and understandings in this age of détente than they were in the Cold War era.

The crises of international Communism can also become internal crises for non-ruling parties. As we have seen, Khrushchev's secret speech, Hungary, Czechoslovakia, and other international events wreaked no small amount of havoc in a number of the Western parties. Illusions were broken, allegiances were shattered, and divisions were deepened. The cumulative crises of international Communism have produced a "God is dead" crisis within many of the Western parties.[2]

One result of this has been a decline in revolutionary fervor and dedication. In many of the Western European parties, the organization is withering and the recruitment of new members, especially young people, is alarmingly unsuccessful. In Norway the NKP's youth organization is insignificantly small, and the majority of the declining Austrian Communist Party's membership is over sixty years of age. In Britain the CPGB organization suffers from high turnover, luke-warm dedication, and major problems in enlisting young people.[3] In 1973 only about sixteen thousand of the nearly thirty thousand members of the Party even paid their dues. Even in

Italy, the PCI's youth federation is now in decline. Seemingly, the best organized parties are the French, Italian, West German, Finnish, Portuguese, and Spanish, which have the funds to hire squadrons of functionaries to supplement party volunteers.

Another result of the crises of international Communism has been the proliferation of rival Leftist movements—Maoist, Stalinist, Trotskyist, New Left, and Anarchist—that have sprung up to challenge the established Communist party in virtually every country of Western Europe. In France the PCF has had to contend with innumerable revolutionary splinter parties and the Italian Communist Party has been faced with opposition from various Left-wing terrorist organizations, but the party facing the greatest challenge is the British Communist Party. Among student and union circles, the CPGB has clearly been outflanked on the Left, particularly by the Trotskyist Workers Revolutionary Movement.

Developments in world Communism other than those directly dealing with the prestige of the Soviet Union and East-West relations also affect Western parties' political fortunes. Events in Portugal, for example, have posed threats to the alliance strategies of Western parties, particularly in Italy and France. For its part, the Italian Communist Party acted swiftly to disassociate itself from the Portuguese Communists, trying to maintain its credibility as a "democratic" potential party of government. In France, where the PCF had pledged its support for the Portuguese Communist Party, the issue was one factor underlying strained relations between the Communists and the Socialists. In Spain the events in Portugal probably worked to delay the legalization of the PCE, and the Spanish Communists moved to disassociate themselves from their Portuguese comrades.

The International Environment and Party Policy

Not only does the international environment affect the receptivity of the Western Communist parties' domestic environment to the initiatives and appeals of the Western parties, but it also places constraints on the actions of the parties themselves. Historically, the domestic and international policies of the Communist parties of Western Europe have been influenced both directly and indirectly by Soviet policy. The various tactics of united front from below, united front, and class against class were in large part conceived and instituted from Moscow, often for reasons of Soviet foreign policy rather than in the domestic interests of the non-ruling parties.

For example, the popular front policy of the French Communist Party was dictated by the Soviet Union. On its surface, the Popular Front in France was the result of fear by French Leftists, particularly the Communists, of the possibility of the establishment in France of a regime similar to the Fascist regimes in Germany and Italy—a fear evidently engendered by the nationalist revolt of February 6, 1934, in Paris. However, according to Célie and Albert Vassart, two well-placed participants in the events of the time, this was not the case. Rather, the Popular Front was a result of the Soviet Union's desire to safeguard its European front by a system of international guarantees, and instructions for the new line came directly from Moscow.[4]

Perhaps the best illustration of the Western Communist parties' historical mimicry of Soviet policies was the gyrations in position revolving around the Nazi-Soviet Pact of 1939 and the beginning of World War II. Before the agreement was made public, the posture of the Western parties was one of support for anti-Fascist popular fronts against the German and Italian Fascist menace. After the German-Soviet agreement, the popular front theme was unchanged, but the Western parties unanimously heralded the pact as a move toward peace. Then when war broke out, the first reaction of the Communist parties in the West was one of "patriotic" and "national" support for anti-Fascist unity. After the Soviet invasion of Poland (and, in at least a few cases, instructions from Moscow) their positions switched. In Britain, the *Daily Worker* headlined the Soviet military action with "Red Army Takes Bread to Starving Peasants."[5] Meanwhile, in Norway, the NKP daily, *Arbeideren,* labeled the war "imperialist" and called for an end to resistance.[6] The Danish Party resorted to blaming Churchill and the Social Democrats for their country's occupation.[7]

Throughout Western Europe, the Communist line changed from anti-Fascist patriotism to "revolutionary defeatism" and even sporadic cooperation with the Nazis. In occupied Denmark, for example, the DKP chose to pursue a policy of strict neutrality towards the Germans, while in France, the PCF sought a *modus vivendi* with the Germans, apparently receiving tacit approval for the publication of *L'Humanité*.

When Germany invaded the Soviet Union in June 1941, Communist policy toward the war somersaulted again. In all of Western Europe, Communist parties became ardent patriots, organizing active resistance against the Nazis. In occupied Norway, Denmark, Belgium, Greece, Holland, Luxembourg, Italy, and France, Communists were in the forefront of the armed resistance effort. Elsewhere, they took their place among the war's most loyal supporters.

After the war, the Western parties continued their policy of cooperation with bourgeois anti-Fascist forces and participated in governing coalitions in several countries. As relations between the Soviet Union and the Western powers cooled, however, so did relations between the Western Communist parties and their coalition partners. Furthermore, in every case, to a greater or lesser extent, the Western parties adopted the role of defenders of Soviet domestic and foreign policies.

Since de-Stalinization, since Hungary, since the Sino-Soviet rift, since East-West détente, and certainly since the Czechoslovakian invasion in 1968, the Western Communist parties have frequently been at odds with the Soviet Union. The differences were invariably on issues on which there is a conflict of interests between the Western parties and the CPSU, that is, issues that affect the political fortunes of the Western parties in their own political spheres such as the Czech invasion and Soviet cultural policy.

On other issues, however, the positions of the CPSU and Western parties are closely parallel. Unanimously, the Western parties deplored United States policy in Viet Nam and all other manifestations of "American imperialism." They tend to applaud Cuban and Soviet involvement in Africa while attacking American initiatives there. All support the Soviet viewpoint (if not Soviet tactics) in the Sino-Soviet ideological dispute.

In sum, the international environment has historically set the parameters for many of the policies of Western Europe's Communist parties. In the last two decades, however, the reins of leadership have fallen slack in Moscow's hands as increasingly the Western parties have taken their heads. What, then, were the factors that constrained the leaders of the Western European Communist parties, once binding them firmly to Soviet designs, and how have these constraints weakened?

The first factor that must be considered is that of direct intervention. To what extent are the Communist parties of Western Europe instructed agents of the Soviet Union? Because of scarcity of reliable information, there is no easy answer to this question. The best estimate is that until 1943 extensive direction came from the Third International (read Moscow) and that after the Comintern's dissolution, instructions continued to come from the Soviet Union although not with so much frequency or detail as before. After the Twentieth CPSU Congress in 1956, however, the Western parties for the most part were free from direct outside control.

After the cresting of the revolutionary wave, the Third International became Moscow's tool for controlling the Western parties and during the period of the Comintern, the Kremlin insisted on complete control over member sections. The evidence of massive and direct Soviet interference into the internal affairs of the non-ruling parties is abundant. In 1923 in Norway, the Comintern Executive forced a split in the Norwegian Labor Party to secure control. In Greece in 1931, the International installed new leadership for the KKE. Even small details of operation of the British Communist Party were dictated by Moscow, and in the Netherlands, the Comintern intervened time and again to force purges and leadership shuffles to secure its will. The examples could be multiplied endlessly. What laxity did exist in the Comintern's control over member sections was due to Moscow's indifference, problems of communication, political naïveté on the part of Western European Communist leaders, and some willful disobedience from Western Communists.

The demise of the Comintern did not mean the end of control from Moscow. In 1947 Stalin created the Cominform as an agency for adjusting the policies of the Western Communist parties, particularly the French and Italian, to the needs of his diplomacy. Although the Cominform was instrumental in spreading the Soviet Union's Cold War line among the Western parties, it is unclear how much direct intervention actually occurred. Again, the evidence is very sketchy and it is difficult to determine which actions on the part of the Western Communist parties were self-motivated and which were the result of direct pressure from Moscow.

Since 1956 Moscow has been unable to exercise direct control of the Western European Communist movement in most countries. Illustrative of this loss of dictatorial control was the World Conference of Communist Parties held in Moscow in June 1969. It is a safe conclusion that the Soviets' goal for the conference was to revive a formal institutional structure for the movement that would include the bulk of the world's Communist parties (omitting, of course, such recalcitrants as the Chinese and Albanians). What Moscow got, however, was a conference whose decisions were not binding on its participants and that, the Soviets had to guarantee, would not be used to purge the movement of deviant parties. Even to achieve this, Moscow had to spend several years intensely proselytizing among Communist parties. Khrushchev set out to convene the Council of Trent; Brezhnev got Vatican II.[8]

Soviet policy itself helps determine the relative freedom of the Western parties to act on their own. In times of international tensions during which Soviet leaders feel threatened—the rise of Fascism in Germany, the Cold War period—Moscow exerts its strongest efforts to harness the policies of the Western parties for the defense of the Soviet Union. At other times, however, there is less need for tight control. Currently, even if the Soviet Union had the potential to dictate policy to the Western parties, the present atmosphere of détente reduces Moscow's need for lockstep conformity in Western Europe. "The fundamental implication of Soviet-American détente . . . is that [the Communists] are today more than ever on their own, without even the old and meaningless dithyrambics about Soviet support in the 'world revolution' to justify acting for the Socialist Motherland above all else."[9]

Perhaps the strongest tie still binding Western Communist parties to Moscow is a psychological one. As the first Socialist state, the Soviet Union embodied the hopes and dreams of Western European Communists, and in its role as ideological, political, and military vanguard of the coming Socialist utopia, the Soviet Union could and did parlay its prestige into control of the non-ruling Communist parties. In the 1920s, the prestige of the Bolshevik

Revolution coupled with the wartime bankruptcy of parliamentary Socialism enabled the CPSU not only to dominate the world movement, but also to have a powerful voice in each of the Western parties. Although collaboration with Nazi Germany from August 1939 to June 1941 tarnished Moscow's image, the sacrifices of the Russian people and the successes of the Red Army considerably enhanced Soviet prestige throughout Western Europe, particularly among the ranks of Western European Communists. Currently, although still powerful in some Western parties and in all parties among many veteran cadres who were socialized into party activity during an age in which the Soviet Union was seen as an anti-Fascist bastion, the prestige of the Soviet Union has been shaken—by purge trials, the Nazi-Soviet Pact, the revelations about Stalin's crimes, Hungary, the Sino-Soviet split, détente, the Czechoslovakian invasion. No longer is the moral, political, and ideological leadership of the Soviet Union unchallenged in the international movement. Consequently, the psychological ties between the Western European Communist parties and the Soviet Union are, in most cases, far weaker in 1978 than they were in 1948 or in 1958.

Another tie between the Soviet Union and West European Communist parties is financial. During the Comintern period, most Western parties received international aid with the possible exception of the Swedish Communist Party.[10] Since the dismantling of the Comintern, however, international aid has apparently become much less.

Although proof is hard to come by, a number of Western parties are likely still at least partially supported from abroad. The Communist Party of Luxembourg is apparently financially dependent on the Soviet Union. It has more money to spend than it can raise domestically and its leading members travel frequently in the Soviet Union and spend their vacations there. Its strong support of Moscow is at least partially the result of these financial ties.

The West German Communist Party has a special relationship with Moscow and the East German Communist Party. During its period of illegality, the KPD was almost totally dependent on East Germany for survival. The bulk of its funds apparently came from the German Democratic Republic and its leaders lived there in exile. Since being reconstituted as the legal DKP, the West German Communist Party has remained financially dependent on outside sources, particularly East Germany.[11] Finally, Moscow has made the continued legality of the DKP a condition of its *rapprochement* with the West German government. Not surprisingly, the DKP's foreign and domestic policies are virtually identical with those of the Soviet Union and East Germany.

Moreover, it is reported that the Communist parties of Austria,[12] Portugal,[13] Ireland, Greece (Exterior),[14] and Spain before 1968[15] received financial assistance from the Soviet Union. Also, in recent years, the Spanish Communists have been receiving funds from their Italian and Romanian cousins.[16]

A number of parties receive indirect financial support from abroad. In Italy, France, and Finland, Communist parties operate commercial enterprises, including export-import concerns and travel agencies that make transactions with Eastern Europe and the Soviet Union on often rather favorable terms. A portion of their profits are thus a form of indirect subsidy.

Again, evidence is scarce, but it is apparent that substantial Soviet financial support is lacking for at least some of Western Europe's Communist parties. In recent years, the British Communist Party, for example, has fallen on hard times. It is perennially short of cash and its daily paper, *Morning Star,* has been running a deficit. In Greece, the KKE Interior is having financial difficulties. Its newspaper, *Avgi,* nearly suspended publication in early 1976 because of inadequate circulation.

The larger mass membership parties with entrenched national positions and reliable domestic sources for funds (members' dues and contributions, state subsidies, salaries of office holders, profits from party enterprises—"Red Capitalism") are potentially less dependent on international aid than the weaker dwarf parties. But even for parties not financially dependent on outside assistance, Soviet funds can still act as a policy restraint. Apparently, Moscow is not above supporting "Stalinist" oppositions to Western parties whose policies take on too much of an anti-Soviet air. Russian and East German money supported Austrian hard liners in the KPÖ's factional struggle following the Czechoslovakian crisis of 1968.[17] Similarly, Russian money apparently helped finance Enrique Líster's pro-Moscow dissident Communist party in its struggle with the established Spanish Communist Party.[18]

Another factor binding Western Communist parties to the Soviet

Union involves the concept of proximity. Geographical distance is part of this, but more importantly, it also pertains to perceptions of historical and political ties between a Western European nation and the Soviet Union. Finland lies in the shadow of the Soviet Union and much of its history turns around the state of its relations with Russia. Consequently, the Soviet Union is relatively salient for the average Finn and particularly salient for Finnish Communists. Thus, Moscow's potential for indirect influence is relatively great. Second, the very fact of geographical closeness makes communication and consultation between the CPSU and the SKP relatively easy. The Kremlin has taken advantage of these circumstances to attempt (unsuccessfully) to mediate the current schism with the SKP.

In contrast to Finland, Iceland is geographically relatively distant to the population centers of the Soviet Union and, historically and politically, quite distant. Consequently, there is little to reinforce preexisting psychological attachments of Icelandic Communists to Moscow and the potential for direct intervention by the Soviets in PA affairs is relatively limited.

During the Comintern days, proximity, ease of communications and Soviet perceptions of party salience helped to determine the amount of attention and instruction a Western party received from the Comintern Executive. The French, German, and British parties were much under the scrutiny of Moscow, while parties off the beaten path in Norway and Iceland enjoyed a measure of benign neglect. In the cases of the Italian and Finnish parties, domestic illegality hampered communications between Moscow and the base of the Party, thus allowing each of these parties more freedom than it would otherwise expect.

In this age of "polycentrism," Communist parties other than the CPSU can also influence the non-ruling parties of Western Europe. The Chinese Communist Party has presented a challenge to the CPSU for political and ideological leadership of the world movement and, in turn, virtually every Western European Communist party has been challenged by internal factions or by splinter parties espousing the Chinese positions.

Although none of the main-line Western European Communist parties supports Peking's ideological position in the Sino-Soviet dispute, the fact of that division has provided the Western parties with a wedge to extract greater autonomy for themselves in the international movement. For one thing, the Chinese rebellion against Soviet dominance in the world movement has given the Western European Communists psychological encouragement for their own independent designs. More concretely, the fact of the schism has provided the Western parties with a currency with which they can bargain their own freedom of action. In exchange for general support of Soviet positions and condemnation of the Chinese, Moscow has been willing to accept a greater independence from the Western parties. At the same time, the Western European parties (the more independent ones, at least) are careful not to go too far in their support of Moscow's position. The last thing they want is a complete victory for the Soviets that would restore Russian hegemony in the international movement and thus threaten their independence.

Relatively successful non-ruling parties have served as models for neighboring parties. The Italian Communist Party has recently served as a model for the Swiss Communists with the two having close ties. Also, the Luxembourg Communist Party has strong links with the French Party.

Finally, a major development in the international relations of Western European Communist parties is increased regional contact and cooperation among like-minded Communist parties in Western and Eastern Europe. Regional cooperation among Communist parties offers a "proletarian internationalist" justification for the Western parties to escape Soviet tutelage.[19] In January 1974, for example, at the rally of Western Communist parties in Brussels, the Western parties successfully resisted Moscow's efforts to call an international meeting to read China and her allies out of the world movement. In late 1975, another indication of a growing regional autonomy among Communist parties in Western Europe appeared as the Italian and French Parties published a common declaration that insisted on the independence of each party. Then in June-July 1976, many of the Western European Communists stood with allies from Yugoslavia and Romania to declare their independence from Soviet authority at the East Berlin Conference of European Communist parties.

In summary: financial dependence on Moscow, strong psychological ties, and what we have termed "proximity" to the Soviet Union all serve to constrain Western Communists toward acceptance of the Soviet line and Soviet direction and toward support for Moscow internationally. On the other hand, financial independence (or potential independence), lack of proximity, and the development of ties to Communist parties other than the CPSU, all mean an absence of constraints.

Notes

1. See the Appendix.

2. François Fejtö, "La crise de l'internationalisme marxiste," pp. 11-40, in *Dictionnaire des partis communistes et des mouvements révolutionnaires* (Paris: Tournai Casterman, 1971), pp. 32-33.

3. Kenneth Newton, *The Sociology of British Communism* (London: Penguin, 1969), p. 5.

4. Célie and Albert Vassart, "The Moscow Origin of the French 'Popular Front,' " pp. 234-52, in Milorad M. Drachkovitch and Branko Lazitch, eds., *The Comintern: Historical Highlights* (Stanford: Hoover Institution, 1966); Daniel R. Brower, *The New Jacobins: The French Communist Party and the Popular Front* (Ithaca: Cornell, 1968), pp. 47-61.

5. *Daily Worker*, 20 September 1939.

6. John Otto Johansen, "Norway," pp. 321-69, in William E. Griffith, ed., *Communism in Europe*, vol. II (Cambridge: MIT, 1965), p. 326.

7. Peter P. Rohde, "The Communist Party of Denmark," pp. 3-33, in A. F. Upton, ed., *The Communist Parties of Scandinavia and Finland* (London: Weidenfeld and Nicolson, 1973), p. 14.

8. Kevin Devlin, "The Interparty Drama," *Problems of Communism* XXIV, no. 4 (July-August 1975): 18-34.

9. Ronald Tiersky, "The French Communist Party and Détente," *Journal of International Affairs* XXVIII, no. 2 (October 1974): 188-205.

10. Franz Borkenau, *The Communist International* (London: Faber and Faber, 1938), p. 347.

11. Richard Loss, "The Communist Party of Germany (KPD), 1956-1968," *Survey* XIX, no. 4 (Autumn 1973): 66-85.

12. Neil McInnes, *The Communist Parties of Western Europe* (London: Oxford, 1975): 148.

13. *New York Times,* 10 June 1975.

14. YICA, 1972; *New York Times,* 31 October 1977.

15. Guy Hermet, *The Communists in Spain* (Lexington, Mass.: Heath, 1974), p. 108.

16. *Rinascita,* 6 February 1970, 23 October 1970.

17. McInnes, *Communist Parties,* p. 148.

18. YICA, 1972.

19. McInnes, *Communist Parties,* p. 154.

chapter 4

DOMESTIC SOCIAL STRUCTURE

Although the international environments of the Western European Communist parties are similar, each party must function in a unique domestic environment. A primary aspect of that domestic environment is the social structure, including in particular the nature and intensity of the ethnic, religious, class, and geographic cleavages in each nation in which a Communist party must function.

Two broad generalizations can be drawn about the relationships between a country's social structure and the policies and positions of its Communist Party. First, the social structure is the soil in which a Communist party must either take root and flourish or wither and die; and that soil varies considerably in its fertility. Second, the programs, policies, and sometimes the organization of the parties are, in part, shaped by the necessity of conforming to or coping with the domestic social structure as it acts as a backdrop for political activity.

Social Structure and Electoral Success

A number of hypotheses have been offered concerning the relationship between social cleavages and Communist party strength. Among these are the crude Leninist proposition that the Communist party is the party of the proletariat,[1] Lipset's argument that those on the lower end of an economic stratification system in poorer countries tend toward political radicalism,[2] and Greene's hypothesis that Communism is strong where there are substantial unmediated cleavages along socioeconomic lines.[3] The evidence, however, indicates that social cleavages alone, be they religious, ethnic, geographical, or economic, do not necessarily lead to a strong Communist movement. Rather, they provide a milieu in which a Communist party can find success by clever exploitation of the cleavages.

Religious Cleavages

In much of Southern Europe, particularly in Italy, France, Spain, and Portugal, Communist success is associated with a traditional clerical-anticlerical cleavage. In Italy one study has found that high scores on a clericalism scale are associated with voting for the Christian Democratic Party and low scores with support for the PCI.[4] (See Table 1.) On the basis of a survey taken in late 1963 and 1964 in Italy, another study discovers that a strong relationship exists between the strength of individuals' religious devotion and political tendency. As can be seen from Table 2, Leftist parties do better among those individuals with weaker ties to the Church than they do with moderate or strict Catholics. Similarly, Tables 3 and 4

Table 1. Christian Democrat and Communist Vote in Italy in 1958, by Clericalism Index and Socioeconomic Status, in Percentages

Score on Clericalism Index	Middle	Lower Middle	Lower
	Percent Voting DC		
Low	9	9	10
High	50	39	14
	Percent Voting PCI		
Low	18	20	31
High	0	3	5

SOURCE: Gianfranco Poggi, *Le preferenze politiche degli italiani: analisi di alcuni sondaggi pre-elettorali* (Bologna: Il Mulino, 1968), p. 34.

Table 2. Political Tendency and Religious Involvement in Italy,
1963–64

	Marginal Catholic	Moderate Catholic	Strict Catholic
Leftist	68%	47%	37%
Centrist	28	34	57
Rightist	4	19	6

Leftist = PCI, Socialists, and Social Democrats
Centrist = Republicans, Christian Democrats
Rightist = Liberal, Monarchists, neo-Fascists

SOURCE: Lawrence E. Hazelrigg, "Religious and Class Bases of Political Conflict in Italy," *American Journal of Sociology* XXV, no. 3 (June 1970): 496–511.

Table 3. Church Attendance in Previous Seven Days, 1956, by
Party, in Percentages

	PCI	PSI	PSDI	DC	PLI	MON	MSI
Yes	29	41	69	86	75	77	56
No	71	59	31	14	25	23	44

PSI = Socialist Party
PSDI = Social Democratic Party
DC   = Christian Democrat Party
PLI = Liberal Party
MON = Monarchist Party
MSI = Neo-Fascist Party

SOUCE: Samuel H. Barnes, "Italy: Religion and Class in Electoral Behavior," pp. 171–226, in Richard Rose, ed. *Electoral Behavior: A Comparative Handbook* (New York: Free Press, 1974), p. 195.

Table 4. Frequency of Church Attendance in 1968, by Party, in Percentages

	PCI	PSIUP	PSI-PSDI	PRI	DC	PLI	MON	MSI
At least once a week	12	20	29	39	69	53	37	39
Often during the year	16	22	28	17	16	16	21	21
Sometimes	24	30	25	17	10	20	21	30
Rarely	24	16	12	10	4	9	7	6
Never	24	12	6	17	1	2	14	4

PSIUP = Italian Socialist Party of Proletarian Unity

SOURCE: Samul H. Barnes, "Italy: Religion and Class in Electoral Behavior," pp. 171–226, in Richard Rose, ed., *Electoral Behavior: A Comparative Handbook* (New York: Free Press, 1974).

indicate that Communist voters in Italy are far less likely to be regular church attenders than are supporters of the Christian Democrat Party. The PCI draws the large majority of its support from individuals with only loose ties to the Church. Finally, in 1972 the less frequently an Italian voter attended church the more likely he was to be a Communist voter (Table 5.)[5]

In France, Communist voters are less likely to claim to be Christians (61 percent to 82 percent) than the electorate as a whole, and PCF voters tend to be less involved in Church-sponsored organizations (11 percent to 25 percent) than the electorate in general.[6]

Table 5. Church Attendance and Party Preference, 1972

	Once a week	Often	Sometimes	Rarely or Never
PCI	5.4%	11.4%	29.7%	32.3%

SOURCE: Giacomo Sani, "Mass-Level Response to Party Strategy: The Italian Electorate and the Communist Party," pp. 456–503, in Donald L. M. Blackmer and Sidney Tarrow, eds., *Communism in Italy and France* (Princeton: Princeton University, 1975), p. 496.

Although anticlericalism has apparently benefitted Communist parties in Southern Europe, it is neither a necessary nor a sufficient condition for a strong Communist party. In other climes, particularly in much of Latin America, anticlericalism has not been associated with strong Communist parties. Conversely, in other countries, Communism has gained a footing without the presence of a clerical-anticlerical cleavage. In Iceland and Finland, for example, Latin anticlericalism is largely unknown, but Communist parties nevertheless flourish.

Strong Communist parties have not emerged from relatively severe religious cleavages in Ireland and Austria, nor from less intense divisions in the Netherlands, Sweden, or Norway. If anything, religious conflict has hampered the development of the Irish Communist Party. In the North, CPI members tend to be from Protestant backgrounds, and in the South, Catholic. Consequently, the CPI has had difficulty defining a "Marxist" solution to the problems of Northern Ireland that does not alienate a major sector of its membership.

Ethnic Cleavages

Although the Communist parties of Western Europe have not ignored ethnic divisions, they have been unable to build much of a power base on such cleavages. In Belgium, a nation with a relatively intense ethnic division, the PCB has courted the minority Walloons by endorsing constitutional revisions that would give them more autonomy. Consequently, the Party's strength is largely concentrated in Wallonia[7] and all of its deputies are elected from there. Nevertheless, although the PCB may be a regional party, in no sense is Wallonia a Communist region. In 1968 only 3 percent of the Walloon voters claimed to prefer the PCB.[8]

Similarly, the Communist Party of Switzerland also has a regional flavor to it. Although the French-speaking cantons have only about 20 percent of the population, the PdA in 1971 gathered 71 percent of its vote and all five of its deputies from them.[9] As with the Belgian case, however, Communist Party strength remains modest in the French-speaking regions.

Finally, ethnic cleavages in the rest of Western Europe have provided little grist for the Communist mills. In Finland and Italy, ethnic minorities tend to support peculiarly ethnic parties. In Britain the CPGB has historically drawn much of its support from the celtic fringe regions, but the recent emergence of sectionalist parties in Britain has diminished this base. In Spain the Basque separatist movement has found expression in organizations other than the Spanish Communist Party.

Regional Cleavages

Although Communist strength often tends toward regional concentrations, it would be incorrect to say that Communist strength to any great extent is *based* on regional cleavages. In much of Scandinavia, the major cleavage has been an urban-rural one. Although Communist parties have strongholds in backwoods sectors of Norway, Sweden, and Finland (in addition to concentrations in industrial areas), Communist support there is more the result of economic insecurity and traditional radicalism than an urban-rural cleavage.[10]

In Italy the major regional cleavage is between the South, the *Mezzogiorno,* and the more prosperous North. Although the PCI has addressed a number of appeals to the problems of the South, one can hardly say that the Communist Party is built on that cleavage.[11]

Finally, throughout the continent, Communist strength tends toward concentrations in urban areas such as Paris, Madrid, Copenhagen, Lisbon, Thessaloniki, and Oslo. The reason for this, however, is less an urban-rural cleavage than the concentration of industrial workers in urban areas.

Class Cleavages

The relationship between class divisions and Communist party strength is complex. First, there is no simple one-to-one relationship between the size of the working class or the poorer classes and Communist party strength. If there were, of course, there would be a strong Communist party in virtually every country of Western Europe, which is not the case. Even in countries with mass Communist parties, larger proportions of the working class are neither party members nor Communist voters. Ecological studies in France and Italy show little correlation between Communist voting and the

percentage population employed in industry.[12] Survey data from a
1968 Italian sample found that only 35 percent of the working class
supported the PCI.[13] (See Table 6.) In 1975, although nearly two-
thirds of the Communists' vote came from skilled and unskilled
industrial workers and farm workers, the Christian Democrats
drew a nearly equal proportion of their vote from these groups.[14]
Similarly, in France in 1976, although more than one-half of the
Communists' supporters were workers, nearly 30 percent of the
Socialists' support came from workers and more than one-fifth of
the supporters of the Gaullists and Independent Republicans were
workers.[15]

In Finland in 1966, 79 percent of the supporters of the Communists' electoral front, the SKDL, were working class. Only 34 percent of the working class voted for the SKDL.[16] In the 1958 parliamentary election in Tampere, Finland, it is estimated that although
94 percent of the Communist voters were workers, two-thirds of the
workers in the city voted non-Communist.[17] Moreover, nationwide
data indicate that only 40 percent of Finnish workers prefer the
SKP.[18]

Neither is Communist support predominantly drawn from the
poorer classes. Communist voters in Finland are of somewhat
lower socioeconomic status than those who vote for the Social
Democrats, but the difference is very slight.[19] A Swedish study
concludes that the trades and occupations showing the highest

**Table 6. Party ID in Italy in 1968, by Occupational Class and
Subjective Social Class, in Percentages**

Occupa- tional Class	Subjec- tive Class	PCI	PSIUP	PSI- PSDI	PRI	DC	PLI	MON	MSI
Middle	Middle	6	1	16	3	43	5	1	3
	Working	5	1	17	1	45	4	1	2
Working	Middle	13	3	15	1	42	1	—	2
	Working	22	3	21	1	32	2	—	1

SOURCE: Samuel H. Barnes, "Italy, Religion and Class in Electoral Behavior,"
pp. 171–226, in Richard Rose, ed., *Electoral Behavior: A Comparative Handbook* (New York: Free Press, 1974).

percentage Communist vote are among the best paid rather than the worst paid. Also, there is no relationship in Sweden between unemployment and the Communist vote.[20] In Italy one ecological study even finds a positive correlation between PCI vote at the commune level and per capita income.[21] Survey evidence from 1968 shows that of the lowest income group, those earning less than 50,000 lira a month, 15 percent voted Communist, but 48 percent supported the Christian Democrats.[22] In France a 1965 survey indicates that of the seven largest electoral organizations, the PCF's electorate had the *lowest* percentage of voters with monthly incomes *below* 500 frances.[23]

Second, Communist party strength has a more diverse base than just the industrial working class. In 1975 skilled workers made up just over 25 percent of the electorate of the Italian Communist Party, and unskilled workers and farm laborers together accounted for more than 40 percent. Small businessmen and professionals made up the remaining 30 percent.[24] In France, too, Communist voters come from a broader spectrum than just the working class. Survey data (Table 7) indicate that only about one-half of the PCF's electorate are workers, and although many of those classified as "inactive" are retired workers, significant portions of the Party's vote comes from other sectors of the population.

A similar pattern holds for other countries where data is available. One study finds that almost 25 percent of the British Commu-

Table 7. PCF Electorate

	1976	1973	1968	1967	Adult Population
Professional	8%[a]	3%	2%	2%	6%
Small business	—	5	5	6	9
Middle class	15	17	18	15	17
Workers	52	51	49	49	32
Inactive	21	19	18	19	24
Agricultural	4	5	8	9	12

SOURCE: *Sondages*, 1973, 1976.

[a] Professional and small business combined.

nist Party are middle class.[25] A 1968 study indicates that more than 25 percent of the Belgian Communist Party's voters are middle class.[26] Unfortunately, no recent data are available for the Spanish Communist Party, but in 1937 the PCE claimed that 35 percent of its members were industrial workers, 30 percent farmers, 25 percent agricultural laborers, 7 percent middle class, and 3 percent professionals and intellectuals.[27]

Third, in countries where the Communist party is strong, one of its soundest bases of support is the industrial proletariat. In France, the PCF has been able to count on certain bastions of strength even in years when the Communist vote has been in decline. Foremost among these are the working-class suburbs of Paris—the "Red Belt."[28] Although the support for the Italian Communist Party is more diffuse, the PCI can also rely on a hard core of working-class support.[29] Like its French and Italian counterparts, the Finnish Communist Party has powerful bases of support in varying economic and social regions, one of which is among industrial workers.[30] In 1975 and 1976 elections, much of the electoral strength of the Portuguese Communist Party was concentrated in the working class districts of Lisbon and Setúbal. Much of the Greek Communist Party's support comes from factory workers in the principal cities. In Iceland and Luxembourg, the Communists enjoy a base among workers. Finally, even in countries where Communism is weak, a large portion of what strength it does have is among workers.

Fourth, in spite of the fact that every Western European Communist party has a core of strength composed of workers, not every national proletariat has even a large minority allied to the Communists. In Norway, Austria, and Ireland, the Communists have made almost no inroads among workers. In Britain, although the CPGB has some strength in certain unions, its success in converting even a minority of rank-and-file workers has been minimal. In Belgium, Denmark, West Germany, the Netherlands, Sweden, and Switzerland, the Communists have only been able to establish a foothold among workers.

Finally, class cleavages, like other types of cleavages, are neither a necessary nor a sufficient condition for Communist party strength. In France, Italy, Spain, and Finland, nations that historically have witnessed severe class cleavages, Communism has flourished among the workers. In contrast, countries such as Britain and Switzerland, which have experienced relatively few class conflicts, have no substantial Communist movement. The working-class movements of Austria and Norway, however, to name two examples, have historically been quite radical, but neither country has a strong Communist movement. Even more difficult to explain on the basis of class cleavages is Iceland. It is a small country with neither political rigidity nor deep class division, but it has one of the stronger Communist parties in Western Europe.

The importance of social cleavages for Western European Communist parties is that they provide fertile soil from which a party may seek nourishment. Although the absence of major social cleavages does not preclude Communist strength (witness Iceland) nor does their presence insure Communist success (witness Austria), cleavages, be they clerical-anticlerical,[31] ethnic, regional, or class, provide bases for Communist parties to build support. A clerical-anticlerical cleavage as in France, Spain, and Italy; a large, isolated industrial proletariat as in much of Europe; or sharp ethnic divisions as in Belgium can all be fertile ground for the development and sustenance of a Communist party that can skillfully exploit the division for its own ends. On the other hand, an overwhelmingly Catholic country such as the Republic of Ireland (where as much as 90 percent of the population are practicing Catholics[32]) or a wealthy, predominantly bourgeois nation such as Switzerland provides little natural support for the Communists.

Giovanni Sartori makes a related argument. Social divisions, he suggests, do not lead directly to social action. There is a gap, for example, between class *conditions* on the one hand, and class *actions* on the other. This missing link, he conjectures, may be an organizational variable: the influence of party and trade union control. Class conditions are only a facilitating factor. "To put it bluntly, it is not the 'objective' class (class conditions) that creates the party, but the party that creates the 'subjective' class (class consciousness)."[33] Therefore, Communist party strength does not follow automatically from social division. Rather, it can exacerbate and deepen these divisions, exploiting them for its own ends. How successful the Communists are in this depends, in part, on the strength of their

competitors and, in part, on the applicability of their party programs, policies, and organization.

Social Structure, Party Policies, and Organization

Whether a Communist party is able to take advantage of the
opportune conditions provided by social cleavages or to flourish
despite relatively consensual surroundings (as in Iceland) depends
on a number of factors, one of which is how well it adapts its
programs, policies, and organization to its domestic environment.
Although the size and strength of non-ruling Communist parties is
not rigidly determined by the social structure, their political success
depends at least in part on how well they adapt their programs to
different socioeconomic groups. The more intense the cleavages, the
better the opportunity for the Communists to find a receptive
audience.

The case of the Icelandic Communist Party demonstrates, however, that the absence of major social cleavages does not condemn a
Communist party to political sterility. In Iceland, Communist success has depended in part on the well-directed exploitation of
certain characteristics of the economic and social development of
the nation. As well as workers' issues and the issue of international
neutrality, the PA has successfully appealed to fishermen and fishing interests by strongly championing the rights of Icelandic fishermen in the "cod war" with Britain.

In Finland, too, the Communists have achieved success in appealing to diverse groups. In the developed industrial areas of the
South and West, the SKP has taken advantage of the traditional
radicalism of Finnish workers to establish a stronghold of support.
In the North and East, however, the Party has found success by
pitching its appeals to displaced, "alienated" workers in economi-
cally backward regions experiencing rapid social change.

No other Western European Communist party has sought to
appeal to a broader range of social and economic groups than the
Italian Communist Party. Once called a "vast Tammany Hall" by
Gunnar Myrdal, the PCI has tailored its brand of Marxism to
attract industrial workers in the North, peasant farmers in the
South, city dwellers, Catholics, and even members of the middle

class. Togliatti saw the PCI as encompassing all but the ruling class. "It is necessary," he declared, "to attract into the party all the active elements that are in the working and intellectual classes and to make of our party a party with a mass character."[34]

In the Italian South, the PCI has courted support through establishing mass organizations and agricultural cooperatives, supporting agrarian reform, and emphasizing local issues and personalities, and its success is reflected in election results for the Chamber of Deputies. In 1946 the PCI won only 10.2 percent of the vote in the South, but in 1976 that figure was 31.4 percent.

The PCI has also exerted strong efforts to reach a *modus vivendi* with the Church and to attract Catholic laymen to the Party. To gain the neutrality if not the support of the Vatican, the Italian Communists agreed to the inclusion of the Lateran Pacts in the postwar Republican constitution, endorsed religious freedom in Italy, and attacked the Soviets for their antireligious campaign of 1963. Since Pope John's *Pacem in Terris* in 1963, the Catholic Church itself has been more receptive to Communist advances and the two great social forces of modern Italy have engaged in a dialogue to reach understanding on common interests.[35] For the PCI, the fruits of its approaches toward the Church have been an increased acceptance among Catholic laymen and, significantly, in the June 1975 regional elections, for the first time, the Church hierarchy refrained from specifically endorsing the Christian Democrats.[36] In 1976, however, the Vatican returned to a position of fervent anti-Communism.

In France, too, the Communist Party presents a platform designed to appeal to peasants, small businessmen, and workers. Like the Italians, the French Communists have pursued a policy of *la main tendue* ("the extended hand") toward Catholics, but the French version has not been so far-reaching. It has been between individual Communists and Catholics, rather than formal spokesmen (as in Italy) and has been more sporadic. Since the purging of Roger Garaudy, the PCF's chief advocate of *rapprochement* with the Church, relations between the Party and the Church have cooled considerably.

The group most receptive to the courtship of the French Communists is the workers. By defending their immediate interests, the

PCF has won the allegiance of a large portion of the French working class. According to a 1966 national survey, more Frenchmen consider the PCF the "party of the workers" (41 percent) than any other single description, such as "grand force of the Left" (17 percent) or "the Party that wants revolution" (7 percent).[37]

Elsewhere, too, Communist parties have attempted to capitalize on social divisions by gearing their programs to appeal to the interests of various social groups. In Belgium the PCB has built most of its modest success on appeals to the minority Walloons and to miners and industrial workers in Wallonia and Brussels.[38] The Communist parties of West Germany and Great Britain direct most of their efforts toward workers and trade unionists.

In a number of Western European Communist parties, the organizational structure of the party mirrors salient social cleavages. Although since 1970 the Communist parties of Northern Ireland and the Republic of Ireland have been unified, the CPI reflects the political and religious cleavages in that divided island. The Executive Committee of the Party is divided into North and South branches with the Party general-secretary, Michael O'Riordan, being from the South, and the Party chairman, Andrew Barr, from the North. With each branch holding a veto, the CPI has found it difficult to make policy decisions on matters involving Northern Ireland and Irish unification.

Like the Irish Party, the Belgian Communist Party is divided along lines reflecting the nation's major social cleavage. Since 1966 the PCB has been divided into Walloon and Flemish branches with each having the right of veto.

Finally, the Swiss Communist Party's structure reflects the nation's multilingual character with each of the three major linguistic groups formally represented on the Central Committee. Of its fifty members, thirty-two are French speaking, fifteen German, and three Italian. Also, both German- and French-speaking members are represented on the five-man secretariat. In Spain the PCE has semi-autonomous branches in Catalonia and the Basque country.

The relationship between social structure and Communist party policy and organization is not that the former determines the latter. The presence of Catholics or peasants or urbanites within a political system does not dictate policy. Rather, the influence of social structure lies in the fact that as a major part of the Communist parties' domestic environment, those parties must in some way deal with it. They must harness the political energy created by social cleavages to their own advantage as in France and Italy or, failing in this, be torn apart themselves by those very cleavages, as in Ireland. Social structure affects Communist parties in that the parties mold their particular brand of Communism and the structure of their organization to appeal to the interests of the different social groups in their domestic environments. Since the domestic social environments of the Western parties differ, each is faced with somewhat different exigencies and, in part, their different policies and programs are the result of these differences. Consequently, although the Western parties' international environment, because of its similarity for each of the parties, makes for similarities in the parties' behavior, their domestic social environments, because of their diversity, make for differences.

Notes

1. In terms of voters if not necessarily in terms of members. The party, of course, is the *vanguard* of the proletariat and thus may be more heterogeneous in its composition.

2. Seymour Martin Lipset, *Political Man* (Garden City: Doubleday, 1960), pp. 45-53. Lipset qualifies this with reference to the rapidity of industrialization, the size of non-Communist reform parties, and regional variations. Ibid., pp. 68-71, 122-26.

3. Thomas H. Greene, "The Electorates of Nonruling Communist Parties," Studies in *Comparative Communism* IV, nos. 3-4 (July-October 1971):68-103.

4. Gianfranco Poggi, *Le preferenze politiche degli italiani: analisi di alcuni sondaggi pre-electtorali* (Bologna: Il Mulino, 1968), quoted in Samuel H. Barnes, "Italy: Religion and Class in Electoral Behavior," pp. 171-226, in Richard Rose, ed., *Electoral Behavior: A Comparative Handbook* (New York: Free Press, 1974), pp. 208-10. A problem with this and other surveys taken in Western Europe is the refusal of many respondents to state a partisan preference. These respondents are usually concentrated on the Left; so the Communist proportion of the sample is invariably underrepresented. Since there is no reason to believe that those Communists who refuse to identify themselves are similar to those who do identify themselves, we must accept survey evidence with at least some reservations.

5. Giacomo Sani, "Mass-Level Response to Party Strategy: The Italian Electorate and the Communist Party," pp. 456-503, in Donald L. M. Blackmer and Sidney Tarrow, eds., *Communism in Italy and France* (Princeton:Princeton University, 1975), p. 196.

6. *Sondages,* 1973. Unfortunately, survey data is unavailable for Portugal and Spain.

7. Seventy-eight percent in 1968. Keith Hill, "Belgium: Political Change in a Segmented Society," pp. 29-107, in Rose, *Electoral Behavior,* p. 48.

8. Ibid., p. 49.

9. Neil McInnes, *The Communist Parties of Western Europe* (London: Oxford, 1975), p. 40.

10. Ibid., pp. 41-43; Ake Sparring, "Introduction," pp. 279-85, in William E. Griffith, ed., *Communism in Europe,* vol. II (Cambridge: MIT, 1964).

11. Sidney G. Tarrow, *Peasant Communism in Southern Italy* (New Haven: Yale, 1967).

12. Steighton Arthur Watts, Jr., *The Influence of Socioeconomic Factors on Party Vote in the Italian General Election of June 7, 1953* (Doctoral dissertation, Michigan State University, 1960), tables 22 and 23; Vittorio Capecchi, Vittoria Cioni Polacchini, Giorgio Galli, and Giordano Sivini, *Il Comportamento Electorale in Italia* (Bologna: Il Mulino, 1968), table 32, p. 389.

13. Barnes, "Italy," p. 206.

14. Giacomo Sani, "The PCI on the Threshold," *Problems of Communism* XXV, no. 6 (November-December 1976):27-51.

15. *Sondages,* 1976.

16. Pertti Pesonen, "Finland: Party Support in a Fragmented System," pp. 271-314, in Rose, *Electoral Behavior,* p. 294.

17. Pertti Pesonen, *An Election in Finland: Party Activities and Voter Reactions* (New Haven: Yale, 1968).

18. Erik Allardt, "Social Sources of Finnish Communism: Traditional and Emerging Radicalism," *International Journal of Comparative Sociology* V, no. 1 (March 1964):49-72.

19. Ibid., p. 56.

20. W. Phillips Davison, "A Review of Sven Rydenfelt's *Communism in Sweden,*" *Public Opinion Quarterly* XVIII, no. 4 (Winter 1954-55):375-88.

21. Giordano Sivini, "Il comportamento elettorale in Italia: Primi risultati di un'analisis ecologica," *Ressegne italiana di sociologia* VIII (January-March 1967):115.

22. Barnes, "Italy," p. 204.

23. *Sondages,* 1965.

24. Sani, "The PCI on the Threshold."

25. Kenneth Newton, *The Sociology of British Communism* (London: Penguin, 1969), p. 72.

26. Hill, "Belgium."

27. Guy Hermet, *The Communists in Spain* (Lexington, Mass.:Heath, 1974), p. 35.

28. Jean Ranger, "L'évolution du vote communiste en France depuis 1945," pp. 211-47, in Frédéric Bon, ed., *Le communisme en France,* Cahiers de la fondation nationale des sciences politiques, 175 (Paris: Armand Colin, 1969).

29. Tarrow, *Peasant Communism,* pp. 131-33.

30. Jaakko Nousiainen, "Research on the Finnish Communism," *Scandinavian Political Studies* III (1968):243-51.

31. But not, apparently, between opposing religious persuasions. In the competition between two dogmas, there is no place for a third.

32. C.K. Ward, "Socio-religious Research in Ireland," *Social Compass* XI (1964):26.

33. Giovanni Sartori, "From the Sociology of Politics to Political Sociology," pp. 65-100, in Seymour Martin Lipset, *Politics and the Social Sciences* (New York: Oxford, 1969), p. 84.

34. Quoted in Tarrow, *Peasant Communism,* p. 123.

35. Neil McInnes, "The Christian-Marxist Dialogue: International Implications," *Survey,* no. 67 (April 1968):57-76; Kevin Devlin, "The Catholic-Communist 'Dialogue,' " *Problems of Communism* XV, no. 3 (May-June 1966):31-38.

36. *New York Times,* 16 June 1975; nevertheless, the Vatican was careful *not* to support the Communists. Ibid., 10 November 1975.

37. *Sondages,* 1966.

38. Louis Van Geyt, "Communal and Power Crisis in Belgium," *World Marxist Review* XVII, no. 9 (September 1974):73-82.

chapter 5

POLITICAL SYSTEM

Perhaps the most important aspect of a Communist party's domestic environment is the political system. The domestic political environment directly affects the Western European Communist parties by determining in part their size and strength. Elements of the political environment indirectly shape party policy because it is upon and within this environment that the Communist parties seek to act.

First, other Left-wing parties compete with the Communists for political resources, thus directly affecting the Communists' political success. At the same time, it is usually these same Leftist competitors who are the primary potential alliance partners for the Communists. Moreover, because of the ambivalent position of Leftist parties as both potential rivals and potential partners of the Communists, they can directly influence the shape of the Communists' policy postures, both domestically and internationally.

Second, Communist parties in Western Europe are affected by the nature of the party systems in which they operate. Party systems differ both in number of parties and in degree of polarity. Depending upon the size of a Communist party, its political prospects are affected by these two aspects of the party system and it may modify its policies accordingly. Indirectly, then, the party system can influence Communist policy positions.

Third, the policies and positions of the Western Communist parties are influenced by the nature and strength of actual and potential party auxiliaries such as unions and youth organizations. On the one hand, Communist parties use auxiliaries to shield themselves from environmental uncertainties, but, on the other, these organizations act as ties between the parties and the political system.

Finally, the political culture in which each Communist party is embedded shapes both the Communists' strength and political position. Political cultures differ in their receptivity to Communism; so different political cultures offer different prospects for Communist party establishment and growth. As with social structure, the political culture indirectly influences party policies in that to be successful, Communist parties find it necessary to appeal to salient characteristics of their domestic political culture.

Left-Wing Political Parties

Social Democratic Parties

Throughout Western Europe, non-ruling Communist parties are faced with a variety of other Leftist parties with whom they sometimes compete and sometimes cooperate. Historically, the most important of these, both as competitors and as allies, have been social democratic parties.

In the 1920s, major Communist parties emerged only in those countries where strong Socialist movements split into social democratic and Communist segments and a significant part of the Socialists' leadership, membership, and organization went over to the Communist camp. In Italy the PCI was formed when a group of radical Socialists seceded from the Socialist Party at its Seventeenth Congress in Livorno and joined the Third International. Less than half of the old Socialist Party rallied to the Communist banner, but, nevertheless, the PCI enjoyed a solid core of organizational and mass support after the split, particularly among workers. Moreover, the Party was blessed with a group of very capable leaders, including Gramsci, Togliatti, Terracini, and Tasca.

In France the PCF began after the Socialist Party split at Tours in October 1921. Eighty-nine of the ninety-six old Socialist federations and 110,000 of the 178,800 members elected to follow the

PCF. Although its strength declined until the 1930s, the Party maintained a firm core of support. Although the Finnish Communist Party was founded in Moscow in 1918, it was composed of the Left wing of the Social Democratic Party whose leaders fled following a bloody civil war. Despite its birth in exile, the SKP held a solid base among émigré working-class leaders in Russia and rank-and-file workers in Finland. Finally, in Germany, the only other Western European nation that saw the emergence of even a moderately large Communist party in the 1920s, the KPD was formed in late 1918 by the Spartacist League which had broken with the Socialist Party in 1917. The core of the KPD's organization, membership, and leadership (including Rosa Luxembourg and Karl Leibknecht) was once part of the Socialist Party, and during the 1920s, the Communists added many former Socialist voters and union militants as well.

Thomas Greene argues the importance of elites' initiative, the manner of party formation, and the timing of that formation:

> Where socialism is strong, but communism weak, the explanation lies in the political choice of left-wing elites at a critical juncture in modern history. Modern CPs are strong only where their early leadership, clientele, and organizational network came directly from strong socialist parties already in existence, and only at the time when the Bolshevik Revolution and organization of the Comintern gave impetus to a splintering of the political left.[1]

Thus, in countries where Communist parties were born as a result of a fusion of small Left-wing groups as in Britain, Greece, and Austria, or were virtually implanted from Moscow, as in Ireland, Communism was initially weak. Communist parties were also weak in countries where Socialist parties avoided the splintering caused by the Bolshevik Revolution as in Sweden, Belgium, Holland, Portugal, and Norway.

In the decades since most Western European Communist parties were founded in the late 1910s and early 1920s, the relative strength of the continent's parties has fluctuated considerably. Although the French, Italian, and Finnish parties are still strong, the KPD's West German successor is far from mighty. Other parties, the Spanish, Luxembourg, Portuguese, and Icelandic, have become at least moderately strong and the last several decades have seen the strength of the Greek Communist Party rise and then fall again. The reasons for this fluctuation of Communist strength in Western Europe are many, but, at least in part, the strength of Communist parties is related to the strength of social democratic parties. First, in general, where Socialism is weak, Communism is weak. Second, where Communism is moderately strong, Socialism is moderately strong. Finally, where Socialism is very strong, Communism is weak.

In countries without strong Socialist traditions (Ireland and the United States, for example), neither Socialism nor Communism prospers. Only in countries with Socialist heritages and consequent historically significant Socialist parties, have Communist parties flourished.[2]

Electorally, Communist strength is strongly correlated with prior Leftist voting patterns. In France much of the Communist Party's vote comes from areas with strong Leftist traditions.[3] One study finds that "almost all the constituencies of the Center and the Southwest which are now casting a heavy ballot for the CP went *montagnard* in the election of May, 1849, creating the first legislative assembly of the Second Republic."[4] Later, these same areas voted Radical, then Socialist, and now Communist.

In Italy, Communist and Socialist Party strength in the 1970s geographically coincides to a large extent with the map of Socialist support in 1919 and, for Central Italy, they match almost perfectly. Historically, the "Red Belt" region of Central Italy has been a bastion of anticlericalism. In 1831 representatives of this region gathered in Bologna to protest the temporal power of the Pope. Today, they elect town councils and regional governments with Left-wing majorities and Bologna has a Communist mayor.[5]

In Finland Communist strength in the South and West is concentrated in regions with traditional Leftist voting patterns. According to Allardt, Communist strength in Finland is to a large extent explained by traditions of radicalism and class conflict.[6] Similarly, in recent elections in Spain and Portugal, Communists did well in areas known for Left-wing radicalism—Andalusia in Spain and the Alentejo region in Portugal.

In countries with large and powerful social democratic parties—Great Britain, West Germany, Norway, Denmark, Sweden,

Austria, and Belgium—Communism is chronically weak. In their competition for Leftist voters, social democratic parties in these countries have swept the field. Through their control of the unions and, at times, local and national governments, the Social Democrats have established themselves as the *only* viable Left-wing alternative to the bourgeois parties. Consequently, they win all but a few die-hard or protest Left-wing votes.

The closest case of an exception to this occurs in Luxembourg where the Socialist Party is one of the nation's largest parties. Despite its size, the Luxembourg Socialist Party has failed to dominate the Left because of its inability to win national power. For fifty-five years, until the May 1974 elections, the conservative Christian Socialists controlled the government. The current position of the Socialists at the head of a Center-Left governing coalition may, however, give them the political leverage to expand their support, thus spelling the possibility of hard times for the Communists.

There are a number of cases where Communist parties prospered after events intervened to weaken their Left-wing rivals. In Finland, for example, the legalized SKP was aided in its emergence as a major political force after World War II by the fact that the Social Democrats had been compromised by wartime association with the bourgeois parties. In Sweden, Norway, and Denmark, the political labor movement became practically identical with social democracy, but defeat in World War II ended a similar development in Finland.[7] Subsequently, the Communist and Social Democratic parties in Finland have been at near equal strength. Also, the emergence and early success of Communist parties in France, Germany, and Italy were facilitated because the Socialist parties in those countries were compromised by their involvement in World War I.

In those countries where both Communist and Socialist parties have been historically strong, the respective strength of Communist and Socialist parties varies positively at times and negatively at times. When there is a general swing to the Left among the electorate, both Socialist and Communist parties will benefit correlatively. During the Popular Front period, for example, the tendency was for both Socialist and Communist parties to prosper. Conversely, both parties decline if there is a national shift away from the Left.

The strength of Communist and Socialist parties varies inversely, however, in the case of a secular shift among Left-wing voters. In such an instance, the relative strength of the Left and Right parties remains the same, but the Socialists gain at the expense of the Communists or vice versa. For example, 1920 to 1934 was a long period of decline for the French Communist Party, but years of moderate growth for the Socialist Party. In the Cold War period, in several countries, the Socialists gained at the Communists' expense. Similarly, postwar gains by the Italian Communist Party have been largely at the expense of the Socialists and other Leftist parties.

Ironically, then, the Communists are often in the fiercest competition with the party with whom they are *not* in fundamental opposition on many issues and with whom they appeal to similar social strata and interests—the Socialists. The two parties often find themselves competing for the same relatively fixed number of Left-wing voters and the success of one is the failure of the other. In alliance, Communists and Socialists ostensibly work together to achieve common electoral and programmatic goals against bourgeois opponents. In opposition, they battle for preeminence among Leftist voters. The rub is that there is no clear demarcation between times of alliance and times of opposition. In different locales and at different times, Communists and Socialists both compete and cooperate. During periods of alliance, the two often find themselves competing both for labor union and electoral dominance. In times of opposition, the two parties often cooperate on the local and regional levels. To quote Kurt Schumacher, Communists and Socialists are brothers, like Cain and Abel.

As competitors, Communist parties have been faced with the problem of differentiating their program on popular grounds from that of the Socialists. In countries such as Sweden and Norway, where the Communists have adopted programs pointing to the peaceful Road to Socialism, and the Social Democrats are themselves relatively radical on many issues, the Communists have been hard pressed to find ground on the Left that has not been preempted by the dominant Socialists—ground other than loyalty to the Soviet Union, usually not a popular position.

As allies or would-be allies, Communist parties have been faced with the problem of modifying their positions to secure Socialist backing while, at the same time, not alienating their own base of support. In France, for example, the PCF has been forced to accept such concepts as multi-partism, alternation of power, and the abandonment of the doctrine of the dictatorship of the proletariat. By doing so, however, the PCF has apparently paid a price among some of its own militants who have evinced displeasure with the Party's moderate stance.

Also, as allies, the Communists have faced the problem of being exploited by their partners. As participants in the 1946 coalition of Communists, Social Democrats, and Agrarians, the politically naïve Finnish Communist Party was thoroughly outmaneuvered by its experienced partners. During its tenure in government, the SKP won only the single concession of airline nationalization. In exchange, it was shackled with part of the blame for a wage freeze and price increases and, when major strikes broke out in the fall of 1946, the SKP could no longer play its usual role as unconditional champion of the workers' demands. Similarly, the SKP's participation in Center-Left governing coalitions from 1966 through March 1971 brought it few tangible benefits. In coalition, the Party was forced to make concessions, accepting "non-Socialist" measures, particularly in the economic field. Consequently, the SKP shared the blame for unpopular economic policies and its own internal divisions were exacerbated. The story was much the same during the SKP's recent sojourn in the government from late 1975 to September 1976.

The Communists' dilemma in alliance with Socialist parties is that without the Socialists, they cannot hope to win national political power in most of Western Europe, but in alliance with the Socialists, they face the danger of losing their separate identity and seeing their support dwindle. In France the PCF took major steps to secure an electoral and programmatic alliance with the Socialist Party, reaching agreement on a Common Program in 1972 that was a major compromise of orthodox Communist philosophy. Mitterrand's very strong showing in the 1974 presidential election illustrated the potency of the electoral combination.

Alarmingly for the Communists, however, the major electoral shift after the formation of the common front was not so much *toward* the Left, but *within* the Left in favor of the Socialists and away from the PCF. In 1969 the Socialist Party appeared a spent and humiliated force. It was declining, divided, and dispirited, but since then, under Mitterrand's leadership, it has become the dominant party of the Left. In the fall by-election after the presidential vote in 1974, the Socialists increased their vote, while the Communist vote declined sharply. Polls showed the Socialists far ahead of the Communists,[8] and an October 1975 partial legislative election in Vienne again followed the trend of an increased first-ballot Socialist vote, apparently gained at the expense of the Communists.[9] In local elections in the spring of 1976, once again the big gainers were the Socialists rather than the Communists, and the pattern held in by-elections in November 1976.[10] In the municipal elections held in March 1977, the Union of the Left presented common lists in most areas, but the Socialists again proved to be the big winners, gaining control of twenty-seven additional cities with a population of thirty thousand or more, while the PCF won only twelve more. The dilemma for the Communists was that if they wished to maintain an electoral alliance with a real chance of winning, they had to appear moderate enough to reassure the voters and Socialists alike of their democratic intentions. If they appeared too moderate, however, they risked alienating some of their own cadres and perhaps declining vis-à-vis the Socialists.

The response of the PCF's leaders to this was to walk a tightrope between maintaining the alliance for electoral purposes and boldly reasserting their Party's separate identity. Although the Communists compromised on the issue of election procedures for the European parliament, they stood firm on the issue of nationalizations in the negotiations with their Left-wing allies to update the Common Program.

Eventually the price of alliance proved too high for the Communists, and they forced a rupture in the fall of 1977. If the Communists' strategy was to cut the Socialists down to size, it succeeded. In the first round of the March 1978 parliamentary elections, the Socialists finished a bare 2 percentage points ahead of the Communists, 22.6 percent to 20.6 percent. Subsequently, the Communists, Socialists, and Left Radicals agreed to support common candidates in the second round run-off.

Another danger facing the Communists in France and elsewhere is that Socialist allies may bridge over the Left-Right political cleavage to form a majority government with the bourgeoisie, thus condemning the Communists to what could be permanent minority status on the Left as well as political isolation. In France the PCF has accused the Socialists of yearning to join a coalition under Giscard.

In Italy, however, the threat has taken concrete form in the famed "Opening to the Left." In the early 1960s, the Italian Socialist Party elected to join the Christian Democrat government of Aldo Moro. The PCI was spared isolation, however, for two reasons. First, the Socialists valued their local and regional ties with the Communists too much to give them up. Second, in the long run, the Center-Left government foundered on its inability to solve Italy's more pressing economic problems.

Socialist People's Parties

In 1959 Axel Larsen, who had been deposed as leader of the Danish Communist Party, joined with a large group of former Communists and other Leftists to form the Danish Socialist People's Party (SF). In the 1960 election it outpolled the DKP 6.1 percent to only 1.1 percent and won eleven seats to the Communists' none. Since then Socialist people's parties have complicated life for Communist parties in much of Scandinavia.

The prototype of the Socialist people's parties, the Danish SF, was something of a halfway house between the Social Democrats and the Communists. Anticapitalist, the SF criticized the Social Democrats for having stopped being a truly Socialist party and for becoming too dependent on the union movement. At the same time, while pledging its own adherence to Danish democratic parliamentary traditions, the SF excoriated the DKP for clinging to the Kremlin.

Electorally, the SF did well for a time, winning 5.8 percent of the vote and ten seats in 1964 and 10.8 percent and twenty seats in 1966. In 1968, however, the SF itself split, with the parent party winning 6.1 percent of the vote and six seats and the splinter party, the VS, registering 2 percent and four seats. In the 1971 election, the VS fell below 2 percent and thus, by Danish electoral laws, lost its seats in the Folketing. The SF, however, improved its representation to seventeen seats and 9.1 percent and, with the Social Democrats, entered the government. In 1973, however, the SF lost heavily, falling to 6 percent and eleven seats with the Communists reaping the benefits. The 1975 election saw the SF's decline continue as it dropped to 4.9 percent and nine seats. The 1977 election was even less encouraging for the SF as its total fell to 3.9 percent and seven seats.

Like their Danish comrades, Communists in Norway have had to contend with a challenge from a Socialist people's party. Contrary to Danish experience, the Norwegian SF was formed by a group of unaffiliated Leftists and former Social Democrats in 1961. Like the Danish SF, however, the new Norwegian party rejected both Peking and Moscow as models, pledged its allegiance to parliamentarism, and attacked the Social Democrats for lacking Socialist vigor. Although the long-range goal of the SF was quite similar to that of the NKP—a democratic transition to Socialism based on Marxism, parliamentarism, and the multi-party system—the SF attacked the Communists as "dogmatic" and "old Marxist." In response the NKP accused the SF of splitting the labor movement.

Electorally, the Norwegian SF has recorded more modest successes than its Danish model. In 1961 the SF won only 2.4 percent of the vote and two seats in the Storting, but did hold the balance of power between bourgeois parties and the Social Democrats. In 1965 the SF upped its total to 6 percent of the votes and two seats; then in 1969, after the defection of its youth wing, the SF declined to 3.4 percent and no seats.

In 1973, however, the SF, the NKP, and a group of dissident Social Democrats formed the Socialist Electoral Alliance, winning sixteen seats, 11.2 percent of the vote, and substantial leverage in a closely balanced Storting. Thereafter, the three members of the Alliance began negotiations aimed at merger into a single Leftist party. Although a loose framework for the formation of a Socialist Left Party (*Socialistisk Venstre parti*—SV) was reached in March 1975, the Communists retreated from the proposed union after a bitter internal debate in late 1975. Subsequently, Reidar Larsen, the Communist Party leader, and a number of his followers left the NKP and now support what remains of the SV.[11]

In Iceland, after the 1967 election, Hannibal Valdimarsson, the chairman of the Communist-dominated People's Alliance and head of the Icelandic Federation of Labor, broke away from the PA along with a group of his followers and began the Union of Liberals and Leftists (ULL), Iceland's equivalent to a Socialist people's party. Valdimarsson's quarrel with the PA involved the issue of internal democracy and there were personality conflicts as well. Meanwhile, he criticized the Social Democrats for lacking Socialist purity. The explicit goal of the ULL was the establishment of an umbrella social democratic party, including the PA, the ULL, and the Social Democrats, with Valdimarsson, of course, at its head.

Following the 1971 election, Valdimarsson achieved part of his goal. In the balloting, the PA won 17.1 percent and ten seats, and the ULL, 8.9 percent and five seats. Together with the Progressives, the three formed a Left-wing government. In the 1974 election, however, the ULL, shaken by factionalism, fell to only two seats and the coalition was broken with each of the parties going its separate way.[12]

For the Communist parties of Denmark, Norway, and Iceland, the Socialist people's parties have been an unwelcome threat. As halfway houses between the Social Democrats and the Communists, the SF parties provide a convenient home both for the dissenting Communists who might not bring themselves to move all the way over to the Social Democrats, and for renegade Left-wing Social Democrats and unaffiliated Leftists who might otherwise join the ranks of the Communists.

By dividing the extreme Left-wing vote, Socialist people's parties have further weakened the relatively impotent Communist parties in Denmark and Norway. In Denmark the DKP's electoral strength dropped alarmingly in face of the SF challenge, only rallying in the 1973, 1975, and 1977 elections. Similarly, the NKP vote fell in competition with the SF in Norway. Not until the formation of the Socialist Electoral Alliance did the fortunes of the Norwegian Communists improve. That improvement was short-lived as the Communists are again out in the cold and the Alliance was crushed in the September 1977 parliamentary election. Only in Iceland, buoyed by a general Leftist swing, did the Communists hold their own against an SF challenge.

Socialist people's parties have also challenged Communists in the union arena and among young people. In Iceland the ULL siphoned off some of the PA's strength in the Icelandic Federation of Labor. Similarly, the SF in Norway has attracted agricultural, forestry, and industrial workers away from the NKP. Also, in both Denmark and Norway in particular, SF parties have attracted youths from the Communist parties.

Because of their ideological proximity, Communist parties have been hard pressed to differentiate themselves from the SF parties. Communists have expended their resources villifying the SF parties as "splitters" dividing the Left and defending themselves against charges of heavy-handed orthodoxy and mimicry of Moscow. Consequently, SF parties provide an impetus to the Communists to liberalize their domestic policies and liberate themselves from ties to Moscow. Ironically, however, because they have tended to siphon off the most progressive elements in the Communist party, particularly in Denmark and in 1975 in Norway, too, the presence of a strong SF party makes the Communists less likely to liberalize.

Socialist people's parties complicate the alliance strategies of Communist parties because the SF parties are more acceptable as possible coalition partners for the Social Democrats, thus threatening the Communists with a narrow isolation on the Left, such as occurred in Denmark in 1971. At the same time, if the Communists wish to come to terms with social democratic parties for purposes of alliance, they must also decide on a policy for dealing with the SF parties. Logically, an alliance between Communists and Social Democrats would include the SF who fall between the two ideologically and often hold an important share of parliamentary power. Consequently, negotiations must be among at least three partners and an alliance, if reached, would usually find the Communists subordinate not only to the Social Democrats but to the SF as well. In Norway, where an electoral alliance was reached among the NKP, the SF, and a group of Social Democrat dissidents, the Communists were clearly the minor partners.

Finally, the SF parties, particularly the Danish SF, have provided a model for the renovation of the Swedish Communist Party. The New Left domestic policy, independent international posture, and internal democratization of the VPK are very much akin to that of the SF parties in neighboring countries.

Ultra-Left Parties

In the last decade, virtually every Communist party of Western Europe has been challenged by a proliferation of Maoist, Marxist-Leninist, Trotskyist, New Left, and Anarchist Left-wing splinter parties. One of the first of these was the Communist Party of Belgium, Marxist-Leninist (PCB-ML), begun in 1963 by veteran Communist Jacques Grippa as a pro-Peking rival to the established PCB. Apparently, the PCB-ML initially took 15 percent of the PCB's members and 10 percent of its vote. Since then, the PCB-ML has split and then split again. Currently, however, the main-line PCB faces challenges from another Maoist party and a growing Trotskyist movement.

In France the PCF has been challenged by dozens of small Leftist movements whose appeals have failed to win mass support, but have attracted numbers of students and intellectuals. Indeed, in May-June 1968, much to the chagrin of the PCF, it was the Maoists, Trotskyists, and Anarchists who manned the barricades in an attempt to put their own revolutionary strategies into operation. Today, however, the influence of most of the ultra-Left parties has diminished significantly.

The British Communist Party is being severely challenged on the Left, particularly by the Trotskyist Workers Revolutionary Party. Complicating the picture for the CPGB is the revival of Scottish and Welsh nationalist groups which, although not Leftist in the traditional sense, pose a major threat to Communist recruitment.

In Spain the PCE has been challenged on the Left from several quarters. In 1970 a pro-Soviet splinter group expelled from the PCE formed the Spanish Communist Workers Party, but in the last few years it has shrunk to insignificance. Currently, the PCE's primary ultra-Left opposition comes from a number of militant groups, including Basque guerrillas and the Maoist Patriotic and Revolutionary Anti-Fascist Front.

In the late 1960s and the early 1970s, the chief Leftist threat to the Italian Communist Party come from the *Il Manifesto* group, an anti-Soviet New Left-oriented coterie of intellectuals expelled from the PCI in 1969 and 1970.[13] Today, the PCI is also being challenged from the extreme Left by a number of terrorist organizations, including *Lotta Continua, Brigate Rosse,* and *Nuclei Armati Proletari,* and a new Left-wing party, *Partito di Unità per il Communismo,* that includes *Manifesto* and other groups.

In other countries, the Swiss Communist Party is faced with opposition from numerous Left-wing organizations, including a rapidly growing New Left party, POCH (The Progressive Organizations, Switzerland). A number of Maoist and other far-Left groups compete with Sweden's VPK. The Portuguese Communist Party is opposed by at least fourteen revolutionary New Left organizations. In the Netherlands, dissident pro-Soviet and pro-Chinese parties challenge the CPN, although most pro-Peking and pro-Chinese cadres have remained in the Party. The Greek Communist Party was opposed by some extreme Left organizations in 1976. In Iceland in 1968, hard-line, pro-Soviet elements defected from the PA to form the Organization of Icelandic Socialists. The Communist Party of West Germany faces opposition from numerous Left-wing splinter groups. In Austria the KPÖ is threatened by tiny Maoist and Trotskyist groups. A number of small ultra-Left movements have attracted youths from the Danish Communist Party. The Belgian Communist Party has to contend with several Trotskyist and Maoist groups. In Finland a pro-Peking party exists, but, as we have seen, most dissidents remain in the SKP itself. Finally, a small group of Trotskyists oppose the Communist Party of Luxembourg.

As with the Socialist people's parties, the ultra-Left parties have plagued the Communists by draining away voters and members. Although not all of the ultra-Left groups have functioned as electoral entities, where they have, they have inevitably split the Communist vote, costing the regular Communist party local and national offices. More seriously, however, the ultra-Left parties have drawn their adherents disproportionately from among young people. Consequently, the Communists have lost many of their more vigorous cadres as well as much of a generation of future leaders to their Leftist challengers. In Belgium, for example, Jacques Grippa's Peking-oriented faction proved particularly adroit at recruiting among students. In Norway the entire youth affiliate of the NKP broke with the parent party in 1967 to join a Marxist-Leninist party. Since the 1976 elections in Italy, the PCI youth affiliate has had difficulty recruiting members.

Not only do the ultra-Left parties threaten the Communists' hold on voters and cadres, but they also threaten the established parties' position in unions and party auxiliary groups. In addition to the Norwegian case, Communist youth affiliates throughout Western Europe have been subverted by Leftist parties and groups. Leftist organizations have also made inroads into Communists' union strength. In Britain, for example, the CPGB's position in the trade union movement is under very serious attack.

In a number of Western countries, the ultra-Left parties have harmed the Communists by actions that reflect unfavorably on the Left as a whole. In Italy, although the PCI has deplored extremist-inspired terrorist violence, its Christian Democrat opposition has attempted to use the ultra-Left violence to discredit the Communists. Although the French Communist Party was among the Leftist revolutionaries' severest critics in May-June 1968, the Gaullists succeeded in saddling the PCF with much of the blame for the disorders and decisively used the issue against the Communists in the 1968 election. In Britain the CPGB has had to share the blame, often unfairly, for political strikes inspired by the Communists' ultra-Left rivals. Similarly, the Spanish Right has tried to blame the Communist Party for Basque and Maoist terrorism.

Standing as a spectre on the Left, ultra-Left parties tend to prevent the Communists from straying too far from Leninist orthodoxy, particularly if the Communist party is relatively weak and if there are large groups in the party not unsympathetic to the Leftists' appeals. For example, since too bold a move away from Moscow or too bold a move against the Chinese could alienate their camp's supporters, driving them to pro-Soviet or pro-Peking parties, the Dutch Communist Party has been careful to observe neutrality in the Sino-Soviet split. In other parties, Communist leaders have moved to modernize their doctrine only cautiously for fear of seeing their conservative cadres exit en masse to a Marxist-Leninist rival.

On the other hand, ultra-Left parties at times have been beneficial to the Western Communist parties because they have siphoned off dissident elements, thus preventing internal friction and schisms and, consequently, giving the Communist leaders more freedom of action. Ultra-Left parties are a far greater check on the main-line parties as *potential* homes for Maoist or Stalinist dissidents than actual homes. After the Maoists and Stalinists have defected, the Communist parties are free to act. In Iceland, for example, the departure of pro-Soviet cadres to form the Organization of Icelandic Socialists freed the PA's leaders to pursue their independent foreign policies. The exodus of pro-Moscow cadres from the Spanish Communist Party to join the expelled Líster in forming an opposition party freed the PCE's leaders from pro-Soviet internal pressures. Throughout Western Europe, ultra-Left parties have tended to bring a measure of stability to the Communist parties by siphoning off individual dissidents and groups of recalcitrants. In countries such as Finland, where, except for a miniature Maoist party, ultra-Left parties have not taken root, and countries such as the Netherlands, where most dissidents have remained in the Party rather than defecting, Communist party leaders must walk a tightrope or see their parties torn by factionalism.

Finally, the presence of ultra-Left parties in the political system can make Communist parties more acceptable to middle-class voters and potential alliance partners. In contrast to the revolutionary rhetoric and actions of many of the ultra-Left groups, the Communist parties appear almost austere and conservative and, consequently, more acceptable to many voters, and to other parties as coalition partners. In places such as Italy where the PCI has gone out of its way to cultivate an image of moderation, the contrast with the extremist parties may be quite beneficial to the Communists.

The Party System

One of the major features of a nation's political system is its party system. For the Communist parties of Western Europe, the party system plays a direct role in determining their political strength and an indirect role in shaping their policy positions. In this, three factors work together: (1) the size of the Communist party; (2) the number of parties in the party system; and (3) the polarity of the party system.

As very minor parties in essentially two-party systems, the Communist parties of Great Britain, Austria, and West Germany find themselves in particularly disadvantageous positions, both electorally and in their alliance prospects. Although the electoral effect of a two-party system is not all-determining, it does tend to work against minor parties. Potential supporters generally opt for one of the major parties rather than wasting their votes on a party they believe cannot win. At least in part, for this reason, Communism in Britain, Austria, and under the Bonn Republic in West Germany has failed to make significant inroads against social democratic parties. In these countries, the two-party system also tends to frustrate the alliance ambitions of the Communists. Because of the two-party nature of the system, one of the parties usually wins a parliamentary majority, requiring no coalition partners. Finally, because of their usual distance from the seats of power, the Communists feel few restraints in shaping their policy positions.

As major parties (or at least moderate-sized parties) in multi-party systems, the Communist parties of Iceland, Finland, Portugal (since 1975), Greece (potentially), Luxembourg, and Spain do, however, have incentives to modify their domestic positions and their postures toward the Soviet Union. Since no one party usually wins a parliamentary majority, it is necessary for governing coalitions to be formed and, as a major or moderate-sized party, the Communists are important potential coalition partners. Consequently, the Communists have incentives to modify their positions to appear more palatable to potential partners. Once in a governing coalition, the Communists are further pushed toward policy modification because of the realities and pressures of office.

The French and Italian Communist parties, as major parties in polarized multi-party systems, have strong incentives to modify their positions. Insofar as each is regarded as the first party of the Left (clearly so for the PCI, now much less clearly for the PCF), it has an incentive to moderate its domestic policies to appear as a realistic alternative to the Right. Because of their major status in a polarized system, the Communists also benefit from support from voters who may not be strongly inclined toward them, but see the Communists as the chief opponent of the Right and the prime vehicle for registering protest against the political system. Their prominent position on the Left also makes the Communist parties of Italy and France prime partners for electoral alliances and governing coalitions at the local and regional level. At the national level, however, the Communists, barring a Left-wing majority, are less likely to be included in a coalition government because of the polarity of the system (a polarity the PCI is trying to reduce).

The position of the Swedish, Norwegian, Danish, Belgian, Swiss, and Dutch Communist parties as relatively minor parties in multi-party systems is one of contradictory impulses. Because of the multiplicity of parties, the Communists are pulled toward forming policies that are differentiated from their Left-wing rivals. On the other hand, since the multi-party system makes coalitions and alliances advantageous, and sometimes necessary to form a government, the Communists are propelled toward policy moderation if they seek alliance. Finally, the multi-party system may help to isolate the Communist party if, as in Denmark, parliamentary parties across the political spectrum oppose it, or it may give the Communists disproportionate strength, as was the case in Sweden, if they find themselves holding the balance of power in a closely divided parliament. An important variable that tends to influence the direction of impulses for a minor Communist party in a multi-party system is the degree of polarization in the system. In a highly polarized system, there will be relatively fewer willing possible coalition partners than in a less polarized system; so the Communists will have fewer incentives for policy adaptation. On the other hand, in a relatively unpolarized system, there will be a comparatively greater chance of the Communists being accepted as alliance partners; so there will be greater incentives for policy modification.

The party system also affects Communist party policy positions. In general, characteristics of the Communist party (particularly size) that would further Communist party leaders' perceptions of their party's nearness to office act as incentives toward policy modification and moderation. If the combination of these characteristics offers little hope for an early ascension to office, however, there will be little incentive toward policy modification.[14] Thus, Communist parties that are major parties in polarized or unpolarized multi-party systems and parties that are minor parties in unpolarized multi-party systems have incentives to moderate their programs. There are fewer incentives, however, for minor Communist parties in predominantly two-party systems or polarized multiparty systems.

Party Auxiliaries

Throughout Western Europe, Communist parties maintain or attempt to maintain networks of auxiliary organizations, including children's groups, women's federations, farmers' cooperatives, workers' organizations, pensioners' unions, peace groups, and friendship societies for the Soviet Union and Eastern Europe. For the Communists, these organizations function as socializing agents for party members and potential members; occasional political weapons to be employed to further party goals; bodies that lend the movement respectability and legitimacy; training grounds for party leaders and cadres; and valuable sources of material and human resources.

In general, Communist party auxiliaries serve as buffers to protect Communist parties from the vagaries of a heterogeneous environment. By creating a "countersociety" (although this is probably an overblown term for most of Western Europe), Communist parties try to shape significant portions of their environment to conform to themselves. At the same time, however, these auxiliary groups that serve to insulate the party also serve to tie the party ever closer to the political system in which it functions. Consequently, the nature and strength of these auxiliaries as well as the Communist party's relationship to them considerably affect the positions, policies, and alliance strategies of the parties. For illustrative purposes, we concentrate on two of the more important areas where Communists attempt to establish auxiliaries—unions and youth groups.

Unions

The Communists' power in the trade union movement is both a reflection and a cause of their national political strength. One of the most important factors in determining the importance of union position for Communist policies is the degree to which their strength is concentrated in a single union federation or union stronghold. In France the PCF is firmly in control of the nation's largest trade union federation, the CGT, with more than half of the top union officials being Communists or closely tied to the party.[15] Although not all workers' unions are Communist controlled in France, the Party must share power with no one in the CGT.[16] As in France, Communist union strength in Sweden is secure, but unlike France, in Sweden it is far more restricted, being confined to a few strongholds, particularly the Norbotten region. The Portuguese Communist Party dominates the union federation Intersyndical, but it is opposed by Socialist- and Popular Democrat-dominated unions. In Spain the Communists and Socialists are competing for influence in the trade union movement. In Italy, Finland, Luxembourg, and Iceland, Communist union strength is broad, as in France, but not exclusive in that Communist parties in these countries share union power *within* union federations. The Italian Communist Party shares strength with the Socialists and other Leftist groups in the CGIL (see Table 8), and the Finnish SKP competes with the Social Democrats for union control. In Luxembourg the PCL shares control of the United Federation of Free Trade Unions with the Socialists. Similarly, in Iceland the PA is entrenched along with the Progressives in the leadership of the Icelandic Federation of Labor. The union strength of the British Communist Party is

Table 8. Party Affiliation of CGIL Executive Committee

	1960	1965	1969
PCI	53%	55%	32%
PSI	47	27	24
PSIUP	—	14	12
Other	—	4	32
	(32)	(22)	(37)

SOURCE: Peter R. Weitz, "The CGIL and the PCI: From Subordination to Independent Political Force," pp. 541–71, in Donald L. M. Blackmer and Sidney Tarrow, eds., *Communism in Italy and France* (Princeton: Princeton University, 1975), p. 555.

similar to the overall strength of Communism in Swedish unions, but it is far more dispersed. In the rest of Western Europe, however, Communist union strength is quite minimal.

Union strongholds, whether broadly based as in France or narrowly confined as in Sweden, act as a conservative influence on Communist party policies. Solidly entrenched trade unionists tend to be veteran cadres for whom old policies are the best policies. Consequently, they tend to oppose innovations in domestic policies and positions toward the Soviet Union. In Sweden, for example, the primary opposition to the VPK's moderate line has come from unionists. Similarly, the PCF's unionists are among that Party's more conservative elements. On the other hand, in Italy, where Communists cooperate with Socialists and sometimes Christian Democrats at the union level, or in Iceland, where Communists and members of the Progressive Party cooperate, the unionists play a moderating role. Because Communist trade union leaders in these countries must compromise to maintain union cooperation, they are not wedded to orthodoxy. Finally, in countries such as Britain, where the Communists' union strength is moderate but dispersed, unionists are often among the Party's more innovative cadres. Because of their precarious union position, CPGB unionist leaders find flexibility a virtue.

Trade union experience with other parties also influences the nature and success of alliance strategies. Cooperation at the union level can provide a training ground for cooperation at the electoral or governmental level. In Iceland, for example, the coalition government between the PA and the Progressive Party was preceded by cooperation at the union level. Similarly, cooperation between Italian Communists and Socialists in the CGIL is paralleled at the level of regional and local government. In contrast, a tradition of conflict in the labor movement can carry over to hinder cooperation at the governmental level. In Finland the relations between the SKP and the Social Democrats have waxed and waned in the union movement, but, in general, they have been conflicting. Partially because of this experience, many of the SKP's union leaders have been among those more opposed to coalition with the Social Democrats.

Youth Organizations[17]

The primary purpose of youth auxiliaries is to train young sympathizers to be capable and loyal cadres. Ironically, in much of Western Europe, Communist youth organizations have withered away or, worse, become hotbeds of opposition to the party. In Britain, Denmark, the Netherlands, Norway, Austria, and, in recent months, Italy, Communist youth affiliates have steadily declined in the face of competition from numerous New Left groups. In other countries, the Communist youth affiliates have expressed some notably independent attitudes and, in some cases, have been captured by ultra-Left rivals of the Communists. After 1968 the Swedish Communist Party lost control of its youth affiliate to pro-Chinese rivals. In 1973 the VPK began a new "loyal" youth affiliate. Before 1958 in France, the Communist Students of France (UEC) was a reliable school for Communists, but after that the PCF began to lose control. In 1963 pro-Italians took control and revisionism was *au courant*. By 1964, however, Bernstein ceded to Trotsky and Rome was replaced by Peking. Then, in 1965, the PCF purged the UEC, retaking control. In the process, it emasculated the organization, as the brightest and most energetic young people defected to ultra-Left groups. In Norway in 1967, the NKP's youth affiliate broke with the Party in support of a party faction that had been purged. Since then, a reconstituted youth auxiliary has failed to grow.[18] One result of the malaise among Communist youth organizations has been a decline in the number of capable young cadres entering party ranks and a shortage of vigorous young volunteers for routine party activities.

Second, because of their formal attachment to the main-line Communist party, renegade youth affiliates can bring the party into disrepute. Although the PCF deplored the students' and workers' riots of May-June 1968, the attachment of the various student (and worker) groups with the PCF, at least in the minds of many voters, worked against the Communists.

Finally, because they received their political socialization in youth affiliates that were often quite flexible and occasionally critical of the parent party, many younger generation party cadres and functionaries come to positions of leadership with attitudes more reflective of New Left sentiments than those of their elders. A 1969 study found that younger cadres who were militants in the Italian Communist Youth Federation during a period in which it displayed a measure of independence toward the PCI were considerably different from older recruits who were socialized into a closed party. Younger members tended to be more freely critical of the Soviet Union and more inclined toward a "revolution from below" approach than their older colleagues.[19]

Political Culture

Communist parties find fertile ground for potential growth in political cleavages. Indeed, Communist voters are more readily differentiated from non-Communist voters on the basis of their political beliefs than their socioeconomic status.[20] As with social cleavages, the mere presence or relative absence of political cleavage neither guarantees nor precludes Communist success. Their importance for Communist party strength (and their indirect influence on party policy positions) depends on how well the Communists can exploit them.

For historical and ideological reasons, Communist parties are particularly equipped to deal with alienated or politically disaffected workers. Consequently, in Italy, France, Spain, Portugal, and Finland, countries with large, historically alienated working classes, there are opportunities for Communist party success. In contrast, countries with less worker disaffection, such as Ireland, Great Britain, Sweden, and Iceland, provide less opportune circumstances for Communist advancement.

A number of studies have pointed to the Communists' identification with workers' political interests in explaining Communist party success. In France in 1966, 41 percent of the PCF's electors identified the Party primarily as the "party of the working class."[21] According to a 1963 survey in Italy, a majority of the PCI's supporters favor that Party's pro-working class posture.[22] Similarly, in a study of the 1958 parliamentary election in Tampere, Finland, it was found that 68 percent of the SKDL's voters pointed favorably to the Communists' pro-labor activity.[23]

By no means are Communist opportunities limited to workers' cleavages and dissaffections. Rather, a whole range of economic and political issues lend themselves to Communist exploitation. Thoughout Western Europe, issues such as Common Market participation, NATO membership, the neutron bomb, American imperialism, the abuses of multinational corporations, unemployment, and inflation have received considerable attention from Communists, often with electoral rewards.

Universally, much of the Communists' appeal is the result of protest voting. As McInnes states regarding the French Communist Party:

> The PCF has espoused the cause not only of workers, wage-earners, and pensioners of every condition but of fishermen, professional footballers, yatchsmen, handicapped children, small shopkeepers, motorists, comic opera artists, refugees from colonies, over-taxed managers, engineers and technicians, expropriated landowners, and even *bouilleurs de cru,* smalltime bootleggers. As Galli says of the PCI, a party that is always complaining about everything will attract all those who have a complaint.[24]

Georges Lavau argues that the French Communist Party fulfills an important function in the French political system by expressing the discontent, denouncing the abuses, and organizing the protests of a significant part of the French political community.[25] In Greece during the 1950s and early 1960s, as much as 90 percent of the vote of the United Democratic Left (EDA), the Communist-dominated Left-wing party, may have come from protest voters rather than hard-core Communists.[26]

In a number of cases, Communist parties have garnered some success by appealing to essentially unique characteristics of the political culture of their respective nations. Historically, the people of Iceland, a small, insular country, have jealously guarded their sovereignty and highly valued their independence from the affairs of Europe and North America. Very adroitly, the Communist Party of Iceland has won support by presenting itself as the champion of Icelandic sovereignty and independence and by vigorously opposing the United States defense base in Keflavik and championing the national cause in the "cod war" with Britain. Also, the PA's notably independent policy vis-à-vis the Soviet Union is very much in keeping with Icelandic political values.

Not only do Communist parties attempt to mold their programs and policies to the national political environment, but they also try to shape that environment to respond favorably to their appeals. Through the control of various agents of socialization—unions, press, and various auxiliary structures—the Communist parties act to insure the loyalty of their partisans and attract new supporters.

Finally, unique aspects of the political cultures of various nations act to disadvantage Communist parties in their search for political influence. In West Germany, for example, the past Nazi experience and present Soviet control of East Germany have combined to make West Germans particularly wary of any political party that can be labeled "extremist." As the only Western nation outside of the Soviet bloc that experienced a period of Russian occupation after World War II, Austria has not offered fertile soil for the growth of indigenous Communism.

Notes

1. Thomas H. Greene, "Non-Ruling Communist Parties and Political Adaptation," *Studies in Comparative Communism* IV, no. 4 (Winter 1973):331-61. Here, we add a temporal qualification to Greene's thesis. Although his proposition thesis is accurate insofar as it describes the conditions under which strong or moderately strong Communist parties emerged in the late 1910s and 1920s, it is not sufficient for explaining the subsequent fluctuations in Communist party strength. In Greece, for example, the KKE became a significant political force during the Resistance despite its formation from a fusion of small Leftist groups. (To be precise, a number of intellectuals and Marxists founded the Greek Socialist Party in 1918. In 1920 it changed its name to the Communist Party.) Original conditions are best used for explaining initial strength; subsequent fluctuations in Communist strength must be explained by other factors as well.

2. Greece *may* be an exception. Although there is a good measure of Leftist radicalism in Greece, it is generally of fairly recent vintage. There was not even a Socialist Party before 1918 and Greece's Leftist traditions hardly compare with those of Italy and France. At the same time, however, the actual electoral strength of Greek Communism has been difficult to measure. During the 1920s and 1930s, the Party achieved few electoral successes. Then came illegality, war, Civil War, and illegality again. The

Party's electoral success came under the guise of the United Democratic Left, EDA. Whether or not that vote reflected true Communist strength, however, is difficult to determine. In any case, the important event in the life of the Greek Communist Party was World War II and the subsequent Civil War. The events of this period had a "radicalizing" effect on many individuals who became ardent Communist supporters. In a sense, then, we can argue that just as the events of the French Revolution helped implant a Leftist tradition among certain groups and in certain areas in France in the nineteenth century, the Resistance and the Civil War implanted a Leftist tradition among many Greeks in the 1940s.

3. Jean Ranger, "L'évolution du vote communiste en France depuis 1945," pp. 211-47, in Frédéric Bon, ed., *Le Communisme en France,* Cahiers de la fondation nationale des sciences politiques, 175 (Paris: Armand Colin, 1969); Henry Ehrmann, *Politics in France* (Boston: Little, Brown, 1968), pp. 210-18; Gordon Wright, "Four Red Villages in France," *Yale Review* XLI, no. 3 (March 1952):361-72.

4. Henry W. Ehrmann, "The French Peasant and Communism," *American Political Science Review* XLVI, no. 1 (March 1952):19-43.

5. Mattei Dogan, "Political Cleavages and Social Stratification in France and Italy," pp. 129-95, in Seymour M. Lipset and Stein Rokkan, eds., *Party Systems and Voter Alignments: Cross-National Perspectives* (New York: Free Press, 1967), pp. 182-84.

6. Erik Allardt, "Patterns of Class Conflict and Working Class Consciousness in Finnish Politics," pp. 97-251, in Allardt and Yrjö Littunen, *Cleavages, Ideologies, and Party Systems* (Helsinki: Academic Bookstore, 1964).

7. Ake Sparring, "Introduction," pp. 279-85, in William E. Griffith, ed., *Communism in Europe,* vol. II (Cambridge: MIT, 1965), p. 282.

8. Thirty-two percent to 20 percent. *New York Times,* 20 June 1977.

9. *Le Monde,* 21 October 1975.

10. Ibid., 16 March 1976, 23 November 1976.

11. Per Egil Hegge, " 'Disunited' Front in Norway," *Problems of Communism* XXV, no. 3 (May-June 1976):49-58.

12. In France the PSU (Parti Socialiste Unifié) has a political position similar to Scandinavia's Socialist people's parties. Its political impact, however, has been marginal.

13. Gordon Adams, " 'On the Pavement Thinking 'bout Government': Notes on *Il Manifesto,*" *Politics and Society* I, no. 4 (August 1971):449-62.

14. One must not place too much stock in the role of the party system in shaping Communist party positions. Other factors including leadership, the party's membership and electorate, and the international environment are often far more important.

15. Gérard Adam, "Elements d'analyse sur les liens entre le PCF et la CGT," *Revue française de science politique* XVIII, no. 3 (June 1968):524-39.

16. Although the Socialists, as part of the alliance agreement, are demanding that they be given a larger share of union influence.

17. For ideological reasons, some Communist parties prefer adding youths to the regular party organization rather than a specialized youth affiliate. (After all, it is argued, young people should have the same objective class interests as their elders.)

18. Unfortunately for the Communists, the problems of Communist youth affiliates also affect other Communist front organizations. Since the Sino-Soviet rift, Communist front organizations have been beset by factionalism as groups of various ideological persuasions have battled for control.

19. Stephen Hellman, "Generational Differences in the Bureaucratic Elite of Italian Communist Party Provincial Federations," *Canadian Journal of Political Science* VIII, no. 1 (March 1975):82-106.

20. Thomas H. Greene, "The Electorates of Nonruling Communist Parties," *Studies in Comparative Communism* IV, nos. 3-4 (July-October 1971):68-103.

21. Ranger, "L'évolution du vote communiste."

22. Cited in Sidney G. Tarrow, *Peasant Communism in Southern Italy* (New Haven: Yale, 1967), pp. 159-60.

23. Pertti Pesonen, *An Election in Finland: Party Activities and Voter Reactions* (New Haven: Yale, 1968), p. 134.

24. Neil McInnes, *The Communist Parties of Western Europe* (London: Oxford, 1975), pp. 163-64.

25. George Lavau, "Le parti communiste dans le systeme politique français," pp. 7-55, in Bon, ed., *Le communisme*, p. 28.

26. Jane Perry Clark Carey and Andrew Galbraith Carey, *The Web of Modern Greek Politics* (New York: Columbia, 1968).

chapter 6

CONSTITUTIONAL FRAMEWORK

A final part of each Western European Communist party's domestic political environment is the constitutional framework within which it must operate. Perhaps the most manipulable of all the sectors of the parties' environment, the constitutional structure affects the political position of the Communist parties by granting or denying them legality and through the workings of the electoral laws. The structures of government provide Communist parties with opportunities for establishing strongholds of political power while, at the same time, Communist participation in government in levels and positions below that of national leadership serves to tie them to the established political order. Finally, the constitutional structures of government may find their parallels in the organization of the Communist parties.

Illegality

Today, Communist parties operate freely and legally everywhere in Western Europe, but this has not always been the case. Following the Finnish civil war of 1918, the Finnish Communist Party was proscribed and only achieved legality in 1944 as an implicit part of the agreement ending Finland's war with the Soviet Union. In Italy the PCI fell victim to Fascist repression as early as 1926 and was forced to remain underground until 1944. The Portuguese Communist Party suffered illegality for most of its existence, from 1926 to

1974. In Spain the PCE was banned by Primo de Rivera in 1924, legalized in 1930, outlawed again by Franco in 1939, and finally legalized once more in 1977. The Greek Communist Party was briefly outlawed for several months in 1926. Then in 1936 it found itself banned by the Metaxas dictatorship and was unable to operate legally again until the end of World War II. In 1947 the KKE was outlawed once more and this time the ban lasted until September 1974.

In 1933 the Communist parties of Austria and Germany were dissolved and remained illegal until the end of World War II. The French Communist Party was outlawed in 1939 for opposing the war effort. In Belgium, Greece, Denmark, Luxembourg, the Netherlands, and Norway, Communist parties were banned by the Germans during their countries' occupation in World War II. Neutral Switzerland's prohibition of pro- and anti-Nazi groups in November 1940 led to the dissolution of the Swiss Communist Party. Finally, the West German KPD lived from 1956 to 1968 under a decree of unconstitutionality until it reemerged in 1968 under a new name.

Although the goal of those who ban Communist parties is to destroy them as a political force, the results of illegality on Western European Communism have been mixed. Electorally, although illegal Communist parties cannot field candidates under their own name, they can resort to front parties. In Finland the Communists operated for several years under the Socialist Workers Party label, winning 15 percent of the vote and twenty-seven seats in the 1923 election. It, too, however, was banned in 1923 and its entire parliamentary group and party committee were arrested. In West Germany, the KPD employed the League of Germans (BdD) in 1957 and the German Peace Union (DFU) in 1961 and 1965 as electoral surrogates, but they achieved no appreciable success at the polls.

In Greece, however, Communist-dominated electoral fronts were more successful in winning votes and gaining political influence than their West German counterparts. In the 1950 election, the Communists supported the Democratic Group, a coalition of non-Communists as well as Communists united in opposition to Greece's entry into NATO and discontent with the status quo. Although the coalition won only 9.7 percent of the vote, its ten seats were the balance of power in a closely divided parliament. The Democratic Group lacked cohesiveness, however, and split after the election. In 1951 the KKE found a new vehicle to carry its electoral ambitions, the United Democratic Left (EDA). It, too, included many non-Communists who joined to protest slow progress in economic rehabilitation and Greece's pro-Western foreign policy. At the polls, the EDA won only ten seats in 1951 and was shut out in 1952 under the newly adopted majority system of election.

In 1956, however, the EDA found allies on the Center and Center-Left, who formed the Democratic Union, adopting a vague and rather general platform. The coalition captured 48 percent of the vote and 132 seats, 18 of which were won by the EDA. Once Parliament began its session, however, this disparate group also broke up. In 1958 the EDA could find no allies; so it ran alone, winning 24.4 percent of the vote and 79 deputies. In 1961 the EDA stood in alliance with a Communist-oriented agrarian group, but lost considerable electoral ground, winning but 15.1 percent of the vote and retaining only 24 seats. The EDA contested the 1963 election alone, winning 14.5 percent of the ballots and 28 seats, but these were enough to give it the balance of power in a closely divided parliament. In 1964 the EDA captured 22 seats and 12 percent of the vote, but lost its strategic position in parliament as the Center Union emerged the clear winner. In 1967 the EDA was outlawed by the Greek military government.

Illegality, then, has often proved an ineffective weapon against Communist electoral ambitions. Communists, it seems, are quite adept at establishing front parties that not only seem to win the traditional Communist vote, but are often more successful at attracting non-Communist supporters and coalition partners than the Communist parties themselves. Only if the regime is willing to persevere in banning Communist-dominated surrogate parties and in prosecuting their functionaries (as in Finland) can a democratic regime succeed in suppressing the electoral strength of a Communist party, and then that suppression may only be temporary.

In extra-electoral matters, illegality has not always meant the end of Communist influence. After its ban the Finnish Communist Party moved to reach workers and other potential supporters through an active participation in public organizations. In mid-1919, the Communists won control of the Social Democratic Youth League and, in September of that year, the SDP's Helsinki organization came under Communist domination. By the end of 1920, the Communists had won a firm foothold in the trades union movement.

Because of their organizational strength and outside support, Communist parties are often better able to survive illegality than other parties. Thus, illegality may prove to have been advantageous to the Communists once that illegality is lifted. The overthrow of the Salazar-Caetano dictatorship in Portugal in April 1974 found the Portuguese Communist Party well-equipped to take advantage of its new freedom. During the long decades of dictatorship, the PCP had carefully built its organization, cultivating strength among workers and, in recent years, among young army officers who had been radicalized by a protracted colonial war in Africa. Consequently, when the dictatorship fell in 1974, the Communists were able quickly to move to a position of near dominance in the government, the media, and the unions, while other parties, the Socialists and Social Democrats (formerly Popular Democrats), were still getting organized. Communist success proved short-lived, however, as the Socialists and others got their political feet on the ground, and moderates gained ascendance in the Armed Forces Movement.

In Spain illegality did not prevent the PCE from developing an efficient organization and establishing a firm base in the Workers Commissions. However, the government's step-by-step policy of democratization enabled other parties to build up their organizations before the PCE was legalized. Consequently, much of the Communists' organizational head-start was erased.

In much of Western Europe, proscription by the Nazis during the German occupation rebounded to the Communists' advantage as the Communists moved to the forefront of Resistance activities. In France, for example, Communist influence rose during the war because, for the first time, the PCF was squarely on the side of the Republic.

For no Western European Communist party, however, was the Resistance more important than it was for Greece's KKE. After the

Germans overran the country in the spring of 1941, the Communists were quick to reorganize cadres, to provoke strikes, and to hamper the recruitment of forced labor. Since the Germans concentrated their occupation forces in the cities and on the main arteries of communication, the countryside was largely left in the hands of Resistance forces, which the Communists dominated under the guise of the National Liberation Front (EAM) and the National Popular Liberation Army (ELAS). Because of their patriotic posture and because they systematically eliminated opposition, the Communists gained undisputed political control over mountain Greece. Consequently, whereas the KKE had been quite weak in the decades before the war, during the Resistance, it built for itself a significant popular base of loyal supporters.

Despite its obvious disadvantages, illegality has not led to the demise of Communism anywhere in Western Europe. Although the German Communist Party has been badly weakened by two long periods of illegality, elsewhere parties have come back from fugitive status with renewed vigor. At the hands of the Nazis and Fascists, illegality proved to be something of a blessing for many parties. Because of the persecution, Communist parties were stripped of all but their most faithful followers who were forced to develop a careful, efficient organization to survive. More importantly, the Communists' suppression at the hands of the hated Nazis and Fascists cast them in the role of national patriots, a role that proved electorally advantageous to them after the defeat of the Axis. Also, as an outlawed party, the Communists were in a position from which they could take maximum advantage of governmental failures.

Because of its illegal status before 1944, the Finnish Communist Party was in an opportune position to criticize the failures of Finnish foreign policy that had led to two major wars with the Soviet Union in five years. Consequently, after the Party's return to legality in 1944, it shared no formal blame for past governmental errors. Similarly, unlike the Republicans and Liberals, the Italian Communists did not bear the stigma of cooperation with the Fascists and consequently faced no postwar backlash.

By no means, however, are all of the effects of illegality beneficial to the Communist parties of Western Europe. Prolonged unconstitutionality, particularly if it is coupled with repression and persecution, can weaken Communist parties by drying up domestic sources of financial and human resources. The German KPD was virtually wiped out by Hitler's Gestapo and, even though the Bonn government was far more benign, the KPD's postwar period of illegality left it almost totally dependent on East Germany for funds and as a headquarters in exile for its leaders. Similarly, the Portuguese Communist Party has long been dependent on Moscow for support. Illegal, persecuted at home, and lacking a large refugee membership to serve as a source of finance, the PCP had to rely on the Soviets for financial support during the long years of illegality (a support that has apparently continued even though the Party is now legal) and as a refuge for the Party's longtime leader Alvaro Cunhal after he escaped from a Portuguese prison in 1960.[1] In light of the PCP's ties to Moscow and the DKP's links to East Germany and the Soviet Union, it is hardly surprising that the Portuguese and West German Communist Parties have been pro-Soviet in their international positions.

Perhaps a more serious side effect of illegality for the Western European Communist parties is that it engenders factionalism, particularly if the illegality is protracted and the party has a substantial exile structure with an émigré leadership in addition to the domestic organization. Over time, the exile leadership loses touch with domestic conditions while growing more dependent on foreign assistance and refuge. Meanwhile, the domestic leadership must cope with the serious problems of illegality. Prolonged exile tends to make émigré leaders more rigid and more inclined toward the ideological and political postures of their foreign hosts. Domestic leaders, however, tend to develop a flexible, pragmatic approach to the problems of survival, seeking allies among other opposition groups.

In Finland in the 1920s and early 1930s, a deep division developed in the SKP between the émigré leadership in Russia and the Party's leaders in Finland and in Stockholm. Out of touch with Finnish realities, the émigré leadership feared an imperialist plot and a Finnish attack on the Soviet Union. Therefore, they called for union militancy and strikes. The only result of this, however, was the strengthening of the Finnish Right and a weakening of the

Communists' position as the government cracked down on the Left. On the other hand, domestic Communists led by N. Wälläri favored a more pragmatic approach, even calling for their Party's freedom from Comintern interference. (After the war, when the SKP was finally legalized, its longstanding factional problem was largely solved, thanks to Stalin. The Finnish Communist organization in Russia had been crushed and many of the émigré leaders liquidated.[2])

In Spain as in Finland, illegality forced the Communist Party into a geographical division as a large part of the PCE's leadership and militants were driven into exile. Whereas the Finnish exiles and émigré leadership were in the Soviet Union, most Spanish refugees went to France and the major PCE leaders divided their time between the Soviet Union, France, Eastern Europe, and, in recent years, Spain (often illegally) and Italy. Consequently, the PCE exile organization was less dependent on Moscow than the Finnish exiles were since many of the Spanish Party's exile cadres were in the West where they could send money to the Party. Moreover, the Italian Communist Party assisted the Spanish Communists financially. As a result, the PCE exile leaders were not constrained to parrot the Soviet line.

If circumstances spared the illegal PCE from dependence on the Soviets, they did not spare it the problems of factionalism. During the long decades of illegality, communications between the leadership abroad and cadres in Spain were often poor and discipline ineffective. A number of schisms developed, including those surrounding the expulsion of Fernando Claudín in 1964, the exodus of young Maoists in 1967, and the ouster of Stalinists under Líster in 1969-70.[3]

No contemporary Communist party in Western Europe has been more severely rent by factionalism than the Greek Party. Since the end of the Civil War in 1949, it has been divided physically. Since the latter half of the 1960s, it has been divided politically and spiritually. Following the Communists' crushing defeat in 1949, many of the Party's militants and leaders retreated to Yugoslavia, Bulgaria, and elsewhere in Eastern Europe. Subsequently, the KKE leadership in exile grew increasingly isolated from Greek domestic affairs and ever more dependent on their Eastern European hosts and Soviet mentors for support. On the domestic front, however, Communists appealed for non-Communist allies to form electoral fronts and adopted relatively pragmatic policies to win electoral support. As time went by, a rift developed and the Party split into two factions: one located in Eastern Europe, loyal to Moscow, and hard line in domestic policy; the other centered in Greece, espousing international autonomy and domestic moderation.

In cases where the Communists' illegality is short-lived or where there is no appreciable party-in-exile, illegality does not lead to factionalism. In most of Western Europe, the Nazi-imposed illegality was too short for party factions to take root. Further, there were few Communist exiles. In Italy the PCI's illegal period was relatively long, but no exile community of Italian Communists developed. In Portugal, although the PCP was outlawed for nearly fifty years, there was no large refugee community of Portuguese Communists and much of the Party's leadership remained in Portugal, either in hiding or in prison. Finally, the German Party was spared factionalism, primarily because the exile leadership was close at hand and the domestic organization was nearly totally dependent on the East Germans for support and guidance.

Electoral Systems

Contrary to Duverger's thesis, the electoral system does not rigidly determine the contours of a party system.[4] Instead, it is the creation of the dominant political forces in the system who design it to their own benefit. Consequently, the electoral system is often constructed to advantage its architects and disadvantage other parties. As perennial outsiders, usually outside of the government, sometimes outside of the system, Communist parties have often been the victims of electoral tinkering by non-Communist and anti-Communist parties.

In France the electoral system "has been treated as a weapon in the struggle between different political camps and between different political forces for the control of State and society."[5] Under the Fifth Republic, the system of proportional representation employed during the Fourth Republic was discarded and France returned to a second ballot plurality system designed to reward second ballot alliances and thus weaken the then isolated Communists. In this the Gaullist system proved immediately successful. Under the Fourth Republican system in 1956, the PCF won 147 seats based on 25.9 percent of the vote. In 1958 with the new system, however, the Communists' vote percentage slipped to 19.2 percent, but their total of seats won plummeted to only ten. Although the electoral fortunes of the PCF have improved since 1958, the Communists are still woefully underrepresented. In 1973, their best showing under the Fifth Republic, they captured only about one-seventh of the seats despite winning more than one-fifth of the popular vote.

Another effect of the modern French electoral system has been to provide a significant incentive to the Communists to form electoral coalitions. For the 1958 election, the Communists stood alone with disastrous results, but in 1962, after reaching an agreement for second ballot withdrawal with the Socialists, the PCF won forty-one seats and 21.8 percent of the popular vote. Thus, the electoral payoffs for the Communists (and Socialists) in forming electoral alliances are relatively great.

On a number of occasions, the Greek Communist Party has felt the effects of changes in the electoral laws. In 1932 the KKE won 4.6 percent of the votes and ten seats in parliament under the system of proportional representation. A majority system was adopted for the 1933 balloting, however, and the Communists failed to elect a deputy even though they won 4.2 percent of the vote. Similarly, the EDA captured ten of two hundred and fifty seats under a system of modified PR in the 1951 election. In 1952 under the majority system, the Party won none of the three hundred seats at stake.

In Italy, too, the electoral system has been used as a weapon in the political battle between the Communists and their bourgeois opponents. Before the 1953 parliamentary election, the Christian Democrats enacted legislation awarding two-thirds of the legislature's seats to any party or list that won 50 percent or more of the popular vote. Then the Christian Democrats proceeded to line up alliances with other Center and Right parties to insure the isolation of the Left. The Christian Democrat coalition fell 0.3 percent short of 50 percent, however, and subsequently the "swindle law," as the Communists called it, was repealed.

Although in many countries the electoral system has not been used as an explicit weapon against the Communists, as smaller parties (which most Western European Communist parties are), the Communists find themselves disadvantaged to some degree by every electoral system in use in Western Europe.[6] In Sweden, Denmark, West Germany, and Norway, a party must register a certain minimum percentage (as low as 2 percent in Denmark, as high as 5 percent in West Germany) to receive representation. Consequently, weak Communist strength, even if it is concentrated in a few districts, is insufficient to win any parliamentary seats. Although the single-seat district as in Britain would benefit parties whose support is geographically concentrated, Britain's plurality system strongly handicaps minor parties. To win any seats, a party must win a plurality in an electoral district. Consequently, voters will be unlikely to "waste" their votes for a minor party that is unlikely to threaten the larger parties' electoral lead. Even under a system of proportional representation and multi-member districts, which, Rae argues, produce more nearly proportional results, Communist parties are disadvantaged when they are minor parties.[7]

What are the long-term effects of electoral laws on the Communist parties of Western Europe? For the dwarf parties, "first-past-the-post" systems and minimum-percentage requirements act as barriers to electoral growth. For minor parties, these relatively mild barriers are insufficient to prevent the Communists from maintaining a parliamentary foothold. For the major parties of Iceland, Luxembourg, Italy, and Finland, the electoral system acts as no handicap and occasionally favors the Communists. In France the Fifth Republican electoral system has consistently shortchanged the PCF, but has failed to destroy the Communists as a major political force.

Although an electoral system can be used to keep a weak Communist party weak and to hamper a strong Communist party, in the long run, the strength of Communism is determined by other factors. Under no electoral system could a weak Communist party such as that in Britain win more than a few seats, and even the highly disadvantageous French system has failed to wreck the electoral prospects of the PCF. What an electoral system can do, however, is to maximize trends already present in the political system, be that the maximization of Communist weakness, as in Britain, or the maximization of Gaullist strength vis-à-vis the Communists, as in France.

Restrictive electoral systems can also act as incentives for Communists to seek electoral alliances. As we have seen, under the Fifth Republic in France, there are strong dividends for electoral cooperation for both Socialists and Communists. Additionally, electoral systems requiring a party to win a minimum percentage of the vote to gain representation make electoral alliances very attractive to small parties which would otherwise face being shut out of parliament. In Norway, for example, the NKP was able to surmount the 2 percent barrier and return to parliament only in alliance with two other Left-wing groups.

Since restrictive electoral systems place premiums on alliance, small Communist parties in such systems will be encouraged to modify their policies to woo possible alliance partners. Unfortunately for the Communists, their bids for electoral alliance have been accepted only by other, small Left-wing parties which are also disadvantaged by the electoral system. In Norway the NKP, emphasizing its independence from Moscow, succeeded in forming a Leftist electoral coalition with the Socialist People's Party and a group of Left-wing Labor Party dissidents. It did not win cooperation with the dominant Labor Party itself, however. Elsewhere, in Sweden, West Germany, and Denmark, other countries with electoral systems penalizing small parties, Communists have failed to win electoral cooperation from larger social democratic parties which would have little to gain from such an alliance.

Constitutional Structures and Communist Participation

Political systems with constitutionally established local and regional governments provide opportunities for Communist parties to secure political office at levels beneath the national government. In virtually all of Western Europe (excepting Ireland), Communists hold at least a few minor local offices. It is in Italy and France, however, that the Communists have their most secure footings in local and regional governments.

There are 251 French cities with a population over 30,000 and, since the municipal elections of March 1977, the Communists have participated in the government of 147 of these cities. Because of governmental centralization, however, municipal government in France has no constitutional autonomy beyond the right of existence. All the powers local government exercises are granted by the central government and decisions of locally elected officials can be annulled by prefects who represent the central government. This does not, however, condemn local officials to passivity. Rather, the mayor bargains incessantly with authorities of the state for approval of municipal actions.

Although as Mark Kesselman contends, the general pattern for local government in France is one of nonpartisanship and consensus building,[8] this is generally not the Communist approach. The PCF seeks to run its municipalities in an openly partisan manner. It consciously attempts to politicize local government and to subordinate local officials to Party discipline, and tries to avoid letting its municipalities become dependent on the services of the prefect. In administration the Communists try to present themselves as efficient public servants responding to the needs of the people, particularly the working class.[9]

To finance their social welfare programs, Communist officials bargain with the prefect and other representatives of the state. Although relations between the two are generally cordial, it is not unusual for the governmental savings bank, the *Caisse des Dépôts et Consignations,* to refuse a loan, or for the prefect to deny permission for Communists' taxing proposals. In practice, however, local government exercises considerable power in local matters.

The Italian Communist Party also enjoys power in local government. Alone or with its allies, the Communists control the municipal governments of every major Italian city and forty of Italy's ninety-four provincial councils. As in the case of its French counterpart, the local Italian Communist governments are limited by central government control, particularly in areas of borrowing, taxation, and spending. Every commune in Italy is administered by a mayor and an executive council, each of which is chosen by the common council (*consiglio comunale*), which is popularly elected. But, as in France, the mayor is both the executive of the commune and an agent of the central government and each commune is under the supervision of the prefect who has virtual veto power over many local actions. It is not unusual for prefectoral controls to be exercised in a partisan manner, often severely against Leftist administrations. Nor is it unusual for the central government to discriminate in the granting of state subsidies and loans that are often necessary because of the communes' inadequate system of taxation.[10]

The relationship between the central government and Communist administration in Italy is generally one of tight but not suffocating supervision. Because of central government control over deficit financing, Communist administrations generally follow quite conservative fiscal policies. Budgets are balanced, borrowing is limited, and fiscal responsibility is the norm.[11] Ironically, the politically discriminatory financial scrutiny by the central government of Left-wing communes has helped to make them the best governed in Italy.

Political power at the local and regional level affects Communist parties in several ways. In the first place, local office is a training ground for national party leaders to learn the skills of exercising power and bargaining with other power holders. In Italy in 1963, for example, nearly 70 percent of PCI party officials had held public posts as communal councillors.[12] The result of this is the moderation of Communist practice. In both Italy and France, the Communist municipal governments stress efficiency, honesty, and sound administration rather than revolutionary upheaval.

Second, political power at the local and regional levels provides a ready source of patronage with which to reward the party faithful. In Italy the PCI is the greatest political employer in the country for all those posts below the level of national government and has been for decades.[13]

Third, local governmental office can serve as a showcase for Communist programs in action. In France Communist municipal administrators carefully accent reformist, social welfare policies. Similarly, the Italian Communists strive mightily to make local and regional governments under their control showplaces for honest, efficient administration.

Finally, local and regional governments serve as redoubts of Communist strength. The Red Belt regions of Italy and France and

Communist strongholds in Finland and elsewhere stand firm for the Party even in the face of national electoral setbacks. Within Communist-controlled cities and towns, the Party press reaches its densest readership and the local administration is quick to credit the Party for all manner of local improvements and to blame the bourgeois central authorities for all setbacks.

In general, local government in Italy, France, and other countries of Western Europe provides Communists with enough political power to exploit for electoral and other "legitimate" political purposes, but not the leeway to create a base for revolution (even if such a base were desired by the Communists). Although local administrations, particularly Communist ones, are carefully circumscribed in the exercise of power, the day-to-day activities of local government are their responsibilities and, in this, local administrations are required to bargain with various institutions of political order—the central government, the courts, the central bank, and the like. Consequently, power in local government acts to socialize Communist leaders and bureaucrats into an understanding and, to an inevitable degree, an acceptance of the established political system. Thus, political power at the local level tends to have a moderating influence on Communist parties. On their part, the Communists have responded by using local power in quite moderate, democratic ways.

Another institutional tie between Communist parties and the political system is the parliament. Although at times Communist parties have played an obstructionist role in parliament (as did the French Communist Party during the 1950s), in general, Communists have played by the rules of the parliamentary game. In Iceland and Finland on several occasions, and in much of Western Europe in the immediate postwar years, Communist parties participated in governing parliamentary coalitions. Moreover, during the Popular Front in France, the PCF lent its support to the government without joining the government, and in Sweden in recent years, the VPK used its votes to keep the Social Democrats in power.

Even in opposition, Communists have frequently cooperated with other parties in parliament. In committee in the Italian parliament, the PCI has cooperated with the governing Christian Democrats often in exchange for acceptance of Communist amendments. Galli reports that between 1948 and 1968, the PCI ended up voting in favor of three-fourths of the laws enacted.[14] Currently, the PCI is part of the Andreotti Government's parliamentary majority although there are no Communists in the cabinet. Additionally, in both France and Italy, Communists participate in parliamentary commissions.

For the Communists, parliamentary participation provides a number of benefits. First, the floor of parliament is an excellent forum for Communists to publicize their policy positions. Second, the emoluments of office, including patronage and members' salaries, supplement the party's material resources. Third, parliamentary office provides individual Communist leaders with personal prestige and stature beyond that which they would receive otherwise.

The effect of parliamentary participation for Communist parties is to tie them to the established order. The more secure the Communist party's position in parliament, the more tangible benefits it will receive from that position and the more committed it will become to the general political framework. Moreover, participation in the affairs of parliament serves as a socializing agent for Communist leaders, training them in the skills of practical politics.

The net effect of Communist participation in the institutions of government, then, be they local, regional, national, parliamentary, or bureaucratic, is to make the Communist party a de facto member of the system. The larger and more successful the party is electorally, the greater the party's ties to the political system. Ironically, then, it is those Communist parties with the greatest potential for political disruption or even insurrection that have the greatest incentives to stay within the system.

Organizational Variations

Finally, the organizational structure of Communist parties tends to vary from the norm of democratic centralism as a reflection of decentralized variations in the structure of Western European governments. In Ireland, for example, the Communist Party's central committee has a dual structure paralleling that country's division. Similarly, the Swiss Communist Party is organized on a cantonal basis mirroring Switzerland's federal structure.

Notes

1. Cunhal also spent time in Prague and other Eastern European capitals.

2. A.F. Upton, "The Communist Party of Finland," pp. 105-352, in Upton, ed., *The Communist Parties of Scandinavia and Finland* (London: Weidenfeld and Nicolson, 1973).

3. Guy Hermet, *The Communists in Spain* (Lexington, Mass.: Heath, 1974).

4. Maurice Duverger, *Political Parties,* trans. Barbara and Robert North (New York: Wiley and Sons, 1954; first pub. 1951).

5. Peter Campbell, *French Electoral Systems* (Hamdon: Archon Books, 1965), p. 17.

6. Douglas Rae, *The Political Consequences of Electoral Laws* (New Haven: Yale, 1967), p. 134.

7. Ibid., p. 138.

8. Mark Kesselman, *The Ambiguous Consensus: A Study of Local Government in France* (New York: Knopf, 1967).

9. Ronald Tiersky, *French Communism, 1920-1972* (New York: Columbia, 1974), pp. 349-63.

10. Robert H. Evans, *Coexistence: Communism and Its Practice in Bologna, 1945-1965* (Notre Dame: University of Notre Dame, 1967), pp. 35-39.

11. Robert C. Fried, "Communism, Urban Budgets, and the Two Italies: A Case Study in Comparative Urban Governments," *Journal of Politics* XXXIII, no. 4 (November 1971): 1008-51. In general, Communist local governments have been more effective in the industrial North than they have been in chronically poor Southern cities.

12. Giorgio Galli and Alfonso Prandi, *Patterns of Political Participation in Italy* (New Haven: Yale, 1970), p. 158.

13. Giorgio Galli, *Storia del partito communista italiano,* 2d ed. (Milan: Schwarz, 1959).

14. Giorgio Galli, *Il bipartismo imperfetto: comunisti e democristiani in Italia* (Bologna: 1966), p. 308-14.

chapter 7

LEADERSHIP

In many respects, leadership is the most important factor shaping the postures and policies of the Communist parties of Western Europe. The environment presents contingencies and opportunities, and the leadership's role is to outline the contours of the party's response. The environment imposes a number of restraints on the Communist party leaders and other restraints emanate from within the party itself. Sometimes these imposed boundaries are narrow; sometimes they are broad. If, for example, a party is dependent on the Soviet Union for financial support, its leaders have little room for maneuver in terms of policy toward the Soviet Union. On the other hand, if a party is financially independent or has significant alternative sources of funds, its leaders have certain leeway in determining policy vis-à-vis Moscow.[1]

Within these boundaries, whose dimensions we have explored in the preceding four chapters and to which we return in the next two, party policy and posture depend on the individuals and groups of men and women composing the party's leadership. In that different individuals have different perceptual lenses, different priority orderings, and different capacities for decision making and implementation, party behavior varies.

In application, however, the seemingly idiosyncratic behavior of individual leaders does not readily lend itself to generalization. How does one account for the stubborn, unimaginative loyalty to the Soviet Union of Maurice Thorez? Or the pragmatic intellectualism of Palmiro Togliatti? Or the heavy-handed direction of the Luxembourg Party's ubiquitous Urbani family? Or the free-wheeling openness of C. H. Hermansson of Sweden's VPK? Undoubtedly, much of the variation in party leadership must be left to biographers and the authors of case studies to explain on the basis of unique individual personality characteristics. Nevertheless, many leadership characteristics (and consequently much of the variation in party behavior) can be explained on the basis of a number of generalizable characteristics, including the backgrounds of the party leaders, the generation of the top leadership, the position of the party leadership vis-à-vis the political system, and the leaders' personal relationships to the Soviet Union.

Backgrounds

Those who become leaders of Western European Communist parties are not a mass of interchangeable individuals, but rather come to their positions of leadership from varying social and career backgrounds. In that different backgrounds provide leaders with varying perspectives with which to perceive party problems, they provide a foundation for different behavior. Consequently, leaders from different social and career milieus tend to differ in their approaches to their leadership roles.

Working Class

Communist leaders from working-class backgrounds tend to be pro-Soviet in outlook for a number of reasons. First, since working-class Communist leaders generally lack the ideological sophistication to fashion and justify their policies with Marxist-Leninist teachings, they are tied to some external source of ideological verities, almost by default. Because of psychological, financial, and other ties, in Western Europe, that source tends more often to be the Soviet Union rather than Peking or Havana.[2] Second, in much of Western Europe, the working class has been imperfectly integrated into the political system. Many working-class political leaders, particularly those from an older generation, have felt shut out of domestic political affairs. Consequently, Communist working-class leaders have historically tended to look to Moscow as a political and ideological fatherland.

During the 1920s and 1930s, the Comintern frequently intervened in the internal affairs of the Communist parties of Western Europe to install leaders more compliant with Soviet wishes, and it was usually from among the working class that Moscow found its most dependable loyalists. In France in 1921, the PCF, continuing the old organizational style and structure of the Socialist Party, was led by a thirty-two-member directing committee, only four of whom could be classified as workers.[3] After 1924, with the Trotskyist struggle in the background, the Soviet Union moved to purge the Western parties of recalcitrants and to compel them to adopt "everything in Russian bolshevism that has international significance."[4] In France this was accomplished with a vigorous measure of anti-intellectualism and an exultation of the cult of the proletariat, so by 1929 fully 70 percent of the Central Committee of the French Communist Party were workers. The PCF became a faithful servant of Soviet policy under the leadership of Maurice Thorez, a mine worker whom Franz Borkenau characterized as "the very type of the completely colourless true-blue 'proletarian' party bureaucrat who could be trusted to carry out orders without thinking too much";[5] Benoit Franchon, a laborer; Gaston Monmousseau, a railroad worker and union leader; and Jacques Duclos, an apprentice pastry cook.[6]

Like its French counterpart, the Communist Party of Great Britain was largely social democratic in organization and leadership in its early years.[7] Throughout the 1920s, however, Moscow moved to strengthen its influence in the CPGB by restructuring its organization to conform to the principles of democratic centralism and purging a number of independent-minded intellectual leaders, including Sylvia Pankhurst. By 1929 a new, predominantly working-class leadership came to power, including Harry Pollitt and William Galacher. Thereafter, the Party was reduced to slavish submission to Moscow.[8]

Similarly, in its early days, the Dutch Communist Party suffered from internal divisions as the largely bourgeois leadership composed of former social democrats quarreled among themselves and with the Comintern over Party policy. In the late 1920s, the International intervened to assert control and in 1930 named a new, younger working-class leadership less tied to the social democratic past.

In Sweden the bourgeois intellectual leadership of Zeth Höglund and later Karl Kilbom was anything but submissive to Comintern wishes. The Swedish Communist Party repeatedly took independent positions, but the last straw came in 1929 when Kilbom sought a *rapprochement* with the Social Democrats instead of pursuing the International's class-against-class line. Subsequently, the Party split and Moscow switched its support to a more compliant, working-class leadership headed by Hugo Sillén and Sven Linderot, who led the Party down more compliant lines.

Middle Class

Western European Communist leaders with middle-class backgrounds tend to be more independently minded and more attuned to domestic concerns than their proletarian counterparts. First, they are better educated than their working-class comrades and thus less dependent on Moscow for ideological underpinnings. Second, since the Western European middle class has been generally integrated into the economic and political system, middle-class Communist leaders feel less of a need to look abroad for models and support than do their working-class cousins. Consequently, Communist leaders from middle-class backgrounds have been generally less pro-Moscow than working-class leaders.

In France, Britain, Sweden, the Netherlands, and elsewhere, many of the less pliable Communist leaders who fell victim to purges during the 1920s were middle class in origin. In France, for example, Marcel Cachin was the son of a policeman and taught high school before rising to leadership in the newly formed French Communist Party.[9] Another early French Communist leader was Albert Treint, a school teacher. Both he and Cachin fell from power during the mid-1920s.[10] In Britain a number of middle-class Central Committee members fell victim to tightening Soviet authority, including Albert Inkpin, Andrew Rothstein, Arthur Horner, and Tom Bell.[11]

Currently, in at least some of the Communist parties of Western Europe, middle-class individuals enjoy prominent positions in the party hierarchy. We can see from Table 9 that individuals from middle-class backgrounds have risen to numerical dominance in the Italian Communist Party. Moreover, 62 percent of official posts at

**Table 9. Socioeconomic Status of PCI National Party Leaders'
Families, 1963**

Lower	30.5%
Lower middle	19.9
Middle	21.8
Upper middle	8.9
Upper	14.4
Not stated	4.5

SOURCE: Giorgio Galli and Alfonso Prandi, *Patterns of Political Participation in Italy* (New Haven: Yale, 1970), p. 152.

the level of party organization in the PCI are held by middle-class individuals, and among the Party's parliamentarians those from middle-class backgrounds outnumber ex-workers three to one.[12] In Greece 60 percent of the KKE's parliamentary delegation in 1936 classified themselves as workers or employees. In 1964 only 4.5 percent of the EDA delegation were from the working class.[13] In Spain, according to figures recently released by the PCE, there are only 22 workers on the Party's 142-member Central Committee.[14] Finally, in France in 1962, of the PCF's 41 deputies, only 18 had been workers. Of 73 in 1973, a mere 27 were former workers.[15]

Intellectual

Although Communism in Western Europe has made consistent and strenuous efforts to gain the support and cooperation of intellectuals, intellectual party leaders tend to be the least dependable allies of the Soviet Union and the most innovative in devising domestic programs and strategies. By definition, intellectuals have the training and predisposition to interpret Marx and Lenin for themselves, rather than relying on Moscow's version of the truth. Consequently, intellectual leaders often find themselves at odds with Moscow's simplistic Marxism.

Historically, Moscow has found more than a few intellectual party leaders to be less than compliant servants of Soviet demands. In Britain Sylvia Pankhurst of the famous suffragette family was expelled from the CPGB because of her independent views.[16] Boris

Souvarine and L. O. Frossard were among France's intellectual Communist leaders who proved unresponsive to Moscow's demands.[17] Zeth Höglund, Karl Kilbom, and other intellectual founders of the Swedish Communist Party left it in the middle 1920s because they did not care to submit blindly to the Comintern's wishes.[18]

Currently, intellectual Communist party leaders are far from submissive to Soviet dictates. Prominent among Western Europe's intellectual Communist leaders is C. H. Hermansson, the head of Sweden's VPK from 1964 to 1975. After joining the Swedish Party in 1941, Hermansson, a university graduate, began to write for *Ny Dag,* the Party newspaper. By 1959 he rose to the post of editor, a position he parlayed into Party chairman in 1964.[19] Under Hermansson's leadership (and with strong support from intellectual circles at Stockholm University[20]), the VPK embarked on a remarkably innovative course in both domestic and international policies.[21]

Two of Western Europe's Communist parties that historically have been more independent vis-à-vis Moscow and more moderate in regards to domestic policies have had traditions of intellectual influence. The Icelandic Communist Party's first chairman, Brynjoflur Bjarnason, earned a degree from the University of Copenhagen and taught in Iceland before rising to Party leadership. Another of the Party's founders and past presidents, Einar Olgeirsson, studied at the University of Reykjavik and the University of Berlin. Later, he taught in Iceland and edited the party paper, *Thjodviljinn.*[22] Finally, Regnar Arnalds, the current chairman of the PA, is a Swedish-educated lawyer.[23]

Intellectuals have long held prominent positions in the Italian Communist Party. Antonio Gramsci, the Party's political and spiritual founder, has a solid reputation as a fresh and original Marxist theoretician whose works are still widely read in Leftist intellectual circles. Along with Gramsci in the leadership of the early PCI were Togliatti, Tasca, and Terracini, all graduates of the University of Turin and all intellectuals in their own right. As Table 10 indicates, the PCI has long had a large proportion of university graduates in its leadership hierarchy (43.5 percent in 1963). Heinz Timmermann argues that the great number of intellectuals in the PCI's leadership

**Table 10. Percentage of University Graduates in PCI
Leadership, 1946–63**

1946	33.0%
1950	36.9
1953	32.9
1957	34.7
1961	42.5
1963	43.5

SOURCE: Giorgio Galli and Alfonso Prandi, *Patterns of Political Participation
in Italy* (New Haven: Yale, 1970), p. 153.

has pushed the Party toward policies of ideological, political, and
even organizational openness.[24]

Similarly, intellectuals hold prominent positions in the leadership
of the Spanish Communist Party. Santiago Carrillo, the Party's
secretary-general, is an intellectual author of a number of books[25]
and Ramón Tamanes, who may be Carrillo's heir apparent, is an
economist.[26] Further, 54 members of the Party's 142-member Central Committee are classified as "intellectuals or professionals."[27]

In a number of cases, moderate, revisionist challenges to hard-
line Communist leadership have been led by intellectuals. In
Austria the progressive minority that lost a power struggle to pro-
Stalinists following the furor surrounding the Warsaw Pact invasion of Czechoslovakia was led by intellectuals such as Ernst
Fisher and Franz Marek, the editor of *Weg und Ziel,* the Party's
theoretical journal.[28] In 1961 in Finland, a group of intellectuals
broke with the SKP to found the journal *Tilanne,* which became a
jousting ground for "noncomformist" Communists, Socialists, and
Leftists.[29] Similarly, in the Netherlands, a mildly revisionist group
that broke with the CPN in 1958 was led by a group of intellectuals
who founded the journal *De Brug.*[30]

Not all intellectual opponents of Soviet orthodoxy have been
revisionists or progressives. By their nature, intellectuals are neither
revisionists nor dogmatists per se. They *are* more difficult to discipline. Consequently, they may be more dogmatic than the party
line demands rather than more progressive. Throughout Western

Europe, ultra-Left parties have sprung up, led in many cases by intellectuals. In Italy, for example, the *Il Manifesto* group was directed by a group of dissident intellectuals, including Rossana Rossanda, Luigi Pintor, and Aldo Natoli.[31] In Belgium in 1963, Jacques Grippa, whose former tenure on the faculty of a school for cadres gives him some credentials as an intellectual theoretician, led a group of dissidents out of the PCB to launch a pro-Chinese party.[32] In France many of the Maoist and anarchist groups opposing the PCF are led by intellectuals.

Individual intellectuals, too, have often dissented against Communist policies. In France well-known intellectuals such as Roger Garaudy, Simon de Beauvoir, Jean Paul Sartre, Claude Roy, Louis Aragon, and others have first embraced the Party and then repudiated it.[33] Another intellectual, Louis Althusser, is among the PCF's foremost Left-wing critics. Yrjö Leino, a former agronomy professor who served as a Communist member of Finland's postwar cabinet, broke with the Party after separating from his wife, Hertta Kuusinen.[34] In Britain, too, individual intellectuals have left the CPGB to become some of its strongest critics.[35]

Apparatchiki

Communist party leaders whose entire careers have been in the party tend to develop strong attachments to it as an institution. Unlike many of their intellectual and proletarian counterparts, apparatchik leaders eschew rigorous orthodoxy be it pro-Soviet or otherwise in favor of policies and practices designed to insure the organizational well-being of their party. Consequently, apparatchik leaders opt for uninnovative, pragmatic policies they believe will maintain and enhance their party's social and electoral position, policies that may or may not follow the Soviet line, depending on the leaders' perceptions of advantageous positions. Thus, apparatchik leaders of the Western European parties tend enthusiastically to endorse Moscow's policy of international détente, for example, because of its value domestically. In contrast, the Soviet intervention in Czechoslovakia in 1968 is regarded by many Western party leaders as an electoral albatross.

An excellent example of an apparatchik Communist leader in Western Europe is Enrico Berlinguer, the current secretary-general of the Italian Communist Party. The son of a wealthy Sardinian family, Berlinguer has been a member of the PCI's apparatus all of his adult life.[36] In his policy positions, Berlinguer has concentrated on policies designed primarily to further his Party's political position rather than promote Soviet policy aims or further the cause of Marxist revolution. Although Berlinguer has endorsed Soviet policies that enjoy domestic popularity such as détente, he has been quick to put his Party on record against Russian policies that are unpopular in Italy such as the Czechoslovakian intervention and Soviet social policies.

Luigi Longo, Berlinguer's immediate predecessor at the head of the PCI, was also very much the organization man. A longtime deputy of Palmiro Togliatti, Longo virtually grew up within the Party. Like his successor, Longo was an ideologue neither of Stalinism nor of revisionism, but pragmatically desirous of enhancing his Party's domestic political position. An organizer rather than a thinker, Longo continued along the path outlined by his predecessor toward Party autonomy.[37]

Similarly, Waldeck Rochet, who led the French Communist Party from 1964 until prolonged illness forced him to turn over the reins of leadership to Georges Marchais in 1971, was an individual totally devoted to the Party apparatus. As Party leader, Waldeck Rochet lacked innovative brilliance, but excelled at keeping the Party together through his organizational skills and emphasis on safe bread-and-butter policies acceptable to the Party's large constituency.[38] Georges Marchais, Waldeck Rochet's successor, is also very much an organization man. He, too, behaves as a man more concerned with his Party's institutional posture than with either political dogma or Soviet foreign policy interests.

Trade Unionist

Communist leaders with trade unionist backgrounds bring perspectives characteristic of their union experience to their leadership roles. Because of the differing nature of unions in different countries and the varying positions of Communist parties vis-à-vis the union movement in different countries, Communist union leaders' perspectives vary. In Britain the CPGB's long experience of trying to increase its influence within generally non-revolutionary unions has produced pragmatic, flexible unionist party leaders such as John Gollan, John Tocher, and Gordon McLennan, the Party's general-secretary.

Similarly, in Italy, where the PCI's union strategy has long been one of cooperation and compromise with the Italian Socialists and other Left-wing parties, the Communist trade union leaders tend to be moderates on domestic policy. Labor unionist leaders Bruno Trentin and Sergio Garavini are advocates of decentralization and democracy in the PCI, and Agostino Novella and Luciano Lama, the past and present secretaries-general of the CGIL, are associated with Giorgio Amendola's group of moderate Party reformers.[39]

In countries where Communist union strength is concentrated in a single union or a single area, whether broadly as in the CGT in France, or narrowly as in Norway and Sweden, where the Communists dominate a few locals in certain regions of the country, trade unionist party leaders cling to conservative positions. In Sweden, where the union strength of the Communists is concentrated in the Norrbotten region, trade union leaders were among Hermansson's more conservative opponents. In Norway opposition to transforming the Left-wing electoral alliance into a party came from hard liners, many of whom were in union posts. Similarly, trade union leaders in France are generally among the PCF's more conservative members.[40]

In Finland, where the Communist union experience has alternated between conflict and cooperation with the Social Democrats, Communist unionists are found among the ranks of hard liners and progressives both. Although many of those who oppose SKP coalition with the Social Democrats are unionists, some of the progressives are also trade unionists (including Arvo Aalto, the Party's general-secretary[41]).

Regardless of whether Communist union militants tend to be conservative and pro-Soviet as in France, or progressive and independent-minded as in Britain, they all tend to be non-revolutionary. In part this is because union status gives these leaders a measure of prestige in the system as it is, a prestige they may not wish to risk. Second, union leaders tend to have had experience bargaining with governmental authorities (and, in some cases, union leaders of other political persuasions) and this tends to socialize them into the political process. Finally, because of their proximity to the day-to-day struggle for bread-and-butter reforms, union leaders tend to lose interest in revolutionary goals.[42]

Generational Differences

Communist leaders from different generations vary in their approaches to their roles because they differ in their political socialization experiences. Older leaders who acquired their political knowledge and beliefs before 1956 were socialized in a period during which the Soviet Union was revered as a bastion of anti-Fascism and the Soviet Union's place at the head of the Communist movement was secure. In contrast, younger leaders earned their political spurs in a period in which the Soviet myth of infallibility was shattered. The Soviets' moral leadership of the Communist world was threatened by the revelations of Stalin's crimes and the crisis of Hungary. Moscow's political leadership was challenged first by Yugoslavia and then, more seriously, by China. Consequently, older leaders tend still to look to the Soviet Union for leadership in international questions and for guidance in domestic politics, and younger leaders tend to be more independent in both their international and their domestic policies.

In Austria the conflict between moderates and hard liners precipitated by the Czechoslavakian crisis was in many respects fought along generational lines. In general the progressives in the Austrian Communist Party were young, many of them intellectuals. In contrast, the KPÖ leaders who stood most firmly behind the Soviet Union were veteran Communists. Similarly, the deep division between pro-Soviets and progressives in the Finnish Communist Party has generational overtones and in Sweden, too, older leaders tend to be among the opponents of Hermansson's reforms. Also, in the latter country, Hermansson's emergence as Party leader in 1964 came largely as a result of his youthful supporters.

Remarkably, the Communist Party of Luxembourg has been led by the same team of leaders for decades, avoiding splits and purges. Its chairman, Dominique Urbani, rose to a position of leadership before World War II and, with the aid of his family (ten of whom hold positions in the Party machine), continues to exercise tight control over the Party. For Urbani and, not coincidentally, the PCL, the infallibility of the Soviet Union and the truth of orthodox Marxist-Leninist doctrine remain very real.

In contrast, the top leadership of the more forward-looking Italian Communist Party is in the hands of younger men. Berlinguer, for one, is in his early fifties. When the founders of the PCI were being arrested by the Fascists, Berlinguer was only an infant. Lars Werner, the new leader of the Swedish Communist Party is in his early forties and Regnar Arnalds, the chairman of the Icelandic Party, is in his thirties.

Although there are some notable exceptions (Togliatti, Carrillo, and others), veteran party leaders tend to become wedded to past policies. In several countries, for example, veteran Communist leaders only reluctantly accepted de-Stalinization and hesitated to enact reforms in their own parties. Holland's veteran leader Paul de Groot, for example, totally refused to accept de-Stalinization. Ironically, this refusal was one of the factors that led de Groot to take his Party out of the international movement.[43]

In several other cases, it took the ascension of new, younger leaders to bring about change. In France, for example, Communist leaders saw de-Stalinization as contrary to many years of training and Thorez, in particular, saw it as a threat to his personal position. Not until Thorez passed from the scene in 1964 did the PCF begin a transformation. Then Waldeck Rochet, the new Party secretary, took a series of wide-ranging and decisive steps designed to lead his Party away from Stalinism. In this effort, Waldeck Rochet was supported by Roger Garaudy, at that time the Party's resident intellectual, and some younger members of the politburo, including Gaston Plissonnier, Roland Leroy, and René Piquet. The opposition, which carried the day, was led by veteran politburo members, such as Jacques Duclos, Etienne Fajon, François Billous, Raymond Guyot, and Jeannette Vermeersch-Thorez.[44] In recent years, the French Party's new leader, Georges Marchais, who is twenty years younger than his predecessor, has led new assaults on the PCF's "neo-Stalinism," and embarked on a policy of independence from the Soviet Union.

In several Western Communist parties, the change of line during the 1950s from Cold War rigidity to united front tactics was accompanied by a leadership turnover. In Belgium in 1954, the PCB's Eleventh Congress not only adopted a new unity of action program, but shuffled the leadership, turning to two younger men to head the Party, Ernest Burnelle, a former school teacher, and René Beelin, a worker. In Great Britain, Harry Pollitt resigned as general-secretary of the CPGB on the same day that the Party acknowledged the seriousness of Stalin's crimes. Before that, the Party had glossed over the controversy.[45]

Position Vis-à-Vis the Political System

The personal position of individual Communist party leaders in relation to the political system is an important part of their individual political socialization. In general, the experience of holding political office tends to moderate Communists' domestic and international attitudes and to increase their acceptance of alliances with non-Communist parties. As office holders, Communist politicians develop an appreciation of cooperation with office holders from other parties. Additionally, Communist leaders with long tenure in governmental office tend to develop an institutional allegiance to the system. Thus, they develop a stake in the established political order.

A collateral effect of office holding that can be particularly important for the more successful parties of Western Europe is that the occupation of office tends to raise the objective class status of its occupants. Although Communist parties typically require office holders to remit all of their pay above the level of the salary of a skilled worker, the privileges and accoutrements of governmental office that cannot be valued monetarily serve to raise the status of Communist parliamentarians, mayors, and other officials above the lower class. In Finland in 1964, for example, although two-thirds of the Communist delegation came from working-class homes, the largest group among them was middle class, objectively speaking.[46] The effect of this upward social mobility on Communist incumbents may well be a tempering of overt dissatisfaction with the political system.

In Italy the leaders of the PCI are represented in local and regional government offices in large numbers. In 1963 nearly 70 percent of Communist Party officials had held the post of municipal councillor, 20 percent as mayor, nearly 30 percent provincial councillors, and 14 percent communal magistrates. Also, many of the PCI's upper echelon leadership are experienced members of parliament. What is more, the more revisionist elements of the PCI are found in areas where the Party is strongly entrenched in local and regional government (Tuscany, Emilia).[47] Party officials in the Red Belt, for example, enthusiastically endorsed the *"compromesso storico."*[48] In Iceland Communist leaders have shared national power as part of a Left-wing coalition government as well as holding some offices in municipal government.

Similarly, in Finland many SKP leaders hold seats in parliament and a number have had governing experience during the periods of SKP participation in coalition governments. Notably, those Communist leaders who participated in the governing coalition tended to be more supportive of continued Communist participation in the government than those who were removed from power.

In France the Communist Party has long held many local offices and its leaders for the most part are experienced parliamentarians. Arthur Mendel, among others, attributes the PCF's conservative, non-revolutionary postures in part to the comfortable position of its leaders.[49] In Luxembourg the PCL leaders have held parliamentary seats and some offices in local government, but have been excluded from national power.

Personal Relationship to the Soviet Union

A final part of an individual Communist leader's political socialization experience that shapes his behavior as a party leader is his personal relationship to the Soviet Union and other Communist countries. In general, the closer an individual leader's personal ties to Moscow, the more likely his personal policy decisions will support Soviet interests.

Leaders of the West German Communist Party have strong personal attachments to East Germany and the Soviet Union. During the Party's fugitive period, they depended upon the German Democratic Republic for shelter and financial support. They were carefully selected by Moscow for Party leadership and literally they owe their careers to the Soviets and East Germans. Consequently, their loyalty to the international positions of the Kremlin is hardly surprising.

Similarly, leaders of the external faction of the Greek Communist Party are bound to the Soviet Union and Eastern Europe. The headquarters and Party cadres of the KKE Exterior are located in Eastern Europe and the leaders' authority is exercised only at the sufferance of their hosts. Further, the Party relies on Moscow for financial assistance. After escaping from a Portuguese prison in 1960, Alvaro Cunhal, the secretary-general of the Portuguese Communist Party, found refuge in Moscow and various East European capitals until he returned to Portugal in 1974. Moreover, during that period, Cunhal developed a close personal relationship with Leonid Brezhnev. Maurice Thorez, the longtime leader of the French Communist Party, owed his career to Soviet patrons who supported him as Party leader against internal challenges.

A number of Western Europe's Communist leaders are personally tied to Moscow by virtue of training. Nikos Zakhariades, the dominant figure in Greek Communist circles during the 1930s, graduated from Moscow's training school for Eastern peoples before being appointed KKE party leader by the Comintern in 1931.[50] Johann Kopelnig, a founder and longtime secretary-general of the Austrian Communist Party, was trained in the Soviet Union. Later, as a Party leader, he followed the Soviet line faithfully. Karl Tomann, another of the founders of the Austrian Communist Party, learned his Marxism while a prisoner in Russia during World War I.[51]

Other Communist leaders developed ties to Moscow while living there in exile. When the exile experience coincided with training, the result was often the development of a firm allegiance to the Soviet Union. This was the case with the Norwegian Communist Party's Emil Løvlien. For others, however, exile in the Soviet Union was a sobering, even fatal experience. Ironically, after the Finnish Communist Party regained legality in 1944, the only available Communist leaders were those who had languished in bourgeois prisons in Finland. Most of the émigré leaders (along with untold numbers of other East and West European Communist leaders in exile) fell victim to Stalin's purges. For others, such as Palmiro Togliatti, the exile experience (as well as his experience as a high functionary in the Comintern Executive) bred an appreciation of the Soviets' raw power, but also an awareness of their ruthlessness. Throughout his career as leader of the Italian Communist Party, Togliatti was pro-Soviet, but not blindly so. In the last years of his life, in particular when Soviet authority was being challenged on the global level from several quarters, Togliatti led his Party in open and active resistance to some aspects of Soviet policy.

Communist leaders without strong personal ties to the Soviet Union have, in many cases, demonstrated considerable independence from Moscow. It is no accident that a number of West European Communist party leaders who went underground during the Nazi occupation rather than fleeing to Moscow later were purged or split with the party. While underground they were generally cut off from instructions from Moscow and thus cultivated the talent of making policy decisions on their own with little outside guidance. Furthermore, the resistance experience taught them skills in bargaining and cooperation with other political groups, thus giving them closer ties with their own political systems. In Denmark Axel Larsen, who broke with the DKP to found the Danish Socialist People's Party, spent the war in Denmark organizing the resistance until captured by the Germans. Paul de Groot, the longtime leader of the Communist Party of the Netherlands, who in the 1960s led his Party out of the Soviet orbit, was a resistance leader. Similarly, Peder Furobotn, who led the Norwegian resistance against the Germans, was purged from leadership in the NKP in 1949 as a "Titoist."

Finally, many of Western Europe's more independently minded Communist leaders lack strong personal ties to the Soviet Union. Sweden's Hermansson, Iceland's Arnalds, and Italy's Berlinguer, among others, have none of the more obvious links to Moscow (financial, training, past residence). At the same time, Spain's Santiago Carrillo is known to have a close personal relationship with Italy's Berlinguer and he lived in France during his long exile rather than Eastern Europe.

Although there is more than a coincidental relationship between background variables and the decision-making behavior of the leaders of the Communist parties of Western Europe, caution should be observed not to exaggerate the conclusions of this chapter, even within the constraints imposed upon this study. First, even if we adopt the philosophical position of environmental determinism, who is to say that only certain aspects of a Communist leader's background—his social origins, occupation, generation, and personal position vis-à-vis the political system and the Soviet Union—shape his behavior? Other, perhaps idiosyncratic, factors may be important also.

Second, for purposes of discussion, we have considered and illustrated each of the background variables in separate sections, but in reality we could present a matrix of background variables for each leader. Dominique Urbani of Luxembourg's PCL, for example, is a veteran Party militant from a working-class background who was active in the Resistance. He has been a parliamentarian since 1944 and also has close personal ties to Moscow. How does one decide which of the background variables or what combination of variables is most important for each individual?

Finally, we must reemphasize that background variables are important in shaping Communist party leaders' behavior only insofar as the leaders are free to act. Each leader is constrained by variables from the environment, and from factors internal to the party. The leader is free to act within these constraints and it is in this realm that background variables play a role in shaping the leader's actions and, consequently, the policies and postures of the party.

Notes

1. Even if a party is financially independent, there are other restraints that may tend to limit the leaders' freedom in determining policy toward the Soviet Union, including the other types of ties discussed in Chapter 3: historical patterns and the nature of the party's electorate and membership. See Chapter 10 for a discussion of how various factors interrelate to produce party policy and behavior.

2. Albania, of course, looks to the Chinese. In Western Europe, however, the Italians are challenging for ideological leadership.

3. David Caute, *Communism and the French Intellectuals, 1914-1960* (London: Andre Deutsch, 1964), pp. 23-25.

4. Witold S. Sworakowski, *World Communism: A Handbook, 1918-1965* (Stanford: Hoover Institution, 1973).

5. Franz Borkenau, *European Communism* (New York: Harper & Brothers, 1953), p. 107.

6. Robert Wohl, *French Communism in the Making, 1914-1924* (Stanford: Stanford University, 1966), p. 398. François Fejtö, *The French Communist Party and the Crisis of International Communism* (Cambridge: MIT, 1967), pp. 4-10.

7. Walter Kendall, "The Communist Party of Great Britain," *Survey* XX, no. 1 (Winter 1974):118-31.

8. Henry Pelling, *The British Communist Party: A Historical Profile* (London: Adam and Charles Black, 1958), pp. 49-52.

9. Branko Lazitch and Milorad M. Drachkovitch, *Biographical Dictionary of the Comintern* (Stanford: Stanford University, 1973).

10. Wohl, *French Communism*, pp. 426, 429.

11. Henry Pelling, *British Communist Party*, p. 52.

12. Neil McInnes, *The Communist Parties of Western Europe* (London: Oxford, 1975), pp. 66-67.

13. Keith R. Legg, *Politics in Modern Greece* (Stanford: Stanford University, 1969), pp. 283-85.

14. *New York Times,* 1 August 1976.

15. McInnes, *The Communist Parties,* p. 67.

16. Pelling, *British Communist Party,* p. 20.

17. Wohl, *French Communism.*

18. Sworakowski, *World Communism.*

19. YICA, 1966.

20. *Economist,* 16 November 1974.

21. Daniel Tarschys, "The Unique Role of the Swedish CP," *Problems of Communism* XXIII, no. 3 (May-June 1974):36-44.

22. Lazitch and Drachkovitch, *Biographical Dictionary.*

23. YICA, 1969.

24. Heinz Timmermann, "National Strategy and International Autonomy: The Italian and French Communist Parties," *Studies in Comparative Communism* V, no. 2 (Summer-Autumn 1972):258-76.

25. Including, *Después de Franco, ¿que?* (Paris: 1965) and *Demain l'Espagne* (Paris:1964).

26. *Le Monde,* 16 October 1976.

27. *New York Times,* 1 August 1976.

28. Kevin Devlin, "Czechoslovakia and the Crisis of Austrian Communism," *Studies in Comparative Communism* II, no. 3 (July-October 1969):9-37.

29. Bengt Matti, "Finland," pp. 371-410, in William E. Griffith, ed., *Communism in Europe,* I (Cambridge: MIT, 1964), p. 309.

30. Frits Kool, "Communism in Holland: A Study in Futility," *Problems of Communism* IX, no. 5 (September-October 1960):17-24.

31. Bodgan Denitch, "The Rebirth of Spontaneity: *Il Manifesto* and West European Communism," *Politics and Society* I, no. 4 (August 1971): 463-77.

32. YICA, 1966.

33. Caute, *Communism and the French Intellectuals.* Sartre and de Beauvoir were never members, only sympathizers.

34. Lazitch and Drachkovitch, *Biographical Dictionary.*

35. Neal Wood, *Communism and British Intellectuals* (New York: Columbia, 1959).

36. Arrigo Levi, "Berlinguer's Communism," *Survey* XVIII, no. 3 (Summer 1972):1-15.

37. William S. Caldwell, "Luigi Long," pp. 503-25, in Rodger Swearingen, ed., *Leaders of the Communist World* (New York: Free Press, 1971).

38. Pierre Delain, "Waldeck Rochet," pp. 489-502, in ibid.

39. Peter R. Weitz, "The CGIL and the PCI: From Subordination to Independent Political Force," pp. 541-71, in Donald L. M. Blackmer and Sidney Tarrow, eds., *Communism in Italy and France* (Princeton: Princeton University, 1975), p. 556.

40. Ronald Tiersky, *French Communism, 1920-1972* (New York: Columbia, 1974), p. 316.

41. Kevin Devlin, "Finnish Communism," *Survey,* no. 74 (Winter-Spring 1970):49-69.

42. Giorgio Galli, "Italian Communism," pp. 301-83, in Griffith, *Communism in Europe,* p. 326.

43. McInnes, *The Communist Parties,* p. 118.

44. Annie Kriegel, "Communism in France," pp. 351-84, in T. J. Nossiter, A. H. Hanson, and Stein Rokkan, eds., *Imagination and Precision in the Social Sciences* (London: Faber & Faber, 1972).

45. Russian Institute, ed., *The Anti-Stalin Campaign and International Communism* (New York: Columbia, 1956).

46. Martti Naponen, *Kansanedustajien sosiaalinen tausta Suomesse* (Porvoo-Helsinki: WSOY, 1964), quoted in Jaakko Nousiainen, "Research on the Finnish Communism," *Scandinavian Political Studies* III (1968):243-51.

47. Giorgio Galli and Alfonso Prandi, *Patterns of Political Participation in Italy* (New Haven: Yale, 1970), p. 158.

48. See statement of Guido Fanti, the Communist president of the

region of Emilia, *Il Mundo,* 29 November 1973; and that of the mayor of Bologna, Renalto Zangheri, ibid., 6 December 1973.

49. Arthur P. Mendel, "Why the French Communists Stopped the Revolution," *Review of Politics* XXXI, no. 1 (January 1969):3-27. See also George Lavau, "Parti et société: *Les communistes français,*" *Critique* XXV, no. 271 (December 1969):1083-94; Denis Berger and Paul-Louis Thirard, "Un parti social-démocrate de type nouveau," *Les temps modernes* XXVI, no. 284 (March 1970):1446-71; Michel Winock, "La contradiction du PCF," *Esprit* XXXVIII, no. 392 (May 1970):884-97; and Annie Kriegel, "Le parti communiste français et la Vᵉ République," *Contrepoint* IX (1973):149-72.

50. Jane Perry Clark Carey and Andrew Galbraith Carey, *The Web of Modern Greek Politics* (New York: Columbia, 1968), pp. 118-19.

51. Lazitch and Drachkovitch, *Biographical Dictionary.* After losing a factional struggle in the KPÖ, Tomann deserted the Party and in World War II acted as an official for the pro-Nazi regime. When the Red Army swept through the area, he was arrested and shot.

chapter 8

PARTY MEMBERSHIP
AND ELECTORATE

Not all constraining factors influencing the actions of Communist party leaders are imposed by the party's external environment or by the personal characteristics of the individual leaders themselves. Other constraints arise from the internal composition and nature of the party itself, including the nature of the party's membership and electorate, which we examine here, and certain characteristics of the party's historical experience, which we explore in the next chapter.

Although in general parlance, we speak of a political party's leaders, members, and voters as if they were distinct, well-defined groups, it is more accurate to picture an individual's relationship to a political party as a continuum based on that individual's psychological and behavioral involvement in the party. In Figure 2, such a continuum has been constructed with labels attached less to indicate clearly differentiated categories than to suggest names for the relative intensities of involvement and attachment to a party that individuals may possess. The least degree of positive association to a party is held by an individual who votes for the party on a more or less regular basis. At a level of greater involvement, the individual self-consciously identifies with the party, occasionally donating his resources to its use. Moving further up the involvement continuum, we find the individuals who more properly may be called party

	supporter		upper leader	
elector	active member	intermediate leader	top leader

Figure 2. Party Involvement.

members. These individuals form the nucleus of each of the party's basic groups. They are the unpaid volunteers who collectively flesh out the party's organizational framework and actively participate in election campaigns. Above these in involvement and participation are the leadership. Intermediate leaders tend to see party work as more vocational (at least potentially) than avocational. Near the higher end of the involvement continuum are the upper leadership and at the highest level of involvement and commitment are the top leadership, including a relatively small number of individuals or perhaps only a single leader.

In this chapter, our interest is concentrated on the left half of the involvement continuum—those who vote, join, and work for the party. Although in our analysis, we employ terms like *member, voter,* and *leader* as if they were clearly distinct groups, we must keep in mind the nature of the qualitative distinction between them and the difficulty of drawing a precise line between groups in the party.

The individuals and groups who compose the electorate and membership of a Western European Communist party are important to the party because it is they, for the most part, who provide the party's primary resources. It is they, particularly the activists, who contribute time, money, votes, and effort in an election campaign. It is they who work for the party in the countryside, the union hall, and the legislature. It is they who contribute the ideals, ideas, and insight that come to comprise the party's program.

Potentially, a party's membership and electorate can act as a powerful restraint on the party's actions. First, a displeased membership may choose to cease contributing their physical and material resources to the party, thus precipitating financial and man-power shortages. They may choose to withhold their electoral support or, worse, vote for a rival, thus reducing the Communists' domestic political strength. Second, discontented militants may opt to support an internal opposition to reverse party policies, creating or enlarging an internal schism. Finally, unhappy members can withdraw from the party to create a rival Left-wing party.[1]

In general, the more active and better informed the participants in the party, the greater the check they impose on party behavior. More active members contribute more to the party; so the with-drawal of their services is a greater blow than the abstention of relatively passive individuals. Further, individuals who are more aware will be a more potent constraint, at least potentially, because they are alert to a broader range of party activities. Consequently, a Communist party's electorate, because of its lesser awareness of internal party decisions and relatively lesser contribution to the party's success, is generally a relatively weaker constraint than the party's militants.

We see, then, that a Communist party's participants—voters, members, militants—can place boundaries on the party's leaders. The nature of these boundaries depends on the character and nature of the membership and electorate of the parties.

Several generalizations can be drawn about the membership and electorate of the Communist parties of Western Europe. First, Communist party voters and members throughout Western Europe tend to support the Communist party in its *"fonction tribunitienne,"* as Georges Lavau terms it. The party fulfills this tribune function, Lavau argues, by expressing the malcontentments, denouncing the abuses, and organizing the protests of the plebian masses it repre-sents.[2] To be sure, the empirical evidence indicates that the "plebian masses" who support the Communist party do tend to be malcon-tents. In general, they tend to oppose bourgeois incumbents and support proposals for political reform. A survey of industrial work-ers in France and Italy in late 1955 and early 1956 finds that many workers (more than 60 percent in each country) see a great deal of injustice around them and that many see the Communist party as the most effective means of making themselves heard by the govern-ment.[3] "The interviews," the study concludes, "made it clear that to a large extent the communist vote expresses protest against the political system. . . ."[4]

In more recent surveys, in France in 1968, 35 percent of the PCF's electors replied that people vote Communist because the Party represents a useful opposition force, and another 38 percent said it is because the PCF translates general discontent.[5] In 1974 the IFOP (*Institute Française de l'Opinion Publique*) asked supporters of the different French political groupings their attitudes on a series of government policies and institutions. As can be seen from Table 11, on almost every question, the Communist voters favor "a great deal of change" in greater proportions than any other political group. Finally, a study based on interviews with PCF delegates at a federation conference in the department of l'Isére in 1974 finds that these activists see the Party's task as that of relieving the misery of men.[6]

The Italian Communist Party benefits from a large bloc of protest voters that differs from other voters largely on the basis of attitudes toward the established government. According to a 1963 survey, only 15 percent of the Communists' supporters favored the

Table 11. Percentage of Each Political Grouping Desiring "A Great Deal of Change" in Various Governmental Policies, 1973

	PCF	Socialists & Radicals	Reformateur	Majority
Tax system	75%	62%	52%	31%
Function of justice	59	56	52	38
Orientation of social policy	71	62	50	29
Gov't. information policy	67	52	33	15
Personalities	73	57	32	6
Role of parliament	60	45	38	12
Orientation of Economic policy	62	47	27	13
Role of president	52	31	16	4

SOURCE: *Sondages*, 1973.

then current government of Christian Democrats, Social Democrats, and Republicans.[7] Many Italians vote for the PCI to protest
the corruption and inefficiency of the Christian Democrats.

In other countries, too, Communist voters tend to differ from
non-Communist supporters on the basis of their attitudes toward
the political system. In the Netherlands in 1947, 79 percent of the
CPN's voters felt the national income distribution was unjust, and
only 50 percent of the whole sample agreed.[8] A study in Finland
reports that when asked what is wrong with Finnish society, 51
percent of the Communist supporters said inequalities, a far greater
proportion choosing that answer than in any other party.[9]

Although Communist voters support their party's role as a tribune for the discontented, there is solid evidence that they would not
endorse an overtly revolutionary role by the Communists. As early
as 1956, only 19 percent of the French workers and 16 percent of
the Italians interviewed said that the political situation would be
changed by revolution rather than evolution.[10] In 1968 an IFOP
poll asked Frenchmen how they characterized the PCF and only 1
percent of Communist electors described the Party as "wanting
revolution."[11] Two years later, Frenchmen were asked the following: "Agree or disagree, if the situation seemed favorable to it, the
PCF would be ready to seize power by revolution." Of the PCF's
electors, 21 percent agreed, but 57 percent disagreed.[12] Similarly,
British Communists are not revolutionaries. That banner is being
carried by the ultra-Left in Britain.[13]

As with individual Communist leaders, socioeconomic characteristics tend to predispose Communist militants and supporters toward favoring certain types of political behavior by the party and
opposing other types. Although individual militants have different
programmatic predispositions that depend, in large part, on unique
personal characteristics, some generalizations can be drawn. First,
along generational lines, a division can be made between militants
socialized politically before 1956, those socialized after 1956, and
younger militants who became active politically in the late 1960s
and early 1970s.[14] During their politically formative years, older
members lived in a time in which the international prestige of the
Soviet Union was preeminent. For younger militants, however, the
gloss has faded both from Moscow's world leadership and from her

domestic infallibility. Consequently, older cadres tend to be loyal to Moscow and younger militants are more likely to emphasize the domestic needs of their own party rather than those of the Soviet Union. A party with a large core of veteran militants will thus be constrained to adhere to traditional allegiance to Moscow. On the other hand, if the party's cadres are predominantly younger, leaders will be free (if not encouraged) to pursue a more "nationalistic" line.

Although younger militants will generally allow the leadership leeway in dealing with the Soviet Union, it is not necessarily true that younger activists will advocate more moderate domestic policies than their elders. Theirs is the generation of May-June 1968, and student violence and ultra-Left militance of the late 1960s and 1970s. Consequently, in some parties, a middle-generation leadership finds itself pressed between a group of older generation cadres who demand that the party maintain unswerving loyalty to Moscow and a group of younger militants who are suspicious of the Soviets, but pressure the leadership to pursue relatively uncompromising domestic policies.

This is the problem faced by the Italian Communist Party. In contrast to a number of other Western European Communist parties, there is no large Stalinist bloc among the Party's leadership. All but a small minority of Cold War Stalinists have been ousted from positions of importance and replaced by individuals more loyal to the Party's *Via Italiana al Socialismo.* There are, however, large numbers of older militants in the PCI and they are reticent about criticizing the Soviet Union. Moreover, the Party has succeeded in attracting many young people to the ranks. (The average member's age in 1970 was less than forty.) Many of the new, younger activists hold radical, "New Left" political views[15] and it is they who are frequently critical of the Party's support for the Andreotti government.

So far, Enrico Berlinguer and the Party's middle-generation leadership have maintained control of their party. Few veteran Stalinists are in positions of authority in the hierarchy and the pro-Soviet cadres among the rank and file have nowhere to go. Similarly, the radical younger militants enjoy little influence in the Party leadership. They can, however, vote with their feet, deserting the PCI for any of a number of ultra-Left alternatives[16] and many of them have done just that. The PCI has found itself strongly challenged by ultra-Left parties that accuse it of selling out to the Christian Democrats and the Communists have begun having difficulties attracting young members.

Not every party is divided by three generations. Because of recruiting problems, some parties have few young cadres. In some parties, older, Stalinist cadres have deserted to form opposition parties. Finally, in other parties, veteran militants dominate.

In France a large number of veteran militants place constraints on the Party leadership. Although the PCF is relatively young, many veteran cadres still exercise considerable power in the Party. According to the PCF's own reports, 69 percent of the membership were under forty years of age in 1976.[17] Survey data indicate that the PCF has a relatively young electorate (34 percent younger than thirty-five, only 16 percent over sixty-five in 1976; see Table 12). In contrast, at the Party's Nineteenth Congress in 1970, 85 percent of the Central Committee had become members of the PCF before 1953, the year Stalin died.[18] Similarly, of the thirty-seven Communist mayors interviewed in a recent study, 82 percent said that they had joined the Party before 1950.[19]

The membership of the rival factions of the Greek Communist Party is divided by generation as well as political posture. The hard core of the KKE Exterior consists of about seventy-five thousand refugees in Eastern European Communist countries who fled Greece in the wake of the Civil War. In contrast, the Interior

Table 12. Age of PCF Electorate

	1976	1973	1967	Population
18–20	9%	—	—	—
21–32	25	31%	38%	29%
35–49	27	32	27	29
50–64	23	22	21	22
65+	16	15	14	20

SOURCE: *Sondages*, 1973.

faction of the KKE recruited its supporters and militants after the Civil War period. Although the militants of the KKE Exterior earned their political spurs during the Civil War, the members of the domestically pragmatic, internationally independent KKE Interior were socialized during a time when their Party was campaigning for a united front.[20] Therefore, the contrasting policy positions of the two factions of the KKE reflect the contrasting political perspectives of their memberships.

In no Western European Communist party are veteran militants more firmly entrenched than in the Austrian Communist Party. During the Soviet occupation of Austria from 1945 to 1955, pro-Soviet militants were firmly established in the KPÖ's organization. Because of the Party's inability to attract younger members, the KPÖ has aged (60 percent are over sixty years old) and the veteran Stalinists have remained in place.

Following the Warsaw Pact invasion of Czechoslovakia in 1968, the initial reaction of the Party's "Centrist-progressive" leadership headed by Franz Muhri was one of explicit condemnation. Although the leadership was enthusiastically supported and encouraged by an intellectual and youth minority led by Franz Marek and Ernst Fischer, the bulk of the party's militants, trained in the comforting simplicities of the Stalinist years, were in no mood for change. At the KPÖ's Twentieth Congress in January 1969, the veteran conservatives flexed their muscle by ousting several progressives from the Central Committee. Ernst Fisher was excluded from the Party and the Congress voted to cut off funds from the youth movement. Only Muhri's energetic efforts at compromise and conciliation prevented a formal split.

The result of the KPÖ's Twentieth Congress was, eventually, a complete victory for the veteran militants. Although Marek and other progressives noisily continued the debate, the overwhelming strength of the Stalinists became apparent to everyone, including the "Centrist" leadership, who quickly perceived that the Party's real center was quite conservative. Thereafter, Franz Muhri sided more frequently with the conservatives who, recognizing their own strength, asserted themselves decisively at the Party's Twenty-First Congress in May 1970, purging progressives from the politburo once and for all and reentrenching the Party's pro-Soviet stand. Subsequently, the KPÖ moved away from its relatively moderate position of the early 1960s, opting for unabashedly hard line, pro-Soviet policies.

The Czechoslovakian crisis and the SKP's reaction to it led to revolt by veteran militants in Finland, too, but with different results. In Austria the strength of the oldtimers was overwhelming, but in the more dynamic and younger Finnish Party (whose average age of forty-nine in 1969 indicates a closer division between older and younger militants),[21] the conservatives were only a minority. As in Austria, the Communist Party in Finland condemned Soviet actions in Czechoslovakia and this condemnation spurred Stalinist cadres to action. With the crisis over Czechoslovakia, an already simmering division between progressives and hard liners came to a boil as the conservatives walked out of the stormy Fifteenth Congress in April 1969 to establish a shadow organization.

As in Austria, the SKP in Finland was divided into progressive and conservative blocs with much of the leadership trying to play a moderating, Centrist role. Unlike the Austrian case, however, in Finland, veteran militants did not win the day. Voting at the Fifteenth Congress proved that the hard liners were only a minority, although a large minority. Progressives were able to elect many of their own to Party posts and in a subsequent compromise, progressives were given majorities on the Party's major decision-making bodies. Consequently, although a stubborn minority of veteran cadres and leaders struggle for control of the Party, the SKP, unlike its Austrian counterpart, has not retreated from its criticism of Soviet actions in Czechoslovakia.

Background Factors

The class and career backgrounds of party militants also act as constraints on party leaders. In general, proletarian backgrounds tend to make for allegiance to the Soviet Union, particularly in countries where class consciousness is relatively high and the working class is relatively alienated. This is because workers, historically denied political participation in their own country, have tended to identify with the Soviet Union, both as a model for the development of their own society and as the fatherland of the international working class. For older workers, of course, this is particularly likely to be true.

For middle-class cadres, however, this is less the case. They are likely neither so alienated nor so disadvantaged as their working-class cousins. Consequently, their identification with Moscow is less. It is not surprising, then, that the Hungarian crisis of 1956 precipitated greater defections in the British Communist Party, for example, among middle-class supporters than among workers.[22]

Intellectuals, too, will in general have fewer ties to Moscow. In times of international crisis—Hungary, Czechoslovakia—they tend to lead the way in criticism of the Soviets (not always, of course, in moderate, revisionist directions) and they also tend to author national plans for policy reform. Almost by definition, intellectuals are more aware of and sensitive to policy changes. Consequently, they react in greater proportions and more dramatically to policy shifts than other party members do. Throughout Western Europe, the unsettling events of 1956 were felt most strongly by Communist intellectuals. In Britain and Italy, for example, the effect of the crisis of 1956 was particularly pronounced, precipitating a policy change in the CPGB and an acceleration of trends toward international autonomy in the PCI. In France, where, unlike Italy and Britain, intellectuals play no decision-making role in the Party, 1956 created only relatively minor internal problems.

Finally, militants with trade union backgrounds tend to hold to perspectives reflecting the union conditions in their particular countries, particularly on the questions of alliance strategies. Where Communist unionists are dispersed and must be flexible to win any concessions, they tend to support the party's flexibility and alliance goals. Also, where the Communists share union power with other parties, Communist union activists will have backgrounds that tend to make them supportive of alliance strategies. On the other hand, where Communist union strength is heavily concentrated within a single federation or a group of locals, the party's union militants will be more conservative in regards to alliance strategies. Finally, where there is a history of intense competition between Communist unionists and Socialist rivals, the Communist cadres may be quite hostile to alliances.

In Britain, then, where the CPGB is about 25 percent middle class and the rest working class, there are relatively few conservative constraints on the Party's leadership. The middle-class cadres tend to welcome the leadership's independent policies and, despite the presence of a core of hard-line militants, the union experiences of many of the proletarian activists predispose them to relative moderation.

More than 40 percent of the French Communist Party are workers, many of whom are associated with the CGT, the union federation controlled by the Communist Party. French workers historically have been both relatively class conscious and relatively prudent, and the PCF is most successful representing the legitimate economic interests of the workers, rather than endorsing revolution. At the same time, because of their class consciousness and historical exclusion from political power, French workers tend to have positive attitudes toward the Soviet Union.[23] Consequently, the mass of workers in the PCF tends to constrain the leadership in its domestic political strategies and its international positions. Domestically, because of their union experiences and historical political isolation, French working-class Communists tend to be reserved about extending alliances. Notably, in the spring 1976 cantonal elections, the PCF was forced to discipline four local party organizations who refused to withdraw candidates in favor of better placed Socialists.[24] At the same time, French workers' innate political conservatism or, perhaps, caution, makes them unlikely foot soldiers for a revolution. Internationally, their traditional allegiance to the Soviet Union supports continued strong ties between the PCF and the CPSU.

Although workers compose the largest single group of Party members in France, other groups make up a significant portion of the membership. About 25 percent of the members are retired individuals (often retired workers) or housewives, with another 10 percent being intellectuals.[25] For the most part, however, these groups are not in positions greatly to affect Party policies in a positive sense. Housewives and retirees are likely only to be a conservative drag on the Party, while intellectuals historically have had notoriously little input into PCF policies, either directly or indirectly.

In Italy the Communist Party has a somewhat broader base than its French counterpart. About 50 percent of its membership are industrial workers, 33 percent artisans, technicians, and technical workers, 10 percent agricultural workers, peasants, and tenant farmers, and 3 percent intellectuals.[26] Although Italian workers are traditionally relatively class conscious, their union experiences of cooperation with other Leftist parties in the CGIL predisposes Communist working-class cadres to support alliance strategies and relatively moderate programs. Additionally, the PCI's large number of middle-class members and its retinue of intellectuals, who have historically been far more influential in the PCI than the PCF, tend to support the Party's internationally independent postures.

The membership of the Icelandic Communist Party is one that tends to be supportive of its leadership's liberal policies. Although the Party has a large number of working-class adherents, their union experiences of cooperation with the Progressives in the Icelandic Federation of Trade Unions tend to make them relatively undogmatic. Also, the PA has attracted a relatively large number of generally moderate teachers and intellectuals as well as a number of fishermen and fish-processing workers whose interests are largely economic. In general, then, the membership of the Icelandic Communist Party is one that would tend not to oppose its leaders' progressive, autonomist policies.

In contrast, the membership of the Swedish Communist Party is divided in its support of Hermansson's and now Werner's policies. Supporting the progressive positions are a number of student and intellectual members centered in the universities; the opposition comes largely from a core of veteran working-class militants concentrated in Communist strongholds in the northern provinces. In the spring of 1977, the leadership of the VPK found itself faced with open rebellion from some conservative militants as Party sections in Göteborg and Malmö split with the VPK to form a new party.

In Finland the SKP has a relatively heterogeneous composition. According to the *World Marxist Review*,[27] 58.5 percent of the SKP in 1972 were workers, 6.6 percent white-collar and service personnel, 7.2 percent peasants, 2.3 percent artisans and small producers, 3 percent students and intellectuals, 12.7 percent pensioners, and 9.7 percent housewives.[28] Considering the strength of workers in the Party and the relatively small number of *active* nonproletarian cadres (more than 20 percent of the Party are pensioners and housewives), it is not surprising that there has been opposition to the Party's break with the Soviet Union over Czechoslovakia.

A number of Western European Communist parties closely aligned with Moscow have large proportions of workers in their ranks. Seventy-five percent of the West German Communist Party are working class.[29] In Ireland 90 percent of the small CPI are working class,[30] and 80 percent of Luxembourg's Communist Party are workers.[31]

Although veteran cadres and working-class militants tend to be relatively conservative, and middle-class supporters and intellectuals more progressive, especially in attitudes toward Moscow, it would be overstating the case to say the socioeconomic distribution of a party's membership in and of itself determines policy. First, the socioeconomic distribution of a party's membership is, in part, the result of party policy. A rigid, Stalinist party will tend not to attract young adherents or intellectuals, thus insuring the dominance of veteran militants and proletarian cadres. Conversely, a progressive party may be quite successful in recruiting middle-class and intellectual members, thus guaranteeing at least a sizable group of these in the ranks. Second, by definition, a party's militants do not set policy, but rather act as potential or actual constraints on party leaders. In Austria the constraining force of a mass of Stalinist activists proved decisive in setting Party policy; in Finland, however, the Stalinists were too few to dominate the Party. In Italy there is only moderate resistance in the ranks to progressive policies, but in France there is a considerable measure of resistance to liberalization from well-placed, veteran, working-class activists. For example, although there is considerable open and latent resistance in the French Party to collaboration with the Socialists,[32] Giacomo Sani in 1972 found the large majority of Italian Communists endorsing a PCI coalition with the Christian Democrats.[33] (See Table 13.)

The importance of a Communist party's socioeconomic distribution is that it provides a possible constraint on the leadership. If the party's militants are older workers and heavily pro-Soviet, the leadership will be forced (to avoid splits and desertions) to soft-pedal reforms and international autonomy. Younger militants allow leeway in dealing with Moscow, but may demand relatively uncompromising domestic policies. If cadres are intellectual or middle class, less firmly tied psychologically to Moscow, leaders

Table 13. Orientation Toward DC-PCI Coalition, 1972

	PCI	DC
Favorable	71%	15.9%
Unfavorable	17.4	56.6
No opinion	11.6	27.5

SOURCE: Giacomo Sani, "Mass Constraints on Political Realignments: Perceptions of Anti-System Parties in Italy," *British Journal of Political Science* VI (January 1976): 1–32.

will be free, even encouraged, to be more national in domestic positions.

Homogeneity of the Electorate

In large part, the validity of a Communist party's electorate as a check or constraint on the actions of the party's leaders depends on its homogeneity. In general, the more homogeneous a party's electorate, the easier it is for the leadership to make policy decisions that will not alienate large portions of it. For example, the Czechoslovakian crisis of 1968 provided a major dilemma for the Communist parties of Western Europe. All of the parties had, to varying extents, a core of working-class supporters, both activists and voters, whose psychological attachment to the Soviet Union would dictate support of Moscow no matter the occasion. For most of the parties, however, there existed in their electorates significant numbers of supporters whose views about the Soviets' actions in Czechoslovakia were far less sanguine. Consequently, for the party to condemn the invasion would be to alienate the former group, while endorsing the invasion would disaffect the latter. For the heavily working-class Communist Party of Luxembourg, however, the dilemma was much less severe. Since most of its supporters were pro-Soviet industrial workers, the Party's leaders hesitated not at all in fully endorsing Moscow's actions.[34]

With a heterogeneous electorate, however, Communist leaders must search for positions designed not to alienate any major sector of it. For the Italian Communist Party, this means satisfying large numbers of industrial workers, agricultural workers, and even middle-class supporters.[35] For the Icelandic Communists, it means pleasing working-class and intellectual supporters as well as workers from the fishing industry. Even for the French Communist Party, it means satisfying large numbers of workers from both the public and private sectors, agriculture workers, and some middle-class tradesmen, artisans, and white-collar employees. (See Tables 14, 15, 16, and 17.)

With such heterogeneous electorates, what type of issues can these Communist parties stress that would appeal to all their diverse groups of support without alienating any of them? Economic, bread and butter issues—precisely those types of issues generally stressed in electoral campaigns by the PCI, PCF, and PA. Although it would be an exaggeration to argue that these Communist parties have become umbrella parties of the social democratic type, it is not unfair to say that the heterogeneous bases of support for these parties tend to constrain their leaders toward emphasis of relatively moderate policies. At the same time, the leaders of parties with homogeneous electorates, such as the West German, Irish, and Luxembourg parties, feel fewer such constraints.[36]

A major dilemma for many of the Communist parties of Western Europe is that their militants, in general, tend to be more working class, more pro-Soviet, and often older than their electorates and potential electorates. Consequently, party leaders often find themselves searching for a balance that will enhance their party's electoral position while not adversely affecting the loyalty of the bulk of militants. Inevitably, for the Western Communist parties with large working-class memberships and more heterogeneous electorates, the issue on which this balance has been most difficult to achieve is

Table 14. Social Composition of the PCI's Electorate, 1973

Agricultural workers	17.6%
Industrial workers	39.5
Middle class	13.1
Retired	14.9
Housewives	11.6

SOURCE: *Rinascita*, 3 November 1972.

Table 15. PCI Support and Status Groups, 1972

Industrialists, landowners, executives, professionals	5.0%
White-collar workers	7.6
Artisans, shopkeepers, small businessmen	13.7
Skilled workers	17.6
Small farmers	8.7
Farm laborers and unskilled workers	25.9
Not ascertainable	10.1

SOURCE: Giacomo Sani, "Mass-Level Response to Party Strategy: The Italian Electorate and the Communist Party," pp. 456–530, in Donald L. M. Blackmer and Sidney Tarrow, eds. *Communism in Italy and France* (Princeton: Princeton University, 1975), p. 469.

that of position vis-à-vis the Soviet Union. In periods in which the position of the Soviets and that of the respective Western European nations coincide, there is little problem of balance. When their interests clash, however, such as during the Cold War period or during the Czechoslovakian crisis of 1968, party leaders face the unenviable task of adopting a policy that will likely either antagonize pro-Soviet militants and voters, or alienate more nationalistic elements in the party and the electorate.

Table 16. Social Composition of Italian Electorate: PCI Voters and DC Voters, 1975

	Electorate	*PCI*	*DC*
Executives, businessmen, professionals	14.3%	10.8%	14.5%
Shopkeepers, artisans, white collar, small businessmen	26.5	21.8	22.5
Skilled workers, farmers	26.4	25.8	31.0
Unskilled workers, farm laborers	32.8	41.6	32.0

SOURCE: Giacomo Sani, "The PCI on the Threshold," *Problems of Communism* XXV, no. 6 (November–December 1976): 27–51.

Table 17. PCF Electorate

	1976	1973	1967	Adult Population
Men	59%	59%	57%	48%
Women	41	41	43	52
18–20	9	—	—	—
21–34	25	31	38	29
35–49	27	32	27	29
50–64	23	22	21	22
65+	16	15	14	20
Professional	8	3	2	6
Small business	—	5	6	9
Middle class	15	17	15	17
Workers	52	51	49	32
Inactives	21	19	19	24
Agricultural	4	5	9	12
Rural	25	23	30	30
<20,000	17	17	14	14
20,000–100,000	11	13	10	14
>100,000	22	24	19	25
Paris	25	23	27	17

SOURCE: *Sondages*, 1973, 1976.

In recent years, this dilemma has been vividly illustrated by the French Communist Party. The Party's leaders, first Waldeck Rochet and now Georges Marchais, have seen that the road to power in France can only be traveled successfully in alliance with the Socialists. To achieve and maintain this alliance, the PCF has had to back away from a number of its more hallowed dogmas, including the doctrine of the dictatorship of the proletariat, and adopt a compromise program. Moreover, both to cement the alliance and to lure the last few percentage points of the electorate needed to put the Left in office, Marchais has taken the bold step of following the lead of his Italian comrades by declaring his Party's independence in the international Communist movement and by attacking various aspects of Soviet domestic and foreign policy. Unquestionably, this has pleased the Socialists and it may attract uncommitted voters to the banner of the Left, but it is a difficult course to follow within the Party. There are still many older generation militants in the PCF whose faith in Moscow remains strong. In 1961 the Party leadership found that its condemnation of Soviet actions in Czechoslovakia was too much for many cadres, and the leaders retreated to luke-warm criticisms. In this and other matters, Waldeck Rochet lost his battle to move the Party away from Stalinism.[37]

Marchais, too, has met heavy resistance to his efforts at moderating the Party line, courting the Socialists, and moving to a posture of international independence, and the result of his efforts remains very much in doubt. So far, Marchais has been able to maintain and even strengthen his personal position, while moving forward with the policy changes he advocates. First, he has alternated moderate actions and statements with hard-line rhetoric. On the one hand, Marchais has joined with Berlinguer and Carrillo to declare his Party's autonomy and to criticize Soviet actions. On the other, he has loudly attacked what he calls the proponents of "anti-Sovietism" and assailed "Western imperialism." In terms of domestic policy, Marchais has buried the old doctrine of the dictatorship of the proletariat, but he has continued to beat the drums about the collapse of capitalism and the threat of international monopolies. In short, Marchais has been trying to appeal to Socialists and non-Communist voters outside of the Party while appeasing militants within the PCF.

Second, Marchais has moved to tighten his own control of the Party. At the PCF's Twenty-First Congress at the end of 1974, Marchais was forced to preach a tougher line to quiet visible dissension over his liberalizing policies. In contrast, the Party's Twenty-Second Congress in early 1976 adopted Marchais' program without a dissenting vote. Ironically, the price of the triumph of Marchais' liberalizing domestic policy and independent international position was the curtailment of any semblance of democracy within the Party itself.[38]

Events of the fall of 1977 indicate, however, that Marchais may not be able both to appease the Party faithful and to continue the Union of the Left. In the negotiations to update the Common Program, Marchais stubbornly insisted that the Socialists and Left Radicals acquiesce to Communist positions on a number of key issues, including the minimum wage, defense policy, and the number of nationalizations a government of the Left would impose. The Socialists and Left Radicals expressed a willingness to compromise, but the PCF insisted that its allies surrender on these matters. This they would not do and negotiations were broken off with a great deal of rancor. After the first round of voting in the March 1978 parliamentary election, the Leftist parties agreed on common candidates for the run-off. It was clear, however, that their differences were not resolved, but merely set aside until after the election.

Notes

1. Although this latter possibility can lead to resource shortages for the original party and an increase in external competition, it can also be, as we have seen (Chapter 5), a blessing in disguise in that it removes an internally divisive element from the party.

2. Georges Lavau, "Le parti communiste dans le systeme politique français," pp. 7-55, in Frédéric Bon, ed., *Le communisme en France,* cahiers de la fondation nationale des sciences politiques, 175 (Paris: Armand Colin, 1969).

3. Hadley Cantril, *The Politics of Despair* (New York: Basic Books, 1958).

4. Charles A. Micaud, *Communism and the French Left* (New York: Praeger, 1963), p. 149.

5. *Le nouvel observateur,* 6-21 February 1968.

6. Jacques Derville, "Les communiste de l'Isére," *Revue française de science politique* XXV, no. 1 (February 1975): 53-71.

7. Sidney G. Tarrow, *Peasant Communism in Southern Italy* (New Haven: Yale, 1967), pp. 159-60.

8. Jean Stapel and W.J. de Jonge, "Why Vote Communist?" *Public Opinion Quarterly* XII, no. 3 (Fall 1948): 390-98.

9. Erik Allardt, "Patterns of Class Conflict and Working Class Consciousness in Finnish Politics," in Allardt and Yrjö Littunen, *Cleavages, Ideologies, and Party Systems* (Helsinki: Academic Bookstore, 1964), pp. 97-131.

10. Cantril, *Politics of Despair*, p. 105.

11. *Sondages*, 1966.

12. *Sondages*, 1968.

13. Kenneth Newton, *The Sociology of British Communism* (London: Penguin, 1969); Brian Crozier, "Britain's Industrial Revolutionaries," *Interplay* IV, no. 1 (January 1971):30,35-36.

14. In Chapter 7 we divided leaders into two generations rather than the three in which we divide militants. This is because the youngest generation is generally not yet represented among the party leadership.

15. Stephen Hellman, "Generational Differences in the Bureaucratic Elite of Italian Communist Party Provincial Federations," *Canadian Journal of Political Science* VIII, no. 1 (March 1975):82-106.

16. Because they are generally anti-Soviet, the ultra-Left parties are no alternative for pro-Moscow militants.

17. *Economist*, 7 February 1976.

18. At the Party's Twenty-Second Congress in 1976, 61 percent of the delegates had joined the Party since 1968. However, one must be cautious about placing too much significance on such figures. The Congress is not a decision-making body in any substantive sense and the Party tends to select delegates for cosmetic, public relations purposes. Consequently, women and young people have recently been well represented at Party congresses.

19. Denis Lacorne, "On the Fringe of the French Political System: The Beliefs of Communist Municipal Elites," *Comparative Politics* IX, no. 4 (July 1977):421-42.

20. Ilios Yannakakis, "The Greek Communist Party," *New Left Review*, no. 54 (March-April 1969).

21. YICA, 1970.

22. Henry Pelling, *The British Communist Party: A Historical Profile* (London: Adam and Charles Black, 1958).

23. Denis Lacorne, "Analyse et 'reconstruction' de stéréotypes: communistes et socialistes face au 'socialisme soviétique,' " *Revue française de science politique* XXIII, no. 6 (December 1973):1171-1201.

24. *Le Monde*, 12 March 1976.

25. Claude Harmel, "Social Composition of the French Communist Party and Its Evolution from 1959 to 1966," *Est & Ouest*, 16-28 February 1967.

26. YICA, 1969.

27. A source that should be accepted only with reservations.

28. *World Marxist Review* XVI, no. 5 (May 1973):129-30.

29. Ibid., 126-27.

30. Ibid., XVII, no. 4 (April 1974):140.

31. Ibid., XVI, no. 10 (October 1973):131.

32. Ronald Tiersky, "Alliance Politics and Revolutionary Pretensions," pp. 420-55, in Donald L.M. Blackmer and Sidney Tarrow, eds., *Communism in Italy and France* (Princeton: Princeton University, 1975).

33. Giacomo Sani, "Mass Constraints on Political Realignments: Perceptions of Anti-System Parties in Italy," *British Journal of Political Science* VI, no. 1 (January 1976):1-32.

34. A subsequent election in December 1968 proved the correctness of their perceptions.

35. Giacomo Sani, "Mass-Level Response to Party Strategy: The Italian Electorate and the Communist Party," pp. 456-503, in Blackmer and Tarrow, eds., *Communism in Italy and France,* p. 469.

36. The question of which comes first, the heterogeneous electorate or the electoral emphasis on bread and butter issues, is answered by the statement that they both come at generally the same time with one reinforcing the other.

37. Annie Kriegel, "Communism in France," pp. 351-84, in T. J. Nossiter, A.H. Hanson, and Stein Rokkan, eds., *Imagination and Precision in the Social Sciences* (London: Faber & Faber, 1972).

38. Ian Campbell, "The French Communists and the Union of the Left: 1974-76," *Parliamentary Affairs* XXIX (Summer 1976):246-63.

chapter 9

HISTORY

A final factor shaping the differences in policies and postures among Western European Communist parties is history. For a political party, history is the collective memory of the past contained in official records, ideology, sacred writings, traditions, myths, written chronicles, and the memory of the party's older participants. Just as men turn to their personal past experiences to guide them in their actions, so do political parties, at the hand of their leadership, turn to their history for guidance in dealing with present contingencies. For a political party, the past that shapes its present actions is the past as the party perceives it rather than objective history. How, then, does the party's perception of history affect its behavior?

No political party exists in a steady state, but rather innumerable perturbations from the environment act on it, forcing it to seek some response. Internationally, there may be a change in Soviet policy such as de-Stalinization or a change in the international Communist movement. Domestically, subtle changes in the social structure may be occurring, such as the emergence of a highly skilled working class, or there may be a change in the national political system, such as the formation of a Socialist people's party. Constitutionally, a new electoral law may be promulgated as under France's Fifth Republic.

In the face of such environmentally imposed contingencies, Communist party leaders look for responses, but, as we have seen, party leaders are not unrestrained in their search. On the one hand, their search is constrained by international factors and domestic political, constitutional, and social factors. On the other hand, their own personal characteristics and backgrounds, and the character of the party's membership and electorate act as constraints. A final constraint, however, is history.

In arriving at courses of action to deal with problems, party leaders turn first to repertories of *action programs* developed through the party's prior experience.[1] *Action programs* are courses of action that are perceived as having once been successful in dealing with party problems. Originally, they develop from the complex interaction of environmental stimuli and constraints and the internal structure of the party. If once successful (or at least perceived to be so), they tend to be maintained in the collective memory of the party to be summoned forth in the future in response to new, similar contingencies. Thus, a party develops certain patterns of behavior that tend to persist. Rather than developing new approaches, *sui generis,* to new problems, a Communist party through its leaders tends to turn to old approaches and to rely on standard operating procedures developed through years of experience. Within the constraints we considered in chapters 3 through 8, a party's past lives in its action programs to shape its present and future behavior, almost by organizational inertia.

Western Communist party policies and postures differ, as we have seen, because the external and internal constraints on them differ, but also because their histories and, hence, action programs, differ. When a party is young, it has no history, no previously developed action programs to which to look for guides to action. Rather, its behavior is a function of the various internal and external constraints imposed upon the party by its environment and the party itself. Since for each party these constraints differ, action programs differ. In later years, a party's actions are shaped by more than just the internal and external contingencies of the environment and the party itself, but also by history, in the form of action programs.

The undogmatic, adaptable character of the Italian Communist Party is, in large part, a reflection of the PCI's historical experience. The importance of intellectuals and intellectualism in the Party is a result, in part, of the early importance of Antonio Gramsci, the intellectual and political father of Italian Communism, and his intellectual entourage. More important than Gramsci's actual role in the Party's early days (which was considerable) is the general perception in the PCI of his importance and the reverence accorded him and his works in the Party. Togliatti repeatedly turned to Gramsci to justify the various turns of Party policy and, by doing so, hallowed both Gramsci and the concept of an Italian interpretation of Marx,[2] a concept that has served well in supporting the Party's progressive stance. For example, following the startling events of the Twentieth Congress of the CPSU in 1956, Togliatti launched his Party more boldly along the way of an Italian Road to Socialism by evoking the aura of the Gramscian heritage:

> The search for an Italian road to socialism has been our constant preoccupation. I believe that I am able to affirm that it has already been the preoccupation of Antonio Gramsci, who in all his political actions, particularly in the latter period of his life, aimed to translate into Italian terms the teachings of the Russian Revolution.[3]

For a number of Western European Communist parties, an early independence toward the Soviet Union has served as a model for contemporary attitudes toward Moscow. Throughout the 1920s, the Swedish Communist Party split and split again over its relations with the Comintern and the Social Democrats. With no apparent financial ties to the International,[4] the recalcitrant Swedes proved hard to control. Although faithful to Moscow, the Party's leaders were no copycats. Since the early 1960s, the Swedish Communists have returned to their early posture of international independence.

In Iceland the Communists have always been rebellious children of the Comintern. Although the Party was formed in 1930 under the watchful guidance of the International, the Icelandic Communists, physically far removed from the centers of European Communism, soon asserted their independence, withdrawing from the Comintern in 1938 to absorb a group of Left-wing Social Democrats. Except for a period after 1949 when pro-Moscow cadres gained temporary ascendance in the Party, the PA has progressively moved to a position of international autonomy.

For other Communist parties, however, history has provided a legacy of subservience to the Soviet Union. Although all Western parties have historical ties to Moscow, for some, these ties are quite strong. The Irish Communist Party, for example, was created at

Moscow's initiative. Since then, the CPI has cultivated a persistent pattern of loyalty to the Soviet Union except for a momentary deviation over Czechoslovakia in 1968.

In Luxembourg, too, the Communist Party has continued and strengthened its ties to Moscow. From the beginning, the PCL was a loyal supporter of the Soviets and continued to be so, even supporting the Soviet invasion of Czechoslovakia in 1968. In different parties, the legacy of the past is continued through different media— myths, norms, writings. In the PCL, however, one primary vehicle has been the person of Dominique Urbani, the Party's veteran leader, and his family, in whom the Party's tradition of lock-step loyalty to the Soviet Union is personified.

Despite an organizational foundation of democratic centralism, a number of Western Europe's Communist parties have traditions of factionalism that serve to legitimize current dissent. In Sweden the division in the VPK has its antecedents in repeated splits and purges in the early Swedish Communist Party. Similarly, the Finnish Communist Party has a heritage of division as two groups of leaders, one centered in Sweden and Finland, the other in Soviet Russia, contested for leadership in the SKP during its illegal period before World War II.

In the Netherlands, a history of factionalism and the memory of its past ill effects on the Party helped to launch the CPN on a course of isolation in the international Communist movement. With the beginnings of a serious division between China and the Soviet Union in the early 1960s, the Dutch Communist Party was still reeling from a domestic Party split of the late 1950s. In 1958 the *De Brug* group, a mildly reformist coterie of militants, bolted the CPN to form an oppositionist party. In the parliamentary election of 1959, the new party won 0.6 percent of the vote, apparently all at the expense of the CPN whose parliamentary delegation fell from seven to only three members. For the leadership of the Dutch Communist Party, then, the spectre of another schism over the issue of the Sino-Soviet conflict was a calamity to be avoided at all costs. Both a large group of unreconstructed Stalinists and a sizable pro-Peking faction were within the Party; so any position the Party took on the issue would be sure to alienate one group and perhaps precipitate another disastrous Party split. In the face of this, Paul de Groot, the Party's leader, elected to steer a neutralist course on the Sino-Soviet conflict. In time, de Groot found that the best way to remain neutral was to stay aloof. Consequently, the CPN's move toward international autonomy was precipitated, at least in part, by its recent experience with factionalism.

The historical relationship between Communists and Socialists has tended, in many countries, to shape action programs that affect the current relationships between the two parties. In Luxembourg, for example, the Socialists and Communists together win a majority of the popular vote, but their long history of enmity works against any parliamentary alliance. In contrast, in Italy the experience of cooperation under Fascism between the PCI and other parties has promoted postwar cooperation particularly at the local and regional levels between Communist and Socialists and, in recent months, Christian Democrats as well.

In Finland and France, Communists have experienced long periods of sometimes bitter conflict with Socialists but, at the same time, have achieved their greatest political success in cooperation with them. Consequently, both Communist parties, the SKP and the PCF, have developed styles of suspicious cooperation with the Socialist parties in their respective countries.

In sum, virtually all aspects of a Communists party's present position and posture are affected by the party's history. Past party policies, both international and domestic, past alliance strategies, past organizational patterns, and past modes of decision making tend to persist in the collective memory of the party and to be reflected in currently operative action programs.

Although a party's history affects a party's present because it establishes patterns of behavior that tend to be retained, it does not *determine* the present. These historically established patterns, these action programs, are not immutable. First, changing environmental constraints can cause modifications in behavior patterns. For example, new electoral systems or laws in several countries have placed a premium on alliances, thus increasing the payoffs for cooperation between Communists and other Leftist parties. Internationally, de-Stalinization and the Sino-Soviet rift have opened the door to the possibility of greater autonomy for the Communist parties of Western Europe. For a number of parties, however, the inability to recruit young people has increased the proportion of older cadres in the party ranks, thus making the assertion of such autonomy more difficult. In a final example, the failure of bourgeois and social democratic governing parties in several countries has provided opportunities for Communists to enhance their electoral position through protest votes.

Second, changes in leaders can lead to breaks with past behavior. Individuals with long tenure in the party apparatus and at its head, such as Luxembourg's Urbani and Portugal's Cunhal, are veritable repositories of historical patterns themselves. When they die, retire, or are replaced, the way is open for new leaders to introduce new patterns of behavior. In France, for example, Thorez's replacement by Waldeck Rochet led to a relaxation of the PCF's rigidity, a relaxation that has gone further under Georges Marchais. C.H. Hermansson's ascension to leadership in the Swedish Communist Party heralded the beginning of a more liberal approach by the VPK.

Third, the dramatic failure of past patterns of behavior can lead to the adoption of new positions. For a number of Communist parties, the twin crises of de-Stalinization and Hungary provided the backdrop for just such a departure. In Britain the shattering events of 1956 led to rising discontent among the CPGB rank and file and mass resignations from intellectuals in particular. No longer did the traditional pattern of alliance to Moscow benefit the Party. Subsequently, autonomous forces in the Party gained ascendance and the British Communist Party moved away from its blind allegiance to the Soviets. Similarly, in Italy, Hungary was one of the catalysts that spurred the PCI to quicken its pace toward independence from the Soviets.

Although the failure of Communist policies tends to lead to their change, the best guarantee of the persistence of a policy is its success. In Italy the electoral success of the PCI has reinforced that Party's flexible, autonomist line. In contrast, the French Communist Party's often uncertain efforts toward policy liberalization are, in part, the result of the setbacks of 1958 and 1968. In Iceland the electoral success of the PA tends to support that Party's brand of Communism, and the hard-line policies of the Luxembourg Communist Party receive endorsement for the PCL's moderate success.

Notes

1. See James G. March and Herbert A. Simon, *Organizations* (New York: Wiley and Sons, 1958). For a specific consideration of organizational theory and political parties, see R. Neal Tannahill, "An Organizational Theory Approach to Political Parties," unpublished manuscript.

2. A.B. Davidson, "The Varying Seasons of Gramscian Studies," *Political Studies* XX, no. 4 (December 1972):448-61.

3. *L'Unità*, 15 March 1956.

4. Franz Borkenau, *The Communist International* (London: Faber & Faber, 1938), p. 347.

PART THREE

CONCLUSIONS AND PROSPECTS

chapter 10

CONCLUSION

We began this study of the Communist parties of Western Europe by examining their differences and similarities. In Chapter 1, we compared the parties in terms of domestic policies and postures, focusing on their size and strength, their alliance strategies, domestic programs, and their organization. In Chapter 2, we examined the relationship between the parties and the Soviet Union, comparing the strength and nature of their ties to Moscow and the international movement.

After outlining the diversity in Western European Communism in Part One, we turned in Part Two to the question of why such allegedly similar parties should be so dissimilar. To answer this, we sketched a model in which a Communist party finds itself affected by (and, in turn, affecting) a diverse environment that we have divided into four sets of factors: the international environment, the domestic social structure, the domestic political system, and the constitutional system. The party, through its leadership, must act *on* and *in* this environment. In so doing, the leadership is affected by a number of constraints, posed by environmental factors and variables internal to the party as well, including the party's membership and electorate, the party's history, and the personality and character of the party leadership.

In chapters 3 through 9, we examined each of the sets of factors influencing the policies and postures of Western Europe's Communist parties individually, but, in reality, these factors affect the

Communist parties simultaneously. The process is dynamic in that the various sets of factors interact to shape the policies and postures of a Communist party that then, in turn, feed back on the environment.

In this chapter, we focus on the dynamic aspects of our model by examining the process shaping Communist party policy in a number of cases. First, we examine this process in two hypothetical ideal types. Then, we turn to actual cases, comparing the factors shaping the policies and postures of Communist parties in three matched pairs of Communist parties.

Two Ideal Types

The Communist parties of Western Europe differ considerably in their domestic and international position, but we can identify two ideal polar types to which the contemporary parties approach to greater or lesser degrees. At one extreme, we find the *Neo-Stalinist Party*. Domestically, it preaches the gospel of hard-line orthodoxy, eschews alliances with other parties except on its own terms, and strives to maintain a small, disciplined party membership organized on the basis of democratic centralism. In terms of international policy, the Neo-Stalinist Party loyally clings to Moscow, attacks the Chinese heretics, and boldly defends the Soviets from all criticism. At the opposite end of the spectrum, we find our other ideal type, which we label the *Eurocommunist Party*. Domestically, it has adopted reformist, pragmatic positions on all major issues; it campaigns for alliances with other parties; organizationally, it allows internal debate and has accepted some internal democratization; and it seeks to be a broad-based mass party. Internationally, the Eurocommunist Party has declared its independence from foreign direction, frequently criticizing the Soviet Union and building ties with other parties in addition to the CPSU.

Now that we have described the two ideal types, the Neo-Stalinist Party and the Eurocommunist Party, what does our model tell us about the process through which these hypothetical parties acquire their postures and positions? What configuration of factors shapes each of these two polar extremes? Looking first to international factors, financial dependence on Moscow and close physical and psychological proximity to the Soviet Union are factors that lead to Neo-Stalinism since party leaders will be constrained to adopt policies in line with the wishes of Moscow. On the other hand, a party that is free of these ties will be able to pursue other policies and will tend toward Eurocommunism. Further, the Eurocommunist Party seeks to strengthen its independence by building ties with like-minded Communist parties in Eastern and Western Europe.

Relatively intense social cleavages, particularly class cleavages, make for hard-line domestic policies as the Communists find it politically advantageous to voice the grievances of the workers. On the other hand, if the domestic social structure affords few cleavages or a number of different cleavages that are not too intense, the policies of the Communist party will tend toward moderation since the party's leaders will find it necessary to appeal simultaneously to diverse interests to win voters and members. Consequently, the Neo-Stalinist Party tends to emerge in an environment with a primary class cleavage that is relatively intense, and the Eurocommunist party emerges from a social structure lacking cleavages or with a number of relatively less severe divisions. The party may even decentralize its organizational structure to take account of some of these divisions.

A number of variables in the political system also influence a Communist party's policy positions. If the Communist party faces stiff competition from Socialist or SF parties, it will tend to adopt hard-line policies to differentiate itself from its opponents. On the other hand, if there is a good chance of a future electoral alliance or governmental coalition between the Communists and the Socialists or SF party, the Communists will tend to moderate their policies to increase the likelihood of alliance. Further, if alliances already exist, the Communist party will tend toward Eurocommunism as it works to maintain those alliances. In contrast, an isolated Communist party with little hope of breaking out of that isolation will tend toward Neo-Stalinism.

The party system is another political variable that shapes Communist policy. Communist parties that are major parties in polarized or unpolarized multi-party systems or minor parties in unpolarized multi-party systems tend toward Eurocommunism since these parties' leaders' perceptions of their nearness to office will lead them to policy modification and moderation. There are fewer incentives for moderation, however, for minor Communist parties in predominantly two-party systems or polarized multi-party systems. These parties, then, tend toward Neo-Stalinism.

Another political factor affecting the Communist parties' policy postures is their position in the unions. Union cooperation with Socialists and others tends to make for policy modification to maintain the alliances, and union experience socializes party leaders toward moderate policies. All of this leads to Eurocommunism. A Neo-Stalinist Party emerges from a union environment of unrelenting competition or Communist dominance. In this case, patterns of conflict rather than cooperation have been ingrained.

A final political factor influencing party behavior is political culture. As with social cleavages, intense political cleavages make for hard-line party policy as the party tries to establish itself as the spokesman for the more radical side. Thus, a single intense political cleavage makes for Neo-Stalinism. Eurocommunism arises when there are multiple cleavages or when there are no intense political cleavages at all.

A number of constitutional factors shape party positions. Prolonged illegality can lead to Neo-Stalinism if it leads to dependence on the Soviet Union and Eastern Europe as a refuge and a source of material aid. On the other hand, illegality can lead to moderation among underground leaders and cadres at home in that it forces them to adopt pragmatic policies and seek alliances to survive. Electoral systems that place a premium on alliances can also lead to policy moderation, since the Communist party will find it necessary to modify programs to win Socialist cooperation. Finally, experience in local and regional governments and in the national government below the executive level also produce Eurocommunist parties. Communist officials gain experience in dealing with the day-to-day problems of government and develop bargaining skills. Individually, they gain a stake in the political system, while the party enjoys patronage and other benefits of office.

Another factor influencing party policy is leadership. At the one extreme, Neo-Stalinist leaders tend to be from older generation working-class backgrounds and to have close personal ties to the Soviet Union. At the other extreme, Eurocommunist leaders tend to be younger intellectuals or party professionals and to hold important positions in local or national government.

Turning to party membership and electorate, a Neo-Stalinist Party tends to have a homogeneous, older, working-class membership and electorate. A Eurocommunist Party, however, tends to have a heterogeneous membership. Younger militants support the Eurocommunist Party's independence from Moscow, but may demand a tougher policy line in domestic affairs.

Finally, history affects Communist party policy. A party that historically has been closely tied to Moscow and that traditionally has preached hard-line policies tends toward Neo-Stalinism. In contrast, a party with a tradition of independence from Moscow and past patterns of policy moderation tends toward Eurocommunism.

In the long run, what are the prospects for the future policy evolution of the Eurocommunist and the Neo-Stalinist parties? First, the current policies of each tend to be reinforcing. Hard-line, pro-Soviet policies attract like-minded members and voters who will support the continuance of such policies and drive away potential members and electors who would advocate other policy positions. A similar process operates in the party advocating progressive domestic policies and international autonomy. Indeed, many of the factors that "cause" Neo-Stalinism or Eurocommunism are also "caused" *by* Neo-Stalinism or Eurocommunism. In many respects, the process is not only dynamic, but self-reinforcing.

Second, the death and retirement of older, generally pro-Soviet cadres and leaders tend to reinforce the policies of the Eurocommunist Party. On the other hand, the Neo-Stalinist Party may either shrink or be pressured into policy modifications to recruit new adherents. Third, political success reinforces each party's current policies, but failure causes a rethinking and a possible policy change. Finally, there are many environmental factors over which the Western European Communist parties have little direct control that can rebound to affect their policies and postures.

Thus, we have outlined the constellation of factors that we hypothesize would shape each of our ideal types, but how effective is our model for explaining the different policies of real Communist parties? We test it by comparing three pairs of Communist parties that are quite similar on a number of grounds, but very different in terms of policy positions—the Icelandic and Luxembourg Communist parties, the Spanish and Portuguese parties, and the Italian and the French Communist parties.

The Icelandic and Luxembourg Communist Parties

Both the Icelandic and Luxembourg Communist parties are moderate-sized parties in multi-party systems in small countries. Yet Iceland's PA is internationally independent and domestically reformist, and Luxembourg's PCL is ardently pro-Soviet internationally and relatively conservative in domestic policy. What factors have produced such policy differences despite surface similarities? First, the Luxembourg Party has significant international ties to Moscow, but the Icelandic Party has virtually none. The PCL apparently receives a sizable financial subsidy from the Soviet Union and its leaders travel frequently and extensively in Eastern Europe. On the other hand, the PA is far distant from Moscow, both geographically and psychologically. The Party apparently receives no aid from the East and psychological ties have worn thin over the years. Little wonder that the PCL is pro-Soviet and the PA is internationally dependent.

Second, each party's electorate and membership help to shape their party's contrasting positions. In Luxembourg the Communist Party's membership and electorate are overwhelmingly working class, and older militants dominate in much of the party structure. Consequently, the rank and file in Luxembourg have supported the Party's posture. The PCL was the only legal Communist party in Western Europe to support the Soviet intervention in Czechoslovakia in 1968 and it was the only party to increase its vote in a national election held shortly after the invasion. In contrast, the membership of the Icelandic Communist Party is far more heterogeneous and younger. It has been atracted to the PA by the Party's independent, nationalistic line. What is more, the walkout in 1969 of Stalinist cadres and members to launch their own party helped insure the continuance of the Party's liberal line.

Third, the two parties have constructed their policy positions in response to differing social and political structures. The Luxembourg Party has drawn upon the industrial working class for support. In Iceland, however, the PA has appealed to a number of diverse groups. Further, Icelanders are fiercely nationalistic, jealous of their sovereignty and independence. Therefore, the PA has had to echo these qualities in its international policies to win support. In Luxembourg, however, there are many workers for whom psychological ties to the Soviet Union remain strong.

Fourth, the leadership of the two parties differs dramatically. The Communist Party of Iceland has long been led by intellectuals and the current leader, Regnar Arnalds, is quite young. In contrast, the PCL has been led by one man, Dominique Urbani, and dominated by his family for decades. Moreover, the leadership of the Icelandic Party has had experience cooperating with leaders of other parties in governing coalitions at the national and municipal level. In Luxembourg, however, the PCL's leaders have had considerably fewer experiences cooperating with Socialists in government.

Finally, each party's relative success has worked to reinforce its policies. Barring unforeseen developments, the Icelandic Party will likely continue its current policies. The Luxembourg Party, however, may face a crisis in the near future. Dominique Urbani cannot live forever and the Party's future course may be altered by his successor.

The Spanish and Portuguese Communist Parties

On the surface, there are many similarities between the two Iberian Communist parties. Each is well organized and commands a sizable following and each has recently won legal status after operating illegally under a dictator's repression for most of its existence. The two parties differ remarkably, however, in their policy postures. The Spanish Communist Party is domestically progressive and highly independent internationally. On the other hand, no Western European Communist Party is more pro-Soviet than the Portuguese Communist Party and its domestic policies are quite conservative. Why are two parties with such similar backgrounds so different in policy?

First, the international ties of these two Communist parties differ considerably. The PCP has long been supported financially by

Moscow and Alvaro Cunhal and other Party leaders found refuge in Eastern Europe during the Party's long period of illegality. In contrast, the Spanish Party has received no aid from the Soviet Union at least since 1968, when Moscow elected to bankroll a Stalinist splinter group. Currently, the Italian Communist Party is giving the PCE financial assistance.

Second, the parties' experiences in illegality differ. After the Spanish Civil War, a large number of Communist militants sought refuge in France and other Western countries where they were able to continue supporting the PCE financially. Also, the Party's leaders spent most of their time in exile in the West. In contrast, there was no large refugee community of Portuguese Communists and the Party had to raise funds domestically or look abroad to Moscow for aid. Further, the PCP's leaders spent the long years of illegality in jail or in exile in Eastern Europe.

Third, the parties differ in terms of leadership. The Portuguese Communist leaders found refuge in Eastern Europe, and their Spanish counterparts spent most of their exile in the West. At least since 1968, when a number of pro-Moscow leaders and militants left the Party to form a pro-Soviet party, the PCE leadership has been dominated by individuals whose interests tend to lie with the PCE rather than Soviet policy. According to figures recently released by the PCE, 111 of the Party's 142 Central Committee members in 1976 were either Party careerists, intellectuals, or professionals.[1] In contrast, the majority of the Central Committee of the Portuguese Party are workers.[2] Further, Alvaro Cunhal, the longtime leader of the PCP, has a close personal relationship with Brezhnev, but the Spanish Party's leader, Santiago Carrillo, was offended by the Soviet leadership in 1968 over the Czechoslovakian invasion and was the object of direct personal attacks by Moscow in 1977.

Finally, the Spanish Communist Party won national power in the 1930s through a popular front. During the Franco dictatorship, the Party continued searching for allies and aimed at winning legality and political power through the same approach. In 1977 the strategy succeeded, as the PCE was legalized and the Party hopes to find ground for cooperation with Spanish Socialists and the Suárez

Government. In contrast, the PCP's experiences with alliances have been far more limited.

The Italian and French Communist Parties

A third contrast between parties in ostensibly similar positions is that between the Italian and the French Communist parties. Each is a major party in a large, predominantly Catholic country in Southern Europe. On the one hand, the Italian Communists have long advocated progressive domestic policies and autonomy from the Soviet Union. In France, on the other hand, the PCF has traditionally followed hard-line domestic policies and loyally supported Moscow internationally. In recent years, however, the French Communist Party has declared its independence from Soviet direction and shed some of its more revered dogmas. What factors account for the historic difference between the PCI and the PCF and why has the French Party adopted many of the positions of its Italian counterpart?

First, there is a long tradition of alliance and cooperation with the Socialist and other Left-wing parties in the PCI, but a history of conflict with the Socialists in France. In Italy the Communists have long cooperated with Socialists and other Leftist parties in local and regional government and in the unions, but in France the Communists and Socialists have often been at each other's throats.

Second, the French Communist Party has a tradition of subservience to Moscow that the PCI does not have. During the 1920s and 1930s, the PCF received and followed instructions from the Soviet Union on matters of major and minor importance. In Italy during the same period, the PCI was outlawed and underground. Consequently, lines of communication were poor and the Party developed patterns of self-sufficiency in policy formation.

Third, the two parties differ in their leadership. In Italy intellectuals such as Gramsci and Togliatti have historically held the major policy-making positions in the PCI. In contrast, the PCF has used intellectuals as window dressing, leaving actual leadership to working-class individuals such as Maurice Thorez. Further, Thorez had strong personal ties to Moscow.

Finally, the membership of the French Communist Party has long been dominated by a large core of pro-Soviet working-class militants who act as a conservative constraint on the Party. In contrast, the membership of the PCI has been younger and more diverse.

Because a number of these factors have changed and because of other factors as well, the French Communist Party has moved in recent years toward more moderate domestic policies and independence from Moscow. First, the PCF's more recent leaders, Waldeck Rochet and Georges Marchais, have been professional party men whose interests have lain in improving their Party's domestic political position. Both tried to free their Party from the doctrinal rigidities of the past, although Marchais has found more success than Waldeck Rochet.

Second, the electoral system in use in the Fifth Republic advantages second ballot alliances; so the Communists have felt incentives to moderate their policies to convince the Socialists to form an electoral front. If the Communists are to win power electorally, it will probably be in alliance.

Third, time has slowly wrought a change in the Party's membership and electorate. The Party militants are more diverse and younger than they were in the 1950s and 1960s. Further, old-line Stalinists are slowly dying out as younger generation militants assume important positions in the Party.

Finally, the notable success of the Italian Communist Party and the failure of the Portuguese Communist Party's thrust for power provide testimony to the benefits of the reformist strategy of the former and the weakness of the dogmatic, militant approach of the latter.

In sum, many of the factors that made the PCF one of the more orthodox, more pro-Moscow Communist parties in Western Europe have changed or are changing. Consequently, the Party has changed. Other factors, however, have not changed or have changed only slowly; so the transformation of the PCF has been unsteady and the future is in doubt. On the one hand, the Party's electorate and membership have grown younger and more diverse, but, on the other hand, many of the Party's activists remain veteran, hard-line militants. Further, the success of the Union of the

Left has encouraged the Communists to continue the alliance, but the remarkable resurgence of the Socialist Party has threatened to relegate the PCF to a secondary role in the alliance and in any future government of the Left.

All of this presents a troubling dilemma to the leaders of the French Communist Party. The Union of the Left and its eventual electoral triumph have been the primary goals of Marchais' leadership, but the price may be too high. The spring 1977 municipal elections indicated that the Left had a good chance of winning a majority in the spring 1978 parliamentary elections, but they also showed that the Socialists would be in a position to dominate the new government. This could be the worst of all possible worlds for the Communists. First, the Communists would lose the luxury of opposition. No longer could they appeal to malcontents of every sort by sniping at government programs. As a party of government, they would be held responsible for government shortcomings. Second, as junior partners to the Socialists, the Communists would not have the last word on government policy. Although the PCF would likely share the blame for the government's mistakes, the Party's ability to shape the government's program would be limited. Finally, internal opposition would surely arise. Many French Communist militants do not trust the Socialists, and the appearance of Communist Party support for a Leftist government with Socialist leadership could split the Party.

Such is the dilemma facing Georges Marchais and the other leaders of the PCF. The leadership's personal stake in the Union of the Left and the Party's new policy positions is great. At the same time, these are organization men. Their first loyalty is to the integrity of the Party as an organization. Can these goals be reconciled?

In the negotiations to update the Common Program, the Communists drove a very hard bargain, insisting that their allies go along with them on a number of points, particularly on the issue of the extent of nationalizations a government of the Left would demand. If the Socialists and Left Radicals capitulated, the Communists could claim a substantial victory and anticipate more than a secondary influence in a Leftist government. The Socialists and Left Radicals offered concessions, but they did not surrender. Negotiations broke off and the Left-wing parties were unable to agree on common candidates for the March 1978 parliamentary elections. The results of the first round of voting demonstrated that the break-up of the alliance damaged the Socialists more than the Communists, as the two parties captured nearly equal shares of the popular vote (22.6 percent for the Socialists, 20.6 percent for the Communists). Subsequently, the Left reunited in time for the second round of voting, but too late to capture control of the parliament.

Notes

1. *New York Times*, 1 August 1976.
2. Ibid., 15 November 1976.

chapter 11

THE FUTURE OF THE COMMUNIST PARTIES OF WESTERN EUROPE

One cannot conclude an examination of the Communist parties of Western Europe without indulging in some informed speculation about their future. Certainly the topic is a timely one, but, more importantly, we cannot leave our model of the factors that shape the policies and postures of Western European Communism without applying it to the task of prediction. Of course, many of the variables that conceivably could influence the course of Communism in Western Europe are unknown and many of them are unknowable; so no prediction is foolproof. On the other hand, many factors are known and others can be anticipated by the extrapolation of present trends. We turn first to an examination of two of the least likely possibilities for the future of Western Europe's Communist parties: that they will launch an armed revolution, and that they will simply disappear.

For the last quarter century (and much longer in most cases), only one Communist party in Western Europe has engineered an armed revolt, rebellion, revolution, or anything resembling one, and in that case, the Portuguese Communist Party failed in its maneuvers to gain political dominance in the wake of the overthrow of the Salazar-Caetano dictatorship. Moreover, in a number of cases, Communists have ignored or tried to stabilize potentially disruptive situations. In Finland in early 1948, at a time of extreme tensions, the best evidence indicates that rather than attempting a coup, the SKP had no designs on an illegal seizure of power.[1] After the Liberation in France, Thorez ordered the Communist *maquis* to disband, and in 1958 the PCF was among the Fourth Republic's last defenders. Finally, May-June 1968 saw the French Communist Party trying to act as a stabilizing force rather than playing the role of *provocateur*. In Italy in 1948, after an assassination attempt on Togliatti, the PCI moved swiftly to calm a potentially explosive situation. Even in Portugal in 1974-1975, the Communists made no effort to launch an armed revolt or insurrection.

If armed revolution is their aim, why did the Communists of France, Italy, Finland, and elsewhere allow these apparent opportunities to slip through their fingers? Although cynics may argue that the Communists have been cleverly lulling everyone into a false sense of security in anticipation of some future uprising, this seems highly unlikely. First, most of these parties have firmly established non-revolutionary patterns of behavior that will not be easily broken. Not only have the Communists refrained from launching a revolution, but, for the most part, their spokesmen persistently disavow any revolutionary intentions. In rhetoric, at least, most of the Western European Communist parties have accepted the peaceful, parliamentary Road to Socialism for more than a decade. Can it be that the Communists have spent decades trying to convince their countries' electorates of their benign intentions and not convinced themselves?

Second, there is little evidence that most Communist militants would support an illegal attempt to seize power and much evidence that they would not. In France, Finland, Italy, and elsewhere, survey evidence indicates that many Communist supporters are drawn to the party for relatively undogmatic, certainly non-revolutionary, economic reasons.[2] Protest voters are not the stuff from which a revolution is made. Further, survey evidence from France, at least, indicates that Communist voters do not consider the PCF to be revolutionary. In 1966 only 1 percent of the Party's electors described it as "the party that wants revolution,"[3] and in 1968 only 23 percent agreed while 57 percent disagreed that the PCF would be ready to seize power by revolution if the situation seemed favorable to it.[4] Indeed, 1974 survey results indicate that a majority of the

PCF's supporters do not even believe that a Leftist electoral victory would mean the end of capitalism. (See Table 18.) It seems very unlikely that Communist leaders supposedly clever enough to disguise a revolutionary intent for decades would launch a takeover effort with such unprepared supporters.

Third, the prospects for international aid are slight. Considering the distance of many of the nations of Western Europe from Soviet borders, the Soviet interest in preserving détente, and the possibility of Western retaliation, there is little probability of Soviet troops marching into Paris or Rome or Lisbon to climax a Communist-led insurrection. Far more likely would be NATO support for established governments in quashing the uprising.

Fourth, to launch a revolution and fail would mean the likely loss for the Communists of established positions in national legislatures, bureaucracies, regional governments, and local administrations, along with all the perquisites of office that go with them. Although the miniature Irish Communist Party would have little to risk, the larger parties such as the Italian, French, and Finnish would have much to lose indeed. At the very least, an abortive coup would mean the loss of any immediate chance at electoral power, a major reduction in elective offices held, and, consequently, losses in patronage and influence on policy. More likely, however, a Communist party guilty of leading an unsuccessful uprising would be proscribed and thus lose its position in the political system and

Table 18. What Would the Union of the Left Do in Power?

Responses (October 1974)	All	PCF
It would replace the capitalist system with a Socialist system.	19%	27%
It would bring some important reforms to capitalism.	34	41
It would make few changes in capitalism.	27	21
Don't know, no response.	20	11

SOURCE: *Sondages*, 3 & 4 (1975), p. 50.

perhaps in the labor movement as well. For individual Communist leaders, the risks would be just as great. As the heads of legal, "democratic" parties, Berlinguer, Marchais, and Saarinen enjoy considerable personal prestige and power that go beyond the boundaries of their own parties. As the leaders of defeated revolutionary forces, however, they would likely face jail or exile.

Finally, barring widespread social disorder, a Communist-led seizure of power would have very little chance of success. The disaster of the Communist-directed Civil War in Greece in the 1940s and the recent failure of the Portuguese Communists' efforts to win political dominance are hardly encouraging precedents. In most of Western Europe, Communist parties are simply too small, too poorly organized, and with militants too poorly placed to be a real threat to seize an established government. Even in France and Italy, where the Communist parties are mass parties, only the support or neutrality of the armed forces would enable the Communists to have a realistic chance of winning power.

The leaders of the Communist parties of Western Europe are simply too conservative, too tied to the establishment, and too sagacious to embark upon the course of revolution. Its chances of success would be slim; its risks great; and, at the same time, most Western Communist leaders show no predisposition for anything so adventurist as an illegal attempt to seize power. The real revolutionaries in Western Europe are found in the ultra-Left movements such as the Baader-Meinhof gang in West Germany and the Red Brigades in Italy, and the established Communist parties regard them as just as much a menace as do the bourgeois authorities.

If the worst fears of anti-Communists are unfounded, so are their greatest hopes. Although the Communist parties of Western Europe may not be in the vanguard of revolution, they are not about to wither away and disappear either. Many in the West once believed that economic growth, social reform, and the integration of the working class into the political process would mean the end of Communism in the West.[5] Of course, it has not happened. Neither the evident decline of ideology[6] nor widespread economic growth following World War II have led to the complete integration of the working class into the political system or the demise of Western European Communism.

Historically, once established, Communist parties have been remarkably resilient and there is no reason to expect otherwise in the future. Only in Ireland, where the party founded in 1921 died, has a Communist party vanished entirely and there it was refounded in 1933. In Italy, Finland, Portugal, Spain, Greece, and Germany, Communist parties survived long periods of illegality to emerge as formidable parties in Italy and Finland; moderately strong parties in Portugal, Spain, and Greece; and in West Germany, the DKP has at least a base of support. Elsewhere, Communist parties have survived long periods of electoral drought, political isolation, and internal divisions.

As for the future, in France, Italy, Spain, Portugal, Finland, Iceland, Greece, and Luxembourg, Communist parties are established parts of the political system with large numbers of loyal adherents and supporters. One cannot imagine a political cataclysm so severe as to lead to their destruction. In other countries, Communist parties are far smaller and less significant in their respective political systems, but they have shown a remarkable staying power. Each has a core of true believers and apparently many can still call on Moscow for financial aid in time of need. Although the party of Ireland (which is quite small and poorly established) and the party of Austria (which is aging at an alarming rate) may eventually pass from the scene, Communist parties will likely be a part of the Western European political panorama for at least the near and middle future.

Assuming the continued presence of Communism as a political force in Western Europe, what is the likelihood of a Communist party winning political power through constitutional means? For even the major parties, winning an outright electoral majority is very unlikely. The Italian Party has enjoyed the greatest electoral success among the Western parties, but even in its finest hour, in the June 1976 parliamentary election, the PCI won just over a third of the popular vote. The French, Icelandic, Luxembourg, and Finnish parties have seldom gathered more than a quarter of the vote, and in other countries, Communist parties are too small even to dream of electoral majorities.

For many of the larger parties of Western Europe, however, the prospects of governmental participation are brighter now than they

have been since the early postwar era when Communists participated in governing coalitions in much of Western Europe. In Finland, Iceland, and Portugal, such an event has already happened
(from 1966 to 1971, late 1975 until September 1976, and since May
1977 in Finland; 1956 to 1958 and 1971 to 1974 in Iceland; and 1974
to 1976 in Portugal). In France the Socialists and Communists
nearly succeeded in electing a presidential candidate in 1974, and in
the 1978 parliamentary election, they won about 49 percent of the
popular vote even though they failed to win a majority of seats in
parliament. In Italy, the Communist Party is now part of the
parliamentary majority, even though no Communists sit in Christian Democrat Giulio Andreotti's government. In Luxembourg the
PCL is large enough so it together with the Socialists could form a
Left-wing majority if an agreement between the two could be
reached. The Suárez Government in Spain has consulted with the
Spanish Communist Party, finding support for a program to deal
with Spain's economic woes. In Portugal the PCP is large enough to
have an influence in a divided parliament. Finally, it is not unthinkable that moderately small Communist parties in Sweden, Greece,
and possibly other countries may enter a future cabinet as minor
partners.

For most of the smaller parties, although prospects of leading or
participating in a ruling coalition are rather slight, the chances of
holding the balance of power in a closely balanced legislature are
far better. Already, in Sweden, Greece, and Norway, Communist
parties at one time or another have found their positions augmented by just such a situation. Everywhere that Communist parties hold even a small number of seats, the possibility of that
number being the balance of power exists. For other parties, however, the British, Irish, Austrian, and perhaps the West German,
with neither parliamentary seats nor much real hope of winning
any, even such a modicum of parliamentary power is beyond reach.

With the increased probability of Communist participation in the
governments of several Western European nations, what will be
some of the likely results of such participation? Considering first the
consequences of a coalition with Communist participation, but not
dominance, we can turn to recent Communist coalition experiences
in Finland and Iceland as well as early postwar coalitions in several

nations of Western Europe. In general, the consequences of government participation for the Communists have been that rather than using their foothold in government to achieve their own ends, in large part, the Communists have found themselves taken advantage of by their coalition partners. Lacking governmental experience, Communist parties in Finland and Iceland, particularly in the former country, won only modest concessions from their partners in terms of foreign and domestic policy, but paid the price of sharing the blame for both unpopular government decisions and for inaction.

The consequences of entering a Western government as a junior coalition partner are not necessarily all to the Communists' advantage, then. Certainly, the standard rewards of governance—patronage, effect on policy, enhanced legitimacy—would accrue to Communist parties as they do to others, but there are also disadvantages. As junior partners, the Communists' impact on policy historically has been small and will likely continue to be limited. Although some of the Communists' more moderate economic reforms, including some nationalizations, may well become government policy, it is unlikely that dominant coalition partners will accede to demands for massive nationalizations or a fundamental realignment in terms of foreign policy.

At the same time, by becoming part of the government, the Communist party loses much of its freedom to criticize. No longer can the bourgeois parties be solely to blame for unfavorable wage conditions, unemployment, inflation, corruption, and other national problems, but the Communists must share in that responsibility. As minor partners, Communists in coalition governments have often found themselves lacking the power to enact their own solutions to problems, but sharing the blame for those problems.

Another dilemma for the Communist party playing the role of junior coalition partner is that of being flexible and moderate enough to maintain the coalition, but not so pragmatic as to alienate the party faithful. In Finland, for example, the SKP as part of the government from 1971 to 1974 found itself in a position of endorsing wage settlements that its union militants found unacceptable. As the SKP discovered, the consequences of such a dilemma can sometimes be a party schism. Similarly, in 1976 the Communists were forced out of the government coalition because of their reluctance to agree to economic austerity measures unpopular with the workers and hard liners within the Party.

With such a mixed bag of benefits and problems, Communist parties may not necessarily be eager to enter a government as junior coalition partners, particularly if there is a possibility of becoming the dominant partner in some future coalition. In Italy, for example, the PCI has indicated its reluctance to jump into a coalition that could do it more harm than good electorally. Indeed, the Party's present posture of propping up the Andreotti government has generated a ground swell of dissent at the base among the rank and file.[7] For the French Communist Party, the problem of satisfying its militants while tempering its policies to cooperate with the Socialists has been extremely difficult indeed. Already, the Party has gone too far for some militants[8] and the leadership may rather see the Union of the Left dissolved than soften its hard line on the Common Program. In Finland, Iceland, Portugal, Greece, Luxembourg, and Spain, the Communists realistically can hope for no more than junior party status in a governing coalition; so they must opt for a small share of governmental power or none at all.

For the Western political systems themselves, what will Communist participation in government mean? In terms of economic and social policy, it offers the hope that organized labor can be persuaded to accept the tough measures needed to enable Western Europe to overcome its economic miseries and that the working class can be more fully integrated into the political process. Negatively, there is the danger that a sharp speculative outflow of capital will coincide with the entry of a Communist party into a Western European government, leading to a worsened economic situation and, possibly, economic and political instability. At worst, this could pose a threat to the democratic system, either from the Communists themselves or from the Right.

Although the effects of Communist participation in a Western European government may be far ranging, their influence on government policy will likely be limited. As we have discussed, Communist parties as junior government partners will not be able to institute sweeping changes against the will of their partners. They will, however, likely win some concessions in terms of economic policies favoring the working class, some nationalizations, and, in foreign policy, perhaps a weakening of ties with the United States.

Just as important, government experience at the national level will serve to change the perceived political position of the Communist party. On the one hand, since the anti-Communists' worst fears will not be realized (for most people in Finland and Iceland, Communist participation in the government did not directly affect their lives one way or the other), the Communist parties' status will be legitimated as political participants. Both in the eyes of the electorate and for the Communists themselves, government participation will help to integrate the Communist party into the system. On the other hand, government participation will denigrate the chiliastic myths the Communists like to foster about their future rule. Inevitably, the Communists' performance, particularly as junior partners in a coalition, will fall short of the expectations of their most enthusiastic followers. Consequently, the aura of the Communist party, both as a threat and as a panacea, will diminish. For better *and* for worse, Communist participation will more fully integrate them into the political system.

For two of Western Europe's Communist parties, those of Italy and France, the possibility of entering the government as the dominant partner of a Left-wing coalition is real. In Italy the PCI is clearly the foremost party of the Left and the possibility of its heading a future government with Socialists and even Left-wing Christian Democrat support is not unthinkable. In France the Communists and Socialists together may command a majority of the voters between them. Whether the PCF could dominate a popular front coalition in France now that the Socialist Party has experienced a rejuvenation, however, is unlikely.

What would be the consequences of a Communist-dominated government in Western Europe? In foreign policy, a Communist government would likely establish close ties to the Soviet Union, but not necessarily enter a formal alliance with the Soviets and certainly not steer the country toward satellite status. As non-ruling parties, the French and Italian parties pay a certain amount of homage to Moscow, traditionally more so for the French than the Italian, but are far from Moscow's obedient servants, especially in the Italian case. What is more, the surest way for the PCF or PCI to alienate their government partners, either the Socialists or Christian Democrats, and precipitate a government crisis, would be by moving too close to Moscow.

The major foreign policy changes enacted by a Communist-led government would be less in regard to the East than to the West. Although many Western European Communists have become chary about too close ties to the Soviet Union, they are downright hostile about close ties, particularly military ties, to the United States. This does not mean a severing of relations with the United States or even a withdrawal from NATO, at least not precipitously. It does mean that Communist-dominated governments in France and Italy would be more reserved in their relations with the United States, more critical of American foreign policy, and, in the long run, likely to withdraw from mutual defense arrangements.

In terms of domestic economic policy, a Western European Communist government would likely increase the number of nationalizations, but, again, the sensitivities of coalition partners would likely prevent the Communists from doing too much too soon. As for agricultural policy, there would probably not be a vast collectivization since that policy has not worked well in Communist bloc countries and, notably, no Western Communist party now recommends such a policy.

As for domestic social policy, ruling Communists would likely champion reforms designed to advantage lower and lower middle classes by reforming the tax structure, building public housing, extending welfare and pension benefits, providing public employment, and the like. At the same time, however, Western European Communist parties have not been renowned for authoring creative social reform programs, particularly the French Party, which has consistently opposed social reform measures at their outset as "reactionary conspiracies."

From a Western democratic standpoint, the most threatening aspect of a Communist-dominated government involves possible encroachments on civil liberties and the democratic process.[9] In Communist-run municipalities and regional administrations in Italy and France, there have been no widespread abuses of civil liberties. This does not guarantee, however, that a Communist party with the reins of the national government in its hands would not move to consolidate its position by restricting opposition parties and silencing critics. The record of Communist governments in Eastern Europe and elsewhere is hardly comforting. Moreover, the actions of the Portuguese Communist Party in 1974-75 were clearly not the actions of a democratic party. Both the Italian and French Communist Parties, the only Communist parties that now have a real chance of acceding to power in Western Europe, pay lip service to democratic freedoms. The PCI, however, has a longer history of pledging respect for democracy and civil liberties than the PCF and in its internal affairs, it has been less autocratically rigid than its French counterpart.

Regardless of the Communists' motives, there are several factors preventing at least early widespread abuses against democratic freedoms. First, coalition partners are certain to be very sensitive to Communist actions that would undercut the democratic process, and, conceivably, threaten the existence of opposition parties. Even if the Communists are bent on subverting the democratic system, they dare not move too far too fast before their position is secure. Second, a Communist-dominated government embarking on a policy of erosion of civil liberties would meet resistance from both the rank and file and from its electorate. In both France and Italy, most members joined and grew up politically in a party pledging its support for democracy. As the extraordinarily high figures of membership turnover show,[10] Communist members are not automatons who comfortably change positions with the party line. Finally, efforts to restrict opposition parties and limit civil liberties could well precipitate action by the military.

Consequently, the dangers of an early end to democracy in a Communist-led Western state are slim. Instead, the threat is one of subtle erosion. Through administrative appointments and regulatory actions, a Communist-led administration could slowly undermine democratic freedoms. Philosophically predisposed to a highly interventionist state, a Communist government could stumble almost incidentally into an enlargement of governmental controls of individuals and groups that many would regard as threats to civil liberties. Whether a Communist government would make its conscious policy one of undercutting democratic freedoms and individual liberties to insure its own persistence in power, however, cannot easily be determined.

A number of factors would shape a ruling Communist party's predisposition to restrict civil liberties. Considering international factors first, a Communist government in Italy or France that made it its policy to undermine democratic freedoms would face the threat of reduced trade and investment from the United States and the rest of the Common Market in exchange for an uncertain increase in trade from the Communist world.

Other factors affecting the Communist party's actions are its membership and electorate. How firmly indoctrinated into the democratic system are they? How likely are they to challenge leaders' policies with which they disagree? On both counts, the younger, more heterogeneous membership and electorate of the Italian Communist Party would be more likely to remain loyal to the democratic system than their older, sometimes sectarian French cousins.

Another major factor to consider is leadership. Are Georges Marchais and Enrico Berlinguer confirmed democrats or disguised autocrats or something in between? Perhaps even they do not know. Each has risen to power in a democratic political system, but through a highly undemocratic party structure. Each is a member of the younger generation of leaders in whose political lifetimes party slogans about the dictatorship of the proletariat have been supplanted by phrases about "advanced democracy." Each is conservative in his political and personal life-style.

A final factor involves history. Traditionally, the PCI has been more open and more flexible and accommodating in dealing with other groups and institutions—the Church, other parties, the EEC—than the PCF. Also, the PCI, because of its long-held cooperative position in the CGIL and in local and regional governments, has perceived itself as being part of the political system longer than the PCF, which has had a tendency to feel (and to be) isolated. Consequently, one would be more inclined to trust the preservation of democracy to the hands of the Italian Communists than their French comrades.

Regardless of the intentions of future Communist heads of government in Western Europe, they will face certain limiting factors restricting them in the execution of domestic and foreign policies. First, as we have seen, even as heads of a coalition, the Communists will not be free to act irrespective of their allies' sensitivities. To maintain their government, Communists will have to compromise their policy differences with coalition partners.

Second, assuming the Communists intend (or are compelled) to continue the democratic system, they must, like other politicians, keep an eye to pleasing their electorates and mass memberships. Just as the diversity and non-revolutionary character of each has constrained Communist parties to offer economic, non-revolutionary, even pragmatic (especially in Italy) approaches while out of power, in power they will constrain the Communist governors from adopting revolutionary solutions necessitating considerable sacrifice and hardship for the masses.

Third, as the lesson of Allende's Chile has taught, too heavy a dose of Socialism applied with too little planning on too broad a scale can wreck an economy, at least in the short run. No head of state, be he Communist or bourgeois, wants to preside over an economic collapse.

Fourth, lurking in the background is the military. Should a Communist-led government move too precipitously in either foreign affairs or domestic policy, the danger exists of an intervention by the more conservative military. The Portuguese Communists gained influence in the Armed Forces Movement because of the radicalizing effects of a protracted colonial war in Africa on the young officers. Nowhere else in Western Europe is there a similar situation.

Finally, Communist regimes face many of the same sorts of resource and time limitations that other regimes face. Economic problems caused by international economic conditions, scarce resources, unbalanced domestic economies, poorly trained labor, and the like are not amenable to quick, easy solutions and, as Eastern European experience has shown, nationalization is far from a panacea. In power Communists will likely find many of their nation's economic, political, and social problems as intractable as their bourgeois predecessors found them. As Mussolini allegedly remarked about the problems of governance, "It's not that it's so difficult to govern Italy, but that it's useless."

For most of the Communist parties of Western Europe, however, the practical problems of government are of little immediate worry because they lack the size to win political power either at the head of a governing coalition or as junior partners in a government. The best they can hope for is to find themselves in the propitious position of holding the balance of power in a closely divided parliament. The Greek Communist Party has found itself in such a favorable position on several occasions, and in the last several years, both the Communist Party of Norway and the Swedish Communist Party have held the balance of power in their respective parliaments. Conceivably, in any country where the Communists are strong enough even to win a few seats, the possibility exists.

How much impact can a Communist party in such a position have? Very little. The lesson of the Swedish VPK's experience is that the Communists can exercise only marginal influence at best. In the first place, only on certain issues will the parliament be polarized along Socialist-bourgeois lines. On matters upon which the two major blocs can agree, Communist votes are not needed. Second, voting against the government means throwing it out of office, but the Communists may find this an unacceptable alternative. In Sweden to vote against the government on a major bill meant tossing the Social Democrats out and installing a bourgeois government—something the Communists were loath to do. Third, if the Communists become too demanding, the government can strike an agreement with another party. In Sweden the Social Democrats finally freed themselves from any reliance on the Communists by enticing the Liberal Party into giving the government its support. Finally, holding the balance of power is a position of weakness in that its continuance depends less on the performance of the party holding the balance than on the fortunes of the other parties. Very likely, the next election will send the Communists back into the parliamentary wilderness.

Turning to the question of political posture, where is Communism in Western Europe going? Are the Communist parties likely to remain outposts for Moscow? Although the West German, Austrian, Portuguese, Greek (Exterior), Irish, and Luxembourg parties are closely tied to the Soviet Union, the other parties, particularly the continent's major Communist parties, exercise a vigorous measure of international autonomy. Also, the long-run trend is in the direction of greater independence for the parties of the West. Centrifugal forces set in motion by the Twentieth CPSU Congress in 1956 and accelerated by the Sino-Soviet rift have worked to free many of Western Europe's Communist parties from Soviet domination. The larger parties are not forced to rely on Moscow for financial aid and as time eliminates the older, pro-Soviet militants and leaders, psychological bonds will be reduced, too. Barring a major increase in international tensions, the bonds that historically have tied the Western parties to the Soviet Union will continue to relax and the domestic interests of each party rather than the foreign policy interests of Moscow will be foremost in the minds of younger leaders and cadres.

If the trend is toward greater autonomy, why is it that the parties of West Germany, Austria, Portugal, Greece (Exterior), Ireland, and Luxembourg have resisted that trend? In each case, the historical bonds remain powerful as veteran, pro-Moscow militants hold significant positions in the organization in each party with much of the leadership of the Austrian, West German, Portuguese, Greek (Exterior), and Luxembourg Parties being from the older generation. Also, at least four of the parties, the West German DKP, Luxembourg's PCL, Portugal's PCP, and Ireland's CPI, are apparently receiving financial assistance from Moscow, while the leadership and many of the cadres of the Exterior faction of the Greek Party received not only financial aid, but refuge as well in Eastern Europe.

What is the prognosis for each of these parties? In terms of membership, the DKP is young and growing. Potentially, it likely can support itself financially and as older cadres and leaders die or retire, younger replacements may well lead the Party along a more independent path. In Luxembourg, too, the PCL is large enough to survive without international aid, but the entrenchment of the Urbani clan in the leadership makes the prospects for a more internationally independent party uncertain. Much depends on the character of the successor to the Party patriarch, Dominique Urbani. In Ireland, however, both the short and the long run are likely to see the CPI closely allied to Moscow. Without international aid, the CPI would likely disappear. Being so small, however, the CPI faces the possible danger of being infiltrated and taken over by ultra-Left groups. The Exterior faction of the Greek KKE is dependent on Moscow and Eastern European Communists for its survival. In the long run, it will likely remain as is. In Portugal the PCP can probably support itself, although not at the level to which it has grown accustomed. Although the Party's recent setbacks have caused some second thoughts within some Party circles, there will likely be no real changes of policy until Cunhal and other veteran leaders pass from the scene. Finally, the future is cloudy for Austria's KPÖ. Because of its unreconstructed pro-Moscow stance, progressives have fled the Party ranks and recruitment of young people has declined precipitously. As a result, the Party is shrinking and aging, giving pro-Soviet militants an even greater voice proportionately. Consequently, the policies that are leading to the KPÖ's decline are being reinforced by the very process of that decline. For the short run, at least, the KPÖ will likely shrink to the status of a small, politically impotent sect, a status which it is fast approaching now.

If, in the long run, traditional ties to Moscow are lessening for most Communist parties of Western Europe, are the parties evolving in the direction of social democracy? Yes, say Berger and Thirard. Speaking specifically of the French Communist Party, they argue that the PCF can be compared to the social democratic parties as they existed before 1914: representing the working class, opposed to the current government, but tied to the society by organization and function.[11]

On the other hand, Annie Kriegel argues that "one has seen Communist parties collapse and disappear . . . or make changes of strategy, tactics, policy, size, language, leaders, or allegiance, but one has never seen them become social-democratic parties." The French Communist Party, she contends, is not a social democratic party "like the others" because of its organizational structure and liaison with the Soviet Union.[12]

Although there is considerable question about the proximity of the PCF to social democracy, other parties are less closely tied to the Soviet Union and more relaxed organizationally—the Swedish, Icelandic, Italian, and the Spanish parties. If international détente continues and major economic crises are avoided in Western Europe, the already present trends toward international autonomy and flexible domestic policies will likely continue, too.

Does this mean, however, that the Communist parties of Western Europe are evolving toward social democracy? Not necessarily. If the Communist parties of Sweden, Iceland, Italy, and Spain are forerunners of late twentieth-century Communism throughout Western Europe, that Communism will not be a "social democratic" Communism. Although Italian, Swedish, Spanish, and Icelandic Communists are no mere agents of the Kremlin or even, necessarily, consistent supporters, their international postures are far more in accordance with those of the Communist world than those of the West. No social democracy here. What is more, the domestic policies of even the most "progressive" Communist party are more radical than those of the social democratic parties. Although not revolutionary in the orthodox Marxist sense, the programs of the Communist parties of Sweden, Iceland, Spain, and Italy call for nationalizations and radical economic reforms that generally go beyond those sponsored by the Social Democrats in Western Europe.

Where, then, is Communism in Western Europe going? For the past two decades, forces have been at work in Western Europe that are making for a new era for Western European Communism, a new era that is already emerging. First, the decline of Soviet authority in the Communist world that began in 1956 and accelerated with the Sino-Soviet split is continuing apace. Although the Communist parties of Western Europe once looked to Moscow for direction in both foreign and domestic matters, increasingly they look inwardly and to each other for direction. As the events of the June-July 1976 European Conference of Communist Parties indicate,[13] polycentrism has become a reality in Western Europe.

Second, with the passing of older Communist militants who were socialized politically during an age of Soviet-directed internationalism, the ranks of the Western parties are becoming dominated by individuals more attuned to Italian or British or Swedish issues rather than Soviet issues. Also, with the emergence of a more highly educated, technically oriented working class, Communist parties will be compelled to speak to their concerns to secure their votes. Consequently, international Communism is being replaced by a national Communism throughout Western Europe.

Third, nothing breeds imitation quite like success and the electoral success of the pragmatically oriented Italian Communist Party is bound to foster imitation elsewhere. Indeed, the French and Swiss parties have moved to more progressive positions in recent years at least partially in response to the success of their Italian comrades.

Finally, new leaders are emerging more attuned to national, domestic issues and to the institutional needs of their own parties than the foreign policy requirements of the Soviet Union. International autonomy is good politics domestically, and increasingly, the Communist leaders of Western Europe are looking to the political interests of their own parties rather than those of the Soviet Union. Dominique Urbani is an anachronism as younger men such as Georges Marchais and Enrico Berlinguer accede to power.

What these changes are leading to is the growth and extension (because it already has emerged) not of a recycled social democracy, but of something new in Western Europe—national Communism. It is a Communism that looks more to domestic conditions than Soviet interests in shaping its policies and it is a Communism that is loosely dogmatic, proposing radical democratic reforms rather than revolutionary solutions.

In its international postures, Western European Communism is moving out of the shadow of Soviet foreign policy. Although the Communist parties of Western Europe continue generally friendly relations with Moscow, the time is fast passing when Soviet interests can dictate domestic policies and when the Soviets can count on the Western parties for uncritical support of their foreign and domestic policies. What is more, the changes now at work in Western Europe and in the Communist world can only further this trend. Although it is unlikely that any of the Western parties will adopt an anti-Moscow posture such as the Albanians have, it is very likely that more and more the Western parties will assert their independence.

This does not mean, of course, that Western European Communist parties will become pro-United States or pro-NATO. Although, following the lead of the Italians, the Western parties will increasingly come to terms with the realities of Western European politics—the Common Market in particular—their attacks on

American foreign policy are not likely to cease. Looser ties to the East do not mean stronger ties to the West, at least not to the United States.

The ties that will be stronger are domestic ones. With Czechoslovakia in 1968, most Western parties determined that their domestic political interests were more important than Soviet foreign policy interests. With the changes in the Western parties and in the international movement that we have outlined, the Western party leaders increasingly will look to the institutional interests, especially electoral interests, of their own parties rather than Soviet international interests in determining their parties' postures.

Domestically, the Western parties are evolving toward less dogmatic positions. With changes in their membership and electorate (both generational changes and increasing heterogeneity in many parties), parties will continue to extend their pattern of calling for radical democratic and social reform within the parliamentary system. The Western parties will continue to endorse genuinely radical reforms—not the radicalism of the ultra-Left parties that call for a revolutionary transformation of society outside of the parliamentary process—but a radicalism that has become enrooted in the parliamentary process.

Western European Communism is the offspring of two ill-sorted partners: European parliamentary Socialism and Russian Bolshevism. After some early growing pains, it was Bolshevik in organization, Russian in foreign policy, and Marxian and generally parliamentary in domestic policies. After more than fifty years, Western European Communism has matured, but it is still much the product of its heritage. Organizationally, it is developing a style of its own in much of Europe, but it still reflects its Bolshevik background. Internationally, it is increasingly asserting its own interests rather than looking abroad for direction. Domestically, it has revised revolutionary Marxism and adapted it to the parliamentary process calling for radical social and economic reforms, but within the democratic political system.

Notes

1. A.F. Upton, "The Communist Party of Finland," pp. 105-352, in Upton, ed., *The Communist Parties of Scandinavia and Finland* (London:

Weidenfeld and Nicolson, 1973), pp. 283-95. Upton outlines convincing evidence to refute an earlier interpretation of the events of May 1948 as an attempted coup. See Hans Peter Krosby, "The Communist Power Bid in Finland in 1948," *Political Science Quarterly* LXXV, no. 2 (June 1960): 229-43.

2. Erik Allardt, "Patterns of Class Conflict and Working Class Consciousness in Finnish Politics," pp. 97-131, in Allardt and Yrjö Littunen, *Cleavages, Ideologies, and Party Systems* (Helsinki: Academic Bookstore, 1964); Pertti Pesonen, *An Election in Finland: Party Activity and Voter Reactions* (New Haven: Yale, 1968); *Le nouvel observateur*, 6-21 February 1968, quoted in George Lavau, "Le parti communiste dans le systeme politique français," pp. 7-55, in Frédéric Bon, ed., *Le communisme en France*, Cahiers de la fondation nationale des sciences politiques, 175 (Paris: Armand Colin, 1969), p. 30; Gabriel A. Almond and Sidney Verba, *The Civic Culture* (Boston: Little, Brown, 1963), pp. 115-16; Hadley Cantril and David Rodnick, *On Understanding the French Left* (Princeton: Institute for International Social Research, 1956).

3. IFOP, December 1966, *Cahiers de cummunisme*, January 1968, quoted in Lavau, "Le parti communiste," p. 23.

4. SOFRES, 10-20 February 1968; quoted ibid., p. 24.

5. Gabriel A. Almond, *The Appeals of Communism* (Princeton: Princeton University, 1954), pp. 183-85.

6. M. Rejai, ed., *Decline of Ideology?* (Chicago: Atherton, 1971).

7. *Le Monde*, 22, 23 October 1976; *L'Unità*, 4 October 1976.

8. Ian Campbell, "The French Communists and the Union of the Left, 1974-76," *Parliamentary Affairs* XXIX, no. 3 (Summer 1976): 246-63.

9. This also concerns French and Italian voters. In October 1975, French voters were asked if they thought Communist participation in government would be "good" or "bad" from a number of viewpoints:

Do you think it would be good or bad if the PC participated in government?

	Good	Bad	No Response
From the point of view of the economy	37%	33%	30%
Point of view of the social plain	54%	20%	26%
Point of view of individual liberties	25%	43%	32%
Point of view of national independence	23%	40%	37%

SOURCE: *Sondages,* 1975, no. 3 and 4, p. 51.

A 1976 survey in Italy also found a concern among voters about the Communists' commitment to freedom:

Percent Agree	DC	PCI
Party wants to defend freedom	60%	39%
Party wants to limit freedom	25	45
Don't know, no answer	15	16

SOURCE: *Bollettino Doxa* (Milan), 1 September 1976.

Similarly, a poll published in *La Stampa* (Turin) on 12 June 1966 finds that 43 percent of the respondents think freedom will be reduced under the Communists, while only 32 percent think there will be the same freedom.

10. Kriegel says the defection rate in the PCF is about 10 percent. Annie Kriegel, *The French Communists: Profile of a People* (Chicago: University of Chicago, 1972), p. 39. Hamrin says the rate is 8.0 to 8.5 percent in the PCI. Harald Hamrin, *Between Bolshevism and Revisionism: The Italian Communist Party 1944-1947* (Stockholm: Scandinavian University, 1975), p. 223.

11. Denis Berger and Paul-Louis Thirard, "Un parti social-démocrate de type nouveau," *Les temps modernes* XXVI, no. 284 (March 1970): 1446-71.

12. Annie Kriegel, "Communism in France," pp. 351-84, in T.J. Nossiter, A.H. Hanson, and Stein Rokkan, eds., *Imagination and Precision in the Social Sciences* (London: Faber & Faber, 1972), p. 371.

13. *Le Monde*, 1 July 1976, 2 July 1976; *New York Times*, 30 June 1976, 1 July 1976.

Size and Electoral Strength of
Western European Communist Parties

Table 19. Austria: Election Results and Party Membership

Parliamentary Election Results (Nationalrat)[1]

ELECTION DATE	KPÖ (%)	SEATS WON	TOTAL SEATS
Oct. 1920	0.9	0	183
Oct. 1923	0.7	0	165
Apr. 1927	0.4	0	165
Nov. 1930	0.6	0	165
Oct. 1945	5.4	4	165
Oct. 1949	5.1	5	165
Feb. 1953	5.3	4	165
May 1956	4.4	3	165
May 1959	3.3	0	165
Nov. 1962	3.0	0	165
Mar. 1966	0.4	0	165
Mar. 1970	1.0	0	165
Oct. 1971	1.4	0	183
Oct. 1975	1.2	0	183

Estimated Membership, Austrian Communist Party (KPÖ)[2]

1919—3,000	1964—36,000	1971—25,000
1927—2,000	1966—35,000	1972—25,000
1945—20,000	1967—35,000	1973—25,000
1961—42,000	1968—27,500	1974—15,000
1962—50,000	1969—27,500	1975—20,000
1963—50,000	1970—25,000	1976—20,000

SOURCES: 1. Thomas J. Mackie and Richard Rose, *The International Almanac of Electoral History* (New York: Free Press, 1974); *Yearbook on International Communist Affairs* (Stanford: Hoover Institution, 1976).

2. *World Strength of Communist Party Organizations*, Bureau of Intelligence and Research, U.S. Department of State, various years; *Yearbook*, various years; Witold S. Sworakowski, *World Communism: A Handbook, 1919–1965* (Stanford: Hoover Institution, 1973).

Table 20. Belgium: Election Results and Party Membership

Parliamentary Election Results (Lower House)[1]

ELECTION DATE	PCB (%)	SEATS WON	TOTAL SEATS
Nov. 1921	0.0	0	186
May 1925	1.6	2	187
May 1929	1.9	1	187
Nov. 1932	2.8	3	187
May 1936	6.1	9	202
Apr. 1939	5.4	9	202
Feb. 1946	12.7	23	202
Jun. 1949	7.5	12	212
Jun. 1950	4.7	7	212
Apr. 1954	3.6	4	212
Jun. 1958	1.9	2	212
Mar. 1961	3.1	5	212
May 1965	4.6	6	212
Mar. 1969	3.3	5	212
Nov. 1971	3.1	5	212
Mar. 1974	3.2	4	212
Apr. 1977	2.7	2	212

Estimated Membership, Belgian Communist Party (PCB)[2]

1924—590	1963—11,000	1971—12,500
1927—1,500	1966—13,000	1972—12,500
1928—500	1967—13,500	1973—12,500
1939—9,000	1968—12,500	1974—12,500
1949—35,000	1969—12,500	1975—12,500
1962—11,000	1970—12,500	1976—20,000

SOURCES: 1. *Yearbook*, various years; Mackie and Rose, *International Almanac; Le Monde*, 21 April 1977.

2. *Yearbook*, various years; *World Strength*, various years; Sworakowski, *World Communism*; Branko Lazitch, *Les partis communistes d'Europe, 1919–1955* (Paris: les Iles d'Or, 1956).

Table 21. Denmark: Election Results and Party Membership

Parliamentary Election Results (Lower House)[1]

ELECTION DATE	DKP (%)	SEATS WON	TOTAL SEATS
Apr. 1920	0.4	0	139
Jul. 1920	0.3	0	139
Sept. 1920	0.4	0	148
Apr. 1924	0.5	0	148
Dec. 1926	0.4	0	148
Apr. 1929	0.7	0	148
Nov. 1932	0.6	2	148
Oct. 1935	0.8	2	148
Apr. 1939	0.9	3	148
Mar. 1943	—	—	—
Oct. 1945	12.5	18	148
Oct. 1947	6.8	9	148
Sept. 1950	4.6	7	149
Apr. 1953	4.8	7	149
Sept. 1953	4.3	8	175
May 1957	3.1	6	175
Nov. 1960	1.1	0	175
Sept. 1964	1.2	0	175
Nov. 1966	0.8	0	175
Jan. 1968	1.0	0	175
Sept. 1971	1.4	0	175
Dec. 1973	3.6	6	175
Jan. 1975	4.2	7	175
Feb. 1977	3.7	7	175

Estimated Membership, Danish Communist Party (DKP)[2]

1921—25,000	1939—9,000	1969—6,000
1922—1,200	1945—7,500	1971—5,000
1924—750	1953—21,000	1972—5,000
1927—969	1962—5,000	1973—6,000
1928—1,341	1963—5,000	1974—8,000
1930—400	1967—6,000	1975—8,000
1934—3,000	1968—6,000	1976—9,500

SOURCES: 1. *Yearbook*, various years; Mackie and Rose, *International Almanac; Le Monde*, 11 January 1975, 17 February 1977.

2. *Yearbook*, various years; *World Strength*; Lazitch, *Les partis communistes.*

Table 22. Finland: Election Results and Party Membership

Parliamentary Election Results (Eduskunta)[1]

ELECTION DATE	SKDL (%)	SEATS WON	TOTAL SEATS
May 1945	23.5	49	200
Jul. 1949	20.0	38	200
Jul. 1951	21.6	43	200
Mar. 1954	21.6	43	200
Jul. 1958	23.2	50	200
Feb. 1962	22.0	47	200
Mar. 1966	21.2	41	200
Mar. 1970	16.6	36	200
Jan. 1972	17.0	37	200
Sept. 1975	19.0	40	200

Estimated Membership, Finnish Communist Party (SKP)[2]

1921—2,500	1956—48,000	1966—50,000
1922—1,200	1957—47,000	1967—49,000
1924—750	1958—48,000	1968—49,000
1927—969	1959—43,000	1969—49,000
1928—1,341	1960—48,000	1971—47,000
1930—400	1961—52,000	1972—47,000
1934—3,000	1962—52,000	1973—49,000
1939—9,000	1963—52,000	1974—48,000
1945—20,000	1964—47,000	1975—48,000
1955—49,000	1965—47,000	1976—48,000

SOURCES: 1. Mackie and Rose, *International Almanac; Le Monde*, 24 September 1975.

2. A.F. Upton, "The Communist Party of Finland," pp. 105–352, in Upton, ed., *The Communist Parties of Scandinavia and Finland* (London: Weidenfeld and Nicolson, 1973); *World Strength*, various years; Lazitch, *Les partis communistes*; Sworakowski, *World Communism*.

Table 23. France: Election Results and Party Membership

Parliamentary Election Results (Chamber)[1]

ELECTION DATE	PCF (%)	SEATS WON	TOTAL SEATS
May 1924	9.8	26	574
Apr. 1928	11.3	14	602
May 1932	8.3	12	605
Apr. 1936	15.3	72	608
Oct. 1945[a]	26.1	148	522
Jun. 1946[a]	26.2	146	522
Nov. 1946	28.6	166	544
Jun. 1951	26.7	97	544
Jan. 1956	25.9	147	544
Nov. 1958	19.2	10	465
Nov. 1962	21.8	41	465
Mar. 1967	22.5	72	470
Jun. 1968	20.0	33	470
Mar. 1973	21.3	73	490
Mar. 1978	20.6	86	491

Estimated Membership, French Communist Party (PCF)[2]

1921—100,000	1933—28,000	1949—787,000[b]
1922—79,000	1934—40,000	1954—506,000[b]
1923—56,000	1935—87,000	1955—389,000[b]
1924—60,000	1936—280,000	1956—430,000[b]
1925—60,000	1937—330,000	1959—425,000[b]
1926—55,000	1938—320,000	1960—414,000[b]
1927—53,000	1939—300,000	1961—407,000[b]
1928—50,000	1940—387,000	1962—250,000
1929—42,000	1945—545,000	1967—290,000
1930—39,000	1946—804,000[a]	1969—275,000
1931—35,000	1947—809,000[a]	1973—275,000
1932—30,000	1948—788,000[a]	1974—330,000

SOURCES: 1. Mackie and Rose, *International Almanac; Yearbook*, various years; *New York Times*, 20 March 1978.

2. Annie Kriegel, *The French Communists: Profile of a People* (Chicago: University of Chicago, 1972); *Yearbook*, various years; *World Strength*, various years.

[a] Constituent assembly.

[b] Cards delivered.

Table 24. Great Britain: Election Results and Party Membership

Parliamentary Elections Results (Commons)[1]

ELECTION DATE	CPGB (%)	SEATS WON	TOTAL SEATS
Nov. 1922	0.2	1	615
Dec. 1923	0.2	0	615
Oct. 1924	0.3	1	615
May 1929	0.2	0	615
Oct. 1931	0.3	0	615
Nov. 1935	0.1	1	615
Jul. 1945	0.4	2	640
Feb. 1950	0.3	0	625
Oct. 1951	0.1	0	625
May 1955	0.1	0	630
Oct. 1959	0.1	0	630
Oct. 1964	0.2	0	630
May 1966	0.2	0	630
Jun. 1970	0.1	0	630
Feb. 1974	0.1	0	635
Oct. 1974	0.1	0	635

Estimated Membership, British Communist Party (CPGB)[2]

1922—5,116	1914—22,700	1967—33,240
1924—4,000	1942—56,000	1968—32,562
1926—10,000	1946—42,000	1969—32,562
1927—7,000	1950—39,000	1971—32,000
1929—3,000	1953—35,000	1972—29,000
1931—6,000	1956—33,000	1973—29,000
1934—5,800	1957—27,000	1974—28,943
1936—11,500	1958—24,670	1975—28,519
1938—15,500	1962—29,000	
1939—17,760	1963—32,500	

SOURCES: 1. Mackie and Rose, *International Almanac; Yearbook*, various years.

2. Henry Pelling, *The British Communist Party: A Historical Profile* (London: Adam and Charles Black, 1958); *Yearbook*, various years; *World Strength*, various years.

Table 25. Greece: Election Results and Party Membership

Parliamentary Election Results (Lower House)[1]

ELECTION DATE	KKE (%)	SEATS WON	TOTAL SEATS
Dec. 1923	2.3	0	397
Nov. 1926	ca. 4	10	286
Aug. 1928	ca. 1	0	250
Sept. 1932	5	10	250
Mar. 1933	4.6	0	248
Jun. 1935	9.9	0	300
Jan. 1936	5.7	15	300
Mar. 1950[a]	9.7	18	250
Sept. 1951[b]	11.2	10	250
Nov. 1952[b]	10.4	0	300
Feb. 1956[b]	[d]	18	300
May 1958[b]	24.4	79	300
Oct. 1961[b]	15.1	24	300
Nov. 1963[b]	14.5	28	300
Feb. 1964[b]	12.0	22	300
Nov. 1974[c]	9.5	8	300
Nov. 1977[e]	9.4	11	300
Nov. 1977[f]	2.7	2	300

Estimated Membership, Greek Communist Party (KKE)[2]

1931—1,500	1968—27,000
1935—8,000	1971—28,000
1965—20,000	1973—28,000

SOURCES: 1. Jane Perry Clark Carey and Andrew Galbraith Carey, *The Web of Modern Greek Politics* (New York: Columbia, 1968); *World Strength*, various years; *Yearbook*, various years; London *Times*, 22 November 1977.

2. D. George Kousoulas, *Revolution and Defeat: The Story of the Greek Communist Party* (London: Oxford, 1965); *Yearbook*.

[a] Democratic Group.

[b] United Democratic Left.

[c] Pan-Democratic Agrarian Front of Greece.

[d] EDA and allies won 48.15 percent and 132 seats.

[e] KKE Exterior.

[f] KKE Interior and allies.

Table 26. Iceland: Election Results and Party Membership

Parliamentary Elections Results (Althing)[1]

ELECTION DATE	PA (%)	SEATS WON	TOTAL SEATS
Jun. 1931	3.0	0	36
Jul. 1933	7.5	0	36
Jun. 1934	6.0	0	49
Jun. 1937	8.4	3	49
Jul. 1942	16.2	6	49
Oct. 1942	18.5	10	52
Jun. 1946	19.5	10	52
Oct. 1949	19.5	9	52
Jun. 1953	16.0	7	52
Jun. 1956	19.2	8	52
Jun. 1959	15.2	7	60
Oct. 1959	16.0	10	60
Jun. 1963	16.0	9	60
Jun. 1967	13.9	9	60
Jun. 1971	17.1	10	60
Jun. 1974	18.3	11	60

Estimated Membership, Icelandic Communist Party (PA)[2]

1930—800	1967—1,000	1973—2,200
1935—500	1968—1,000	1974—2,000
1953—1,500	1969—1,000	1975—2,500
1962—1,000	1971—1,000	
1963—950	1972—1,500	

SOURCES: 1. *Yearbook*; Mackie and Rose, *International Almanac*.

2. *Yearbook*, various years; Sworakowski, *World Communism*; Lazitch, *Les partis communistes*.

Table 27. Italy: Election Results and Party Membership

Parliamentary Election Results (Chamber)[1]

ELECTION DATE	PCI (%)	SEATS WON	TOTAL SEATS
May 1921	4.6	15	535
Jun. 1946	18.9	104	556
Apr. 1948	31.0[a]	131	574
Jun. 1953	22.6	143	590
May 1958	22.7	140	596
Apr. 1963	25.3	166	630
May 1968	26.9	177	630
May 1972	27.2	179	630
Jun. 1976	34.4	227	630

Estimated Membership, Italian Communist Party (PCI)[2]

1945—1,371,000	1955—2,090,000	1968—1,531,000
1946—1,603,500	1956—2,035,400	1969—1,500,000
1947—1,817,200	1957—1,825,200	1971—1,500,000
1948—1,922,300	1958—1,818,600	1972—1,521,000
1949—2,027,300	1959—1,787,300	1973—1,596,000
1950—2,134,100	1960—1,793,000	1974—1,600,000
1951—2,097,800	1961—1,728,600	1976—1,006,000
1952—2,093,500	1962—1,630,600	
1953—2,134,300	1963—1,500,000	
1954—2,145,000	1967—1,575,000	

SOURCES: 1. Mackie and Rose, *International Almanac; Le Monde*, 23 June 1976.

2. *World Strength*; Giorgio Galli and Alfonso Prandi, *Patterns of Political Participation in Italy* (New Haven: Yale, 1970).

[a] In coalition with Socialist Party.

Table 28. Luxembourg: Election Results and Party Membership

Parliamentary Election Results (Assembly)[1]

ELECTION DATE	PCL (%)	SEATS WON	TOTAL SEATS
May 1922[a]	na	0	25
Mar. 1928[a]	na	0	46
Jun. 1928[a]	—	—	—
Jun. 1931[a]	1.3	0	27
Jun. 1934[a]	6.4	1	29
Jun. 1937[a]	—	—	—
Oct. 1945	13.5	5	51
Jun. 1948[a]	2.5	0	26
Jun. 1951[a]	16.9	4	26
May 1954	8.9	3	52
Feb. 1959	9.1	3	52
Jun. 1964	12.5	5	56
Dec. 1968	15.5	6	56
May 1974	10.4	5	59

Estimated Membership, Communist Party of Luxembourg (PCL)[2]

1921—500	1954—800	1971—500
1925—210	1962—500	1972—500
1945—5,000	1963—500	1973—500
1948—3,000	1967—500	1974—500
1950—1,500	1968—500	1975—500
1953—500	1969—500	1976—600

SOURCES: 1. Mackie and Rose, *The International Almanac: Yearbook*, various years.

2. *Yearbook*, various years; Sworakowski, *World Communism; World Strength*; Lazitch, *Les partis communistes*.

[a] Partial election.

Table 29. Netherlands: Election Results and Party Membership

Parliamentary Election Results (Lower House)[1]

ELECTION DATE	CPN (%)	SEATS WON	TOTAL SEATS
Jul. 1918	2.3	2	100
Jul. 1922	1.8	2	100
Jul. 1925	1.2	1	100
Jul. 1929	2.0	2	100
Apr. 1933	3.2	4	100
May 1937	3.4	3	100
May 1946	10.6	10	100
Jul. 1948	7.7	8	100
Jun. 1952	6.2	6	100
Jun. 1956	4.7	7	150
Mar. 1959	2.4	3	150
May 1963	2.8	4	150
Feb. 1967	3.6	5	150
Mar. 1971	3.9	6	150
Nov. 1972	4.5	7	150
May 1977	1.7	2	150

Estimated Membership, Dutch Communist Party (CPN)[2]

1919—500	1950—33,000	1973—10,000
1922—2,500	1952—25,000	1974—10,000
1924—1,700	1962—12,000	1975—10,000
1927—1,400	1963—12,000	1976—10,000
1929—1,100	1967—12,000	
1931—1,600	1968—11,500	
1932—3,700	1969—11,500	
1938—10,000	1971—11,000	
1946—53,000	1972—10,000	

SOURCES: 1. Mackie and Rose, *International Almanac; Le Monde*, 27 May 1977.

2. *Yearbook*, various years; Sworakowski, *World Communism; World Strength*, various years; Lazitch, *Les partis communistes*.

Table 30. Norway: Election Results and Party Membership

Parliamentary Election Results (Storting)[1]

ELECTION DATE	NKP (%)	SEATS WON	TOTAL SEATS
Oct. 1924	6.1	6	150
Oct. 1927	4.0	6	150
Oct. 1930	1.7	0	150
Oct. 1933	1.8	0	150
Oct. 1936	0.3	0	150
Oct. 1945	11.9	11	150
Oct. 1949	5.9	0	150
Oct. 1953	5.1	3	150
Oct. 1957	3.4	1	150
Sept. 1961	2.9	0	150
Sept. 1965	1.4	0	150
Sept. 1969	1.0	0	150
Sept. 1973	11.2[a]	1	155
Sept. 1977	0.4	0	155

Estimated Membership, Norwegian Communist Party (NKP)[2]

1921—98,000	1945—4,500	1969—2,500
1922—48,000	1947—30,000	1971—2,000
1924—16,000	1953—13,000	1972—2,250
1925—16,000	1962—4,500	1973—2,500
1927—8,000	1965—4,500	1974—2,500
1930—2,985	1967—2,500	1975—2,500
1922—5,272	1968—2,500	1976—2,000

SOURCES: 1. *Yearbook*; Mackie and Rose, *International Almanac; Le Monde*, 15 September 1977.

2. *Yearbook*, various years; *World Strength*; Lazitch, *Les partis communistes*.
[a] Total for Socialist Electoral Alliance.

Table 31. Portugal: Election Results and Party Membership

Parliamentary Elections Results (Lower House)[1]

ELECTION DATE	PCP (%)	SEATS WON	TOTAL SEATS
Apr. 1976	14.6	40	263

Estimated Membership, Portuguese Communist Party (PCP)[2]

1965—2,000	1973—1,000
1968—2,000	1975—75,000–100,000
1971—2,000	1976—100,000–120,000

SOURCES: 1. *Le Monde*, 28 April 1976.

2. Stanley Pastrik, "Portugal's Dangling Revolution," *Dissent* XXII, no. 2 (Fall 1975): 331–35, 338, 344; *New York Times*, 5 May 1976; *Yearbook*, various years; *World Strength*, various years.

Table 32. Spain: Election Results and Party Membership

Parliamentary Election Results (Cortes)[1]

ELECTION DATE	PCE (%)	SEATS WON	TOTAL SEATS
Jun. 1931	4.4	0	446
Apr. 1933	2.4	1	473
Feb. 1936	—	16[a]	454
Jun. 1977	9.4	19	350

Estimated Membership, Spanish Communist Party (PCE)[2]

1931—3,000	1965—5,000
1932—5,000	1968—5,000
1934—10,000	1969—5,000
1936—35,000	1971—5,000
1937—300,000	1973—5,000
1964—5,000	1975—5,000

SOURCES: 1. Guy Hermet, *The Communists in Spain* (Lexington, Mass.: Heath, 1974); *Le Monde*, 18 June 1977.

2. Hermet, *Communists*; Sworakowski, *World Strength*.

[a] Communists alloted 16 of the 256 seats won by the Popular Front. The Front won about 47 percent of the vote.

Table 33. Sweden: Election Results and Party Membership

Parliamentary Elections Results (Riksdag)[1]

ELECTION DATE	VPK (%)	SEATS WON	TOTAL SEATS
Sept. 1921	4.6	7	230
Sept. 1924	3.6	4	230
Sept. 1928	6.4	8	230
Sept. 1932	3.0	2	230
Sept. 1936	3.3	5	230
Sept. 1940	3.5	3	230
Sept. 1944	10.3	15	230
Sept. 1948	6.3	8	230
Sept. 1952	4.3	5	230
Sept. 1956	5.0	6	231
Jun. 1958	3.4	5	231
Sept. 1960	4.5	5	232
Sept. 1964	5.2	8	233
Sept. 1968	3.0	3	233
Sept. 1970	4.8	17	350
Sept. 1973	5.3	19	350
Sept. 1976	4.7	17	349

Estimated Membership, Swedish Communist Party (VPK)[2]

1921—14,000	1946—53,000	1971—17,000
1924—12,000	1948—53,000	1972—17,000
1927—14,000	1951—34,256	1973—17,000
1929—6,000	1957—28,000	1974—17,000
1932—11,000	1962—25,000	1976—14,500
1933—20,000	1963—25,000	
1937—20,000	1967—29,000	
1939—19,000	1968—29,000	
1944—58,000	1969—29,000	

SOURCES: 1. *Yearbook*, various years; Mackie and Rose, *International Almanac; Le Monde*, 24 September 1976.

2. *Yearbook*, various years; *World Strength*, various years; Lazitch, *Les partis communistes*; Sworakowski, *World Communism*.

Table 34. Switzerland: Election Results and Party Membership

Parliamentary Election Results (Lower House)[1]

ELECTION DATE	PDA (%)	SEATS WON	TOTAL SEATS
Oct. 1922	1.8	2	198
Oct. 1925	2.0	3	198
Oct. 1928	1.8	2	198
Oct. 1931	1.5	2	187
Oct. 1935	1.4	2	187
Oct. 1939	2.6	4	187
Oct. 1943	—	—	—
Oct. 1947	5.0	7	194
Oct. 1951	2.7	5	196
Oct. 1955	2.6	4	196
Oct. 1959	2.7	3	196
Oct. 1963	2.2	4	200
Oct. 1967	2.9	5	200
Oct. 1971	2.6	5	200
Oct. 1975	2.5	4	200

Estimated Membership, Swiss Communist Party (PdA)[2]

1930—12,000	1968—4,000	1976—7,000
1938—1,000	1969—4,000	
1945—13,500	1971—3,500	
1953—8,000	1972—3,500	
1962—6,000	1973—3,000	
1963—6,000	1974—4,500	
1967—4,000	1975—5,000	

SOURCES: 1. *Yearbook*, various years; Mackie and Rose, *International Almanac; Le Monde*, 29 October 1975.

2. *Yearbook*, various years; Sworakowski, *World Communism; World Strength*, various years; Lazitch, *Les partis communistes*.

Table 35. West Germany: Election Results and Party Membership

Parliamentary Elections Results (Reichstag)[1]

ELECTION DATE	KPD DKP (%)	SEATS WON	TOTAL SEATS
Jun. 1920	2.1	4	459
May 1924	12.6	62	472
Dec. 1924	8.9	45	493
May 1928	10.6	54	491
Sept. 1930	13.1	77	577
Jul. 1932	14.5	89	608
Nov. 1932	16.9	100	584
Mar. 1933	12.3	81	647
Aug. 1949	5.7	15	402
Sept. 1953	2.2	0	487
Sept. 1957	—	—	—
Sept. 1961	—	—	—
Sept. 1965	—	—	—
Sept. 1969	—	—	—
Nov. 1972	0.3	0	496
Oct. 1976	0.3	0	496

Estimated Membership, German Communist Party (KPD/DKP)[2]

1962—35,000	1971—22,500	1976—42,453
1967—7,000	1972—33,400	
1968—7,000	1973—35,000	
1969—7,000	1974—40,000	

SOURCES: 1. Mackie and Rose, *International Almanac; Le Monde,* 5 October 1976.

2. *Yearbook,* various years; *World Strength,* various years.

SELECTED BIBLIOGRAPHY

I. Newspapers and Periodicals

A. General

    Le Monde
    New York Times
    Times of London
    World Marxist Review

B. Communist Party Publications

1. Austria
   Volksstimme, Weg und Ziel
2. Belgium
   La Drapeau Rouge, Cahiers Marxistes
3. Denmark
   Land og Folk
4. Finland
   Kansan Uutiset, Kommunisti
5. France
   L'Humanité, France Nouvelle, Cahiers de communisme
6. Great Britain
   Morning Star (nee *Daily Worker*)
7. Greece
   Avgi (KKE-Interior), *Rizospastis* (KKE-Exterior)
8. Iceland
   Thjodviljinn
9. Ireland
   Unity

10. Italy
    L'Unità, Rinascita
11. Luxembourg
    Zeitung
12. Netherlands
    De Waarheid
13. Norway
    Friheten
14. Portugal
    Avante
15. Spain
    Mundo Obrero
16. Sweden
    Ny Dag
17. Switzerland
    La Voix Ourvière
18. West Germany
    Unsere Zeit

II. Articles and Books

A. General

Almond, Gabriel S. *The Appeals of Communism.* Princeton: Princeton University Press, 1954.

The Anti-Stalin Campaign and International Communism. New York: Columbia University Press, 1956.

Ascher, William, and Sidney Tarrow. "The Stability of Communist Electorates: Evidence from a Longitudinal Analysis of French and Italian Aggregate Data." *American Journal of Political Science* XIX, no. 3 (August 1975): 475-500.

Benjamin, Roger W., and John H. Kautsky. "Communism and Economic Development." *American Political Science Review* LXII, no. 1 (March 1968): 110-23.

Bennet, Edward M., ed. *Polycentrism: Growing Dissidence in the Communist Bloc?* Pullman: Washington State University Press, 1967.

Birchall, Ian. *Workers Against the Monolith: Communist Parties Since 1943.* London: Pluto Press, 1973.

Blackmer, Donald L.M., and Sidney Tarrow, eds. *Communism in Italy and France.* Princeton: Princeton University Press, 1975.

Borkenau, Franz. *European Communism*. London: Faber, 1953.
———. *World Communism*. Ann Arbor: University of Michigan Press, 1962.
Bowles, Chester. "Is Communist Ideology Becoming Irrelevant?" *Foreign Affairs* XL, no. 4 (July 1962): 553-65.
Burks, R.V. *The Future of Communism in Europe*. Detroit: Wayne State University Press, 1968.
Cantril, Hadley. *The Politics of Despair*. New York: Basic Books, 1958.
Carrère D'Encausse, Hélène. "Communisme et nationalisme." *Revue française de science politique* XV, no. 3 (June 1965): 466-98.
Cornell, Richard. "The Communist Parties of Scandinavia." *Survey* XXI, no. 4 (Autumn 1975): 107-20.
———. "Comparative Analysis of Communist Movements." *Journal of Politics* XXX, no. 1 (February 1968): 66-89.
———. *Youth and International Communism*. New York: Walker & Co., 1965.
Dallin, Alexander, Jonathan Harris, and Grey Hodnett. *Diversity in International Communism: A Documentary Record, 1961-1963*. New York: Columbia University Press, 1963.
Deakin, F.W., H. Shukman, and H.T. Willetts. *A History of World Communism*. London: Weidenfeld and Nicolson, 1975.
Degras, Jane. *The Communist International, 1919-1922*. Oxford: University of Oxford Press, 1960.
———. *The Communist International, 1922-1928*. Oxford: University of Oxford Press, 1960.
———. "United Front Tactics in the Comintern, 1921-1928." In *International Communism*, edited by David Footman, pp. 9-22. Carbondale: Southern Illinois University Press, 1960.
Devlin, Kevin. "The Catholic-Communist 'Dialogue,' " *Problems of Communism* XV, no. 3 (May-June 1966): 31-38.
———. "The Challenge of Eurocommunism." *Problems of Communism* XXVI, no. 1 (January-February 1977): 1-20.
———. "The Interparty Drama." *Problems of Communism* XXIV, no. 4 (July-August 1975): 18-34.
Drachkovitch, Milorad M., ed. *The Revolutionary Internationals, 1864-1943*. Stanford: Stanford University Press, 1966.
Eckstein, Harry. "Economic Development and Political Change in Communist Systems." *World Politics* XXII, no. 4 (July 1970): 475-95.

Einaudi, Mario. "Communism in Western Europe: Its Strength and Vulnerability." *Yale Review* LXI, no. 2 (December 1951): 234-46.

——. "Western European Communism: A Profile." *American Political Science Review* XLV, no. 1 (March 1951): 185-208.

——, Jean-Marie Domenach, and Aldo Garosci. *Communism in Western Europe.* Ithaca: Cornell University Press, 1951.

Evans, John L. *The Communist International, 1919-1943.* Brooklyn: Pageant-Poseidon, 1973.

Fejtö, François. *Dictionnaire des partis communistes et des mouvements révolutionnaires.* Paris: Tournai Casterman, 1971.

——. "L'Evolution des partis communistes de l'Europe de l'Est et de l'Ouest." *International Journal* XXVII, no. 1 (Winter 1971-72): 73-97.

——. "Le mouvement communiste international: l'évolution des relations entre les partis communistes." *Etudes internationales* IV (December 1972): 451-72.

——. "Les organisations internationales communistes en crise." *Revue de défense nationale* XXVI, no. 1 (January 1970): 106-22.

Ferrari, Pierre, and Herbert Maisl. *Les groupes communistes aux assembleés parlementaires italien et français.* Paris: Presses Universitaires Français, 1969.

Fleming, D.F. *The Cold War and Its Origins, 1917-1960.* 2 vols. London: Allen and Unwin, 1961.

Forrer, J.O. "The Sources of Communist Appeal." *World Politics* XVI, no. 3 (April 1964): 521-38.

Gati, Charles. "The 'Europeanization' of Communism?" *Foreign Affairs* LV, no. 3 (April 1977): 539-53.

Gausmann, William C. "Communism in Western Europe." *Problems of Communism* XIII, no. 2 (March-April 1964): 94-97.

Gilberg, Trond. "Patterns of Nordic Communism." *Problems of Communism* XXIV, no. 3 (May-June 1975): 20-35.

Goldsborough, James O. "Communism in Western Europe." *Atlantic Community Quarterly* XIV, no. 2 (Summer 1976): 172-77.

——. "Eurocommunism After Madrid." *Foreign Affairs* LV, no. 4 (July 1977): 800-14.

Greene, Thomas H. "A Comparative Note on the Study of Non-Ruling Communist Parties." *Studies in Comparative Communism* VI, no. 4 (Winter 1973): 455-59.

———. "The Electorates of Nonruling Communist Parties." *Studies in Comparative Communism* IV, nos. 3 and 4 (July-October 1971): 68-103.

———. "Non-Ruling Communist Parties and Political Adaptation." *Studies in Comparative Communism* VI, no. 4 (Winter 1973): 331-61.

Griffith, William E., ed. *Communism in Europe.* 2 vols. Cambridge: MIT Press, 1964-65.

Hobsbaum, E.J. *Revolutionaries.* London: Weidenfeld and Nicolson, 1973.

Holt, Robert T. "Age As a Factor in the Recruitment of Communist Leadership." *American Political Science Review* XLVIII, no. 2 (June 1954): 486-99.

Howe, Irving. "Socialists and Communists in European Politics." *Dissent* XXII, no. 4 (Fall 1975): 382-86.

Kaplan, Frank L. "The Communist International's Press Control from Moscow." *Journalism Quarterly* XLVIII, no. 2 (Summer 1971): 315-25.

Kautsky, John H. "Comparative Communism versus Comparative Politics." *Studies in Comparative Communism* VI, nos. 1 and 2 (Spring-Summer 1973): 135-70.

———. "The New Strategy of International Communism." *American Political Science Review* XLIX, no. 2 (June 1955): 478-86.

Kendall, Walter. "The Communist Parties of Western Europe." *European Community,* no. 120 (February 1969): 6-8.

Kissinger, Henry A. "Eurocommunism: A New Test for the West." *New Leader* LX, no. 15 (July 18, 1977): 8-14.

Kohák, Erazim. "European Communists and European Defense." *Dissent* XXIII, no. 3 (Summer 1976): 273-78.

Kolarz, W. *Books on Communism.* 2nd ed. Princeton: Ampersand, 1964.

Korpi, Walter. "Working Class Communism in Western Europe: Rational or Nonrational." *American Sociological Review* XXXVI, no. 6 (December 1971): 971-84.

Labedz, Leopold, ed. *International Communism after Khrushchev.* Cambridge: MIT Press, 1965.

———, ed. *Revisionism: Essays on the History of Marxist Ideas.* London: Allen & Unwin, 1962.

Laqueur, Walter, and Leopold Labedz, eds. *Polycentrism.* New York: Praeger, 1962.

Lazitch, Branko, and Milorad M. Drachkovitch. *Biographical Dic-*

tionary of the Comintern. Stanford: Hoover Institution Press, 1973.

————. *Les partis communistes d'Europe, 1919-1955.* Paris: Les iles d'or, 1956.

Leites, N. *A Study of Bolshevism.* New York: Free Press, 1953.

Leonhard, Wolfgang. "International Communism: The Present Phase." In *International Communism,* edited by David Footman, pp. 128-49. Carbondale: Southern Illinois University Press, 1960.

Leoni, F. "La legislación anticomunista en los países del mundo libre." *Revista de politíca internacional,* no. 108 (March-April 1970): 35-43.

Library of Congress. *World Communism, 1964-1969: A Selected Bibliography.* Washington, D.C.: U.S. Government Printing Office, 1972.

————. *World Communism, 1967-1969: Soviet Efforts to Reestablish Control.* Washington, D.C.: U.S. Government Printing Office, 1972.

Lichtheim, George. *Marxism: An Historical and Critical Study.* New York: Praeger, 1961.

————. "Social Democracy and Communism: 1918-1968." *Studies in Comparative Communism* III, no. 1 (January 1970): 5-30.

Lindemann, Albert S. *The Red Years: European Socialism versus Bolshevism.* Berkeley: University of California Press, 1974.

Lowenthal, Richard. "The Ideological Crisis of International Communism." *Yearbook of World Affairs* XII (1958): 29-54.

————. "The Prospects for Pluralistic Communism." In *Marxism in the Modern World,* edited by Milorad M. Drachkovitch. Stanford: Stanford University Press, 1965.

McCauley, Martin, ed. *Communist Power in Europe 1944-1949.* London: Macmillan, 1977.

McInnes, Neil. "The Christian-Marxist Dialogue: International Implications." *Survey,* no. 67 (April 1968): 57-76.

————. *The Communist Parties of Western Europe.* London: Oxford University Press, 1975.

————. "The Communist Parties of Western Europe and the EEC." *World Today* XXX, no. 2 (February 1974): 80-88.

————. "East-West Relations Within the Communist Movement." *Survey* XXII, nos. 3 and 4 (Summer-Autumn 1976): 102-05.

McNeil, Robert H., ed. *International Relations Among Communists.* Englewood Cliffs: Prentice-Hall, 1967.

Mackie, Thomas T., and Richard Rose. *International Almanac of*

Electoral History. London: Macmillan, 1974.

Macridis, Roy C. "Eurocommunism." *Yale Review* LXVII, no. 3 (Spring 1978): 321-37.

Marsh, Robert M., and William L. Parish. "Modernization and Communism: A Re-Test of Lipset's Hypothesis." *American Sociological Review* XXX, no. 6 (December 1965): 934-42.

Morris, Bernard S. "Communist International Front Organizations: Their Nature and Function." *World Politics* IX, no. 1 (October 1956): 76-87.

——. *International Communism and American Policy.* New York: Atherton, 1966.

——. "Some Perspectives on the Nature and Role of Western European Communist Parties." *Review of Politics* XVIII, no. 2 (April 1956): 157-69.

Mortimer, Edward. "The Left in 'Latin Europe.' " *Round Table,* no. 265 (January 1977): 9-19.

Nollau, Gunther. *International Communism and World Revolution.* London: Hollis and Carter, 1961.

di Palma, Giuseppe. "Eurocommunism?" *Comparative Politics* IX, no. 3 (April 1977): 357-75.

Petersen, William, ed. *The Relations of World Communism.* Englewood Cliffs: Prentice-Hall, 1963.

Pipes, Richard. "Liberal Communism in Western Europe?" *Orbis* XX, no. 3 (Fall 1976): 595-600.

Popov, Milorad. "The International Communist Movement: Conflict of Priorities." *World Today* XXIX, no. 1 (January 1973): 34-42.

Rice, George W. "The Electoral Prospects for Non-Ruling Communist Parties." *American Journal of Political Science* XVII no. 3 (August 1973): 597-610.

——. "Nonruling Parties and the 'Peaceful Path.' " *Problems of Communism* XXII, no. 4 (July-August 1973): 56-71.

Salloch, Roger. "International Communism." *Survey,* nos. 70-71 (Winter-Spring 1969): 32-55.

Selznick, Philip. *The Organizational Weapon: A Study of Bolshevik Strategy and Tactics.* New York: McGraw-Hill, 1952.

Sheldon, Charles. "Public Opinion and High Courts: Communist Party Cases in Four Constitutional Systems." *Western Political Quarterly* XX, no. 2 (June 1967): 341-60.

Shulman, Marshall. *Stalin's Foreign Policy Reappraised.* Cambridge: Harvard University Press, 1963.

Sontag, John P. "International Communism and Soviet Foreign

Policy." *Review of Politics* XXXII, no. 1 (January 1970): 78-90.

Starobin, Joseph R. "Communism in Western Europe." *Foreign Affairs* XLIV, no. 1 (October 1965): 62-77.

Steinkühler, Manfred. "Unity and Diversity of Communism in Europe." *Aussen Politik* XXVII, no. 4 (1976): 383-407.

Stern, Geoffrey. "The Crisis of Communism—the First World Political Creed." *International Affairs* XLVI, special issue (November 1970): 72-87.

Strausz-Hupé, Robert. "The Crisis of International Communism." *Confluence* VI, no. 3 (Fall 1957): 228-44.

Swearingen, Rodger, ed. *Leaders of the Communist World.* New York: Free Press, 1971.

Sworakowski, Witold S. *The Communist International and Its Front Organizations: A Research Guide and Checklist of Holdings in American and European Libraries.* Stanford: Hoover Institution Press, 1965.

———, ed. *World Communism: A Handbook, 1918-1965.* Stanford: Hoover Institution Press, 1973.

Tannahill, R. Neal. "The Future of the Communist Parties of Western Europe." *World Affairs* CXXXIX, no. 2 (Fall 1976): 414-54.

———. "Leadership as a Determinant of Diversity in Western European Communism." *Studies in Comparative Communism* IX, no. 4 (Winter 1976): 349-68.

Timmermann, Heinz. "West European Communism in Flux." *Problems of Communism* XXV, no. 6 (November-December 1976): 74-78.

Trager, F.N., and R.F. Bordonaro. "The Ninth CCP Congress and the World Communist Conference: Their Meaning for Asia." *Orbis* XIII, no. 3 (Fall 1969): 736-67.

Tucker, H.J. "Measuring Cohesion in the International Communist Movement: 1957-70." *Political Methodology* II, no. 1 (1975): 83-112.

Tucker, R.C. "Culture, Political Culture, and Communist Society." *Political Science Quarterly* LXXXVIII, no. 2 (June 1973): 173-90.

———. "On the Comparative Study of Communism." *World Politics* XIX, no. 2 (January 1967): 242-57.

Uliassi, Pio. "Communism in Western Europe." In *The New Communisms,* edited by Dan Jacobs, pp. 274-98. New York: Harper & Row, 1969.

U.S. Department of State. Office of Intelligence Research. *World Strength of the Communist Party Organizations.* Washington, D.C.: U.S. Government Printing Office, various years.

Upton, A.F. *The Communist Parties of Scandinavia and Finland.* London: Weidenfeld and Nicolson, 1973.

Yearbook on International Communist Affairs. Stanford: Hoover Institution Press, 1966-77.

B. Austria

Devlin, Kevin. "Austrian Communism after Czechoslovakia." *Survey,* no. 73 (Autumn 1969): 165-77.

———. "Czechoslovakia and the Crisis of Austrian Communism." *Studies in Comparative Communism* II, no. 3 (July-October 1969): 9-37.

Muhri, Franz. "A Democratic and Socialist Alternative for Austria." *World Marxist Review* XVII, no. 4 (April 1974): 16-23.

C. Belgium

Huggett, Frank E. *Modern Belgium.* London: Pall Mall, 1969.

Van Geyt, Louis. "Communal and Power Crisis in Belgium." *World Marxist Review* XVII, no. 9 (September 1974): 73-82.

Verkade, Willem. *Democratic Parties in the Low Countries and Germany.* Amsterdam: Universitaire pers Leiden, 1965.

Weil, Gordon L. *The Benelux Nations: The Politics of Small Country Democracies.* New York: Holt, Rinehart, and Winston, 1970.

D. Denmark

Borre, Ole. "Denmark's Protest Election of December 1973." *Scandinavian Political Studies* IX (1974): 197-203.

Cornell, Richard. "The Communist Parties of Scandinavia." *Survey* XXI, no. 4 (Autumn 1975): 107-20.

Riis, Ole. "The General Election and the Formation of Government in December 1971." *Scandinavian Political Studies* VII (1971): 251-58.

Upton, A.F. *The Communist Parties of Scandinavia and Finland.* London: Weidenfeld and Nicolson, 1973.

E. Finland

Allardt, Erik. "Institutional versus Diffuse Support for Radical Political Movements." *Transactions of the Fifth Congress of Sociology* (1962): 369-80.

————. "Patterns of Class Conflict and Working Class Consciousness in Finnish Politics." In *Cleavages, Ideologies, and Party Systems,* edited by Allardt and Y. Littunen, pp. 97-131. Helsinki: Academic Bookstore, 1964.

————. "Social Sources of Finnish Radicalism: Traditional and Emerging Radicalism." *International Journal of Comparative Sociology* V, no. 1 (March 1964): 49-72.

Billington, James H. "Finland." In *Communism and Revolution: The Strategic Uses of Political Violence,* edited by C.E. Black and T.P. Thorton, pp. 117-44. Princeton: Princeton University Press, 1964.

Brodin, Katarina. "Finland's Government: The Return of the Communists." *Survey,* no. 62 (January 1967): 129-40.

Cornell, Richard. "The Communist Parties of Scandinavia." *Survey* XXI, no. 4 (Autumn 1975): 107-20.

Devlin, Kevin. "Finnish Communism." *Survey,* no. 74 (Winter-Spring 1970): 49-69.

Hodgson, John C. *Communism in Finland.* Princeton: Princeton University Press, 1967.

————. "Finnish Communism and Electoral Politics." *Problems of Communism* XXIII, no. 1 (January-February 1974): 34-45.

————. "The Finnish Communist Party." *Slavic Review* XXIX, no. 1 (March 1970): 70-85.

————. "The Finnish Communist Party and Neutrality." *Government and Opposition* II, no. 2 (January-April 1967): 269-87.

Hynynen, Pertti. "The Popular Front in Finland." *New Left Review,* no. 57 (September-October 1969): 3-20.

Jacobson, Max. *Finnish Neutrality: A Study of Finnish Foreign Policy Since the Second World War.* New York: Praeger, 1968.

Krosby, Hans Peter. "The Communist Power Bid in Finland in 1948." *Political Science Quarterly* LXXV, no. 2 (June 1960): 229-43.

Kuusisto, Alan. "The Paasikivi Line in Finland's Foreign Policy." *Western Political Quarterly* XII, no. 1 (March 1959): 37-49.

Marshall, F. Ray. "Communism in Finland." *Journal of Central European Affairs* XIX, no. 4 (January 1960): 375-88.

Nousiainen, Jaakko. *The Finnish Political System.* Cambridge: Harvard University Press, 1971.

————. "Research on the Finnish Communism." *Scandinavian Political Studies* III (1968): 243-52.

Pesonnen, Pertti. *An Election in Finland: Party Activities and Voter Reactions.* New Haven: Yale University Press, 1968.

————. "The 1972 Parliamentary Election in Finland." *Scandinavian Political Studies* II (1972): 266-71.

———— and Onni Rantala. "Current Election Studies in Finland." *Scandinavian Political Studies* II (1967).

Rantala, Onni, "The Political Regions in Finland." *Scandinavian Political Studies* II (1967): 117-40.

Rintala, Marvin. "The Problem of Generations in Finnish Communism." *American Slavic and East European Review* XVII, no. 2 (April 1958): 190-202.

Saarinen, Aarne. "Leading Force of Democratic Development." *World Marxist Review* XVII, no. 11 (November 1974): 38-43.

————. "The Strategic Aim of Finnish Communists." *World Marxist Review* XVIII, no. 9 (September 1975): 93-95.

Schöpflin, George. "Finnish Communists in Disarray." *World Today* XXV, no. 6 (June 1969): 231-34.

Upton, A.F. *The Communist Parties of Scandinavia and Finland.* London: Weidenfeld and Nicolson, 1973.

F. *France*

Adam, Gérard. "Eléments d'analyse sur les liens entre le P.C.F. et la C.G.T." *Revue française de science politique* XVIII, no. 3 (June 1968): 524-39.

Allen, Luther. "The French Left and Russia: Origins of the Popular Front." *World Affairs Quarterly* XXX (July 1959): 99-121.

Barjonet, André. *La C.G.T.* Paris: Editions du Seuil, 1969.

————. *Le parti communiste français.* Paris: Didier, 1970.

Barron, Richard. *Parties and Politics in Modern France.* Washington, D.C.: Public Affairs Press, 1959.

Berger, Denis, and Paul-Louis Thirard. "Un parti social-démocrate de type nouveau." *Temps modernes* XXVI, no. 284 (March 1970): 1446-71.

Bernard, J.-P. "Le parti communiste français et les problèmes littéraires (1920-39)." *Revue française de science politique* XVII, no. 3 (June 1967): 520-44.

Blackmer, Donald L.M., and Sidney Tarrow, eds. *Communism in Italy and France.* Princeton: Princeton University Press, 1975.

Bloch-Michel, Jean. "The French Left—Uneasy Relations." *Dissent* XX, no. 3 (Summer 1973): 289-90.

————. "Rumblings on the French Left." *Dissent* XXII, no. 1 (Winter 1975): 12-14.

Bon, Frédéric, ed. *Le communisme en France.* Cahiers de la fondation nationale des sciences politiques, 175. Paris: Armand Colin, 1969.

Bourricaud, François. "The French Student Revolt." *Survey*, no. 68 (July 1968): 29-37.

Brayance, Alain. *Anatomie du Parti communiste français.* Paris: Denöel, 1952.

Brower, Daniel R. *The New Jacobins.* Ithaca: Cornell University Press, 1968.

Calvez. J.-Y. "Incertitude doctrinales du Parti communiste français." *Lumière et vie* XXVIII (July 1956): 23-50.

Campbell, Ian. "The French Communists and the Union of the Left: 1974-76." *Parliamentary Affairs* XXIX, no. 3 (Summer 1976): 246-63.

Cantril, Hadley. *The Politics of Despair.* New York: Basic Books, 1958.

————, and David Rodnick. *On Understanding the French Left.* Princeton: Institute for International Social Research, 1956.

Caute, David. *Communism and the French Intellectuals: 1914-1960.* London: Andre Deutsch, 1964.

————. "Marxism in France." *Problems of Communism* XVI, no. 3 (May-June 1967): 55-58.

Cetrat, Maurice. *La trahison permanente: parti communiste et politique russe.* Paris: Spartacus, 1948.

Charlton, Sue Ellen M. "European Unity and the Politics on the French Left." *Orbis* XIX, no. 4 (Winter 1976): 1448-70.

Cotta, Michéle. "Oú en sont les communistes?" *L'Express*, no. 1321 (1-7 November 1976): 34-37.

Deli, Peter. "The Soviet Intervention in Czechoslovakia and the French Communist Press." *Survey* XXII, no. 2 (Spring 1976): 96-117.

Derville, Jacques. "Les communistes de l'Isére." *Revue française de science politique* XXV, no. 1 (February 1975): 53-71.

Duclos, Jacques, and François Billous. *Histoire du parti communiste français—manuel.* Paris: Editions Sociales, 1964.

Duhamel, Alain. "Le Parti communiste et l'élection présidentielle." *Revue française de science politique* XVI, no. 3 (June 1966): 539-47.

Duverger, Maurice. *Political Parties.* Translated by Barbara and Robert North. New York: John Wiley & Sons, 1954 (1951).

Ehrmann, Henry W. "The French Peasant and Communism." *American Political Science Review* XLVI, no. 1 (March 1952): 19-43.

————. "The French Views on Communism." *World Politics* III, no. 1 (October 1950): 141-51.

Fauvèt, Jacques. *Histoire de Parti communiste français.* 2 vols. Paris: Fayard, 1964.

Fejtö, François. *The French Communist Party and the Crisis of International Communism.* Cambridge: MIT Press, 1967.

————. "The French Communist Party and Polycentrism." *Osteuropa* XII, no. 7 (July 1962): 459-67.

Ferrari, Pierre, and Herbert Maisl. *Les groups communistes aux assemblées parlementaires italiennes et françaises.* Paris: Presses Universitaires Françaises, 1969.

Ferret, André. *Histoire du Parti communiste français.* Paris: Bureau d'Editions, 1931.

García, Ruiz. "Garaudy y la transformación del socialismo." *Boletín informativo ciencia política* V (December 1970): 49-71.

Godfrey, E.D. "The Communist Presence in France." *American Political Science Review* L, no. 2 (June 1956): 321-38.

Goldey, D. D., and D. S. Bell. "The French Municipal Election of March 1977." *Parliamentary Affairs* XXX, no. 4 (Autumn 1977): 408-26.

Goguel, F. "Esquisse d'une description sociologique du Parti communiste français." *Lumière et vie* XXVIII (July 1956): 7-22.

Greene, Thomas H. "The Communist Parties of Italy and France: A Study in Comparative Communism." *World Politics* XXI, no. 1 (October 1968): 1-38.

Harmel, Claude. "Social Composition of the French Communist Party and Its Evolution from 1959 to 1966." *Est & Ouest* XIX (16-28 February 1967): 4-12.

Hayward, Jack, and Vincent Wright. " 'Les Deux France' and the French Presidential Election of May, 1974," *Parliamentary Affairs* XXVII, no. 3 (Summer 1974): 208-36.

————. "Governing from the Centre: The 1977 French Local Elections." *Government and Opposition* XII, no. 4 (Autumn 1977): 433-54.

Jacquot, Sylvie. "Le Parti communiste français: la fin du ghetto?" *Etudes* (February 1973): 163-87.

Johnson, Richard. *The French Communist Party Versus the Students.* New Haven: Yale University Press, 1972.

Johnson, R.W., and A.R. Summers. "The Communist Campaign in Asnières." *Parliamentary Affairs* XX, no. 3 (Summer 1967): 239-43.

Kanapa, Jean. "A 'New Policy' of the French Communists?" *Foreign Affairs* LV, no. 2 (January 1977): 280-94.

Kogan, Norman. "The French Communists—And Their Italian Comrades." *Studies in Comparative Communism* VI, no. 1 (Spring-Summer 1973): 184-95.

Kriegel, Annie. "Communism in France." In *Imagination and Precision in the Social Sciences,* edited by T.J. Nossiter, A.H. Hanson, and Stein Rokkan, pp. 351-84. London: Faber, 1972.

———. "Les communistes français: l'ordre et la subversion." *Projet,* no. 41 (1970): 20-32.

———. "La dimension internationale du P.C.F." *Politique etrangère* XXXVII, no. 5 (1972): 639-69.

———. *The French Communists: Profile of a People.* Translated by Elaine P. Halperin. Chicago: University of Chicago Press, 1972 (1968).

———. "The International Role of the French Communist Party Since World War II." In *The International Role of the Communist Parties of Italy and France,* edited by Donald L. M. Blackmer and Annie Kriegel, pp. 37-61. Harvard Studies in International Affairs, 33 (1975).

———. "Notes sur l'idéologie dans le Parti communiste. *Contrepoint* III (1971): 95-104.

———. *Les origines du communisme français.* 2 vols. Paris: Mouton, 1964.

———. "Le Parti communiste français sous la Troisième République (1920-1939). Evolution de ses effectifs." *Revue française de science politique* XVI, no. 1 (February 1966): 5-35.

———. "Le parti communiste français et la Vᵉ République." *Contrepoint* IX (1973): 159-72.

———. "The Present Theory of Power and the French Communist Party." *Government and Opposition* II, no. 2 (February 1967): 253-68.

Lacorne, Denis. "Analyse et 'reconstruction' de stéréotypes: communistes et socialistes face au 'socialisme soviétique,' " *Review française de science politique* XXIII, no. 6 (December 1973): 1171-1201.

———. "On the Fringe of the French Political System: The Beliefs of Communist Municipal Elites." *Comparative Politics* IX, no. 4 (July 1977): 421-41.

Lavau, Georges. "Parti et société: *Les communistes français.*" *Critique* XXV, no. 271 (December 1969): 1083-94.

————. "A la recherche d'un cadre théorique pour l'étude du Parti communiste français." *Revue française de science politique* XVIII, no. 3 (June 1968): 445-66.

Lecoeur, Auguste. *Le Parti communiste français et le resistance: août 1939-juin 1941.* Paris: Plon, 1968.

Lefranc, Georges. *Histoire du Front populaire.* Paris: 1965.

Libbey, Kenneth R. "The French Communist Party in the 1960s: An Ideological Profile." *Journal of Contemporary History* XI, no. 1 (January 1976): 145-65.

Ligon, Daniel. *Histoire du socialisme en France, 1871-1961.* Paris, 1961.

Machin, Howard, and Vincent Wright. "The French Left under the Fifth Republic." *Comparative Politics* X, no. 1 (October 1977): 35-68.

Macridis, Roy C. "The French CP's Many Faces." *Problems of Communism* XXV, no. 3 (May-June 1976): 59-64.

————. "The Immobility of the French Communist Party." In *Political Parties,* edited by Macridis, pp. 184-204. New York: Harper & Row, 1967.

————. "Pompidou and the Communists." *Virginia Quarterly Review* XLV, no. 4 (August 1969): 579-94.

Mendel, Arthur. "Why the French Communists Stopped the Revolution." *Review of Politics* XXXI, no. 1 (January 1969): 3-27.

Micaud, Charles A. "The Basis of Communist Strength in France." *Western Political Quarterly* VIII, no. 3 (September 1955): 354-66.

————. *Communism and the French Left.* New York: Praeger, 1963.

Monnerot, Jules. *Sociology and Psychology of Communism.* Boston: Beacon Press, 1953.

Naville, P. "Le parti communiste et le front uni ouvrier." *Temps modernes* X, nos. 112-13 (May 1955): 1906-21.

Percheron, A. "A propos de l'application du cadre théorique d'Easton à l'étude du Parti communiste français." *Revue française de science politique* XVII, no. 5 (October 1967): 944-58.

Perrel, J. "La gauche classique et la Parti communiste en Limousin." *Revue française de science politique* XVII, no. 5 (October 1967): 944-58.

Pickersgill, J.W. "The Front Populaire and the French Elections of 1936." *Political Science Quarterly* LIV, no. 1 (March 1939): 69-83.

Pickles, Dorothy. "The Communist Problem in France." *International Affairs* XXVIII, no. 2 (April 1952): 162-69.

——. "France in 1968: Retrospect and Prospect." *World Today* XXIV, no. 9 (September 1968): 393-402.

——. "The French Elections." *World Today* XXIX, no. 4 (April 1973): 138-48.

Platone, François, and François Subileau. "Les militants communistes à Paris: pratique militantes." *Revue française de science politique* XXVI, no. 2 (April 1976): 260-85.

Ranger, Jean. "L'électorat communiste dans l'élection présidentielle de 1969." *Revue française de science politique* XX, no. 2 (April 1970): 282-311.

——. "L'évolution du Parti communiste français. Organisation et débats idéoligiques." *Revue française de science politique* XIII, no. 4 (December 1963): 951-65.

——. "L'évolution du Parti communiste français et ses relations avec la SFIO." *Revue française de science politique* XIV, no. 1 (February 1964): 72-86.

——, and G. Adam. "Les liens entre le PCF et la CGT. Eléments d'un débat." *Revue française de science politique* XIX, no. 1 (February 1969): 182-87.

Rieber, Alfred J. *Stalin and the French Communist Party: 1941-1947.* New York: Columbia University Press, 1962.

Rossi, Angelo. *A Communist Party in Action.* New Haven: Yale University Press, 1955.

——. *Les communistes français pendant le Drôle de Guerre.* Paris: Iles d'Or, 1951.

——. *La guerre des papillons, 1940-1944.* Paris: Iles d'Or, 1954.

——. *Physiologie du Parti communiste français.* Paris: Self, 1948.

Serfaty, Simon. "An International Anomaly: The United States and the Communist Parties in France and Italy, 1945-1947." *Studies in Comparative Communism* VIII, nos. 1 & 2 (Spring-Summer 1975): 123-46.

Shirk, Albert E. "Communism in France." *Problems of Communism* XIV, no. 5 (September-October 1965): 59-61.

Sommet, Jacques. "Marxisme d'aujourd'hui." *Projet,* no. 83 (March 1974): 257-70.

Stoetzel, Jean. "Voting Behavior in France." *British Journal of Sociology* VI, no. 2 (June 1955): 104-22.

Talbot, Emile J. "Bourgeois Communism in France." *Commonweal* C, no. 19 (August 1974): 446-50.

Tiersky, Ronald. *French Communism, 1920-1972.* New York: Columbia University Press, 1974.

———. "French Communism in 1976." *Problems of Communism* XXV, no. 1 (January-February 1976): 20-47.

———. "The French Communist Party and Détente." *Journal of International Affairs* XXVIII, no. 2 (October 1974): 188-205.

———. "Le P.C.F. et la détente." *Esprit* LXII, no. 2 (February 1975): 218-41.

Timmermann, Heinz. "National Strategy and International Autonomy: The Italian and French Communist Parties." *Studies in Comparative Communism* V, no. 2 (Summer 1972): 258-76.

Touchard, Jean. "Le Parti communiste français et les intellectuals (1920-39)." *Revue française de science politique* XVII, no. 3 (June 1967): 468-83.

Vassart, Célie, and Albert Vassart. "The Moscow Origin of the French 'Popular Front.' " In *The Comintern: Historical Highlights,* edited by Milorad M. Drachkovitch and Branko Lazitch, pp. 234-52. Stanford: Hoover Institution Press, 1966.

Vree, Dale. "Coalition Politics on the Left in France and Italy." *Review of Politics* XXXVII, no. 3 (July 1975): 340-56.

Walter, Gérard. *Histoire du Parti communiste français.* Paris: Somogy, 1948.

Winock, Michel. "La contradiction du PCF." *Esprit* XXXVIII, no. 392 (May 1970): 884-97.

Wohl, Robert. *French Communism in the Making, 1914-1924.* Stanford: Stanford University Press, 1966.

Wright, Gordon. "The Communists and Peasantry in France." In *Modern France,* edited by Edward Earle, pp. 219-31. Princeton: Princeton University Press, 1951.

———. "Four Red Villages in France." *Yale Review* XLIV, no. 3 (Spring 1952): 361-72.

Zartman, I.W. "French Communist Foreign Policy 1952-54: A Propaganda Analysis." *Western Political Quarterly* IX, no. 2 (June 1956): 344-62.

Zévaès, Alexandre. *Histoire du socialisme et du communisme en France, 1871-1947.* Paris: France-Empire, 1947.

G. *Great Britain*

Arnot, R. Page. *Twenty Years: The Policy of the C.P.G.B. from Its Foundation, July 31, 1920.* London: Lawrence & Wishart, undated.

Bell, T. *The British Communist Party: A Short History.* London: Lawrence & Wishart, 1937.

British Communist Party. *The British Road to Socialism.* London: BCP, 1958.

Crook, W.H. *Communism and the General Strike.* Hamden: The Shoestring Press, 1960.

Crozier, Brian. "Britain's Industrial Revolutionaries." *Interplay* IV, no. 1 (January 1971): 30, 35-36.

Darke, B. *The Communist Technique in Britain.* London: Collins, 1953.

Denver, D.T., and J.M. Bochel. "The Political Socialization of Activists in the British Communist Party." *British Journal of Political Science* III, no. 1 (January 1973): 53-71.

Ferris, Paul. *The New Militants: Crisis in the Trade Unions.* London: Penguin, 1972.

Gallacher, William. *The Case for Communism.* Harmondsworth: Penguin, 1949.

————. *Last Memoirs.* London: Lawrence and Wishart, 1972.

Grainger, G.W. "Oligarchy in the British Communist Party." *British Journal of Sociology* IX, no. 2 (June 1958): 143-58.

Hobsbaum, E.J. "The British Communist Party." *Political Quarterly* XXV, no. 1 (January-March 1954): 30-43.

Jones, M. "Why Britain Needs the Communists." *Twentieth Century* CLXII, no. 1017 (Spring 1963): 50-60.

Kendall, Walter. "The Communist Party of Great Britain." *Survey* XX, no. 1 (Winter 1974): 118-31.

Lenin, V.I. *On Britain.* Moscow: Foreign Language Publishing House, 1959.

Macfarlane, L.J. *The British Communist Party: Its Origin and Development Until 1929.* London: MacGibbon & Kee, 1966.

Morton, A.L. *Socialism in Britain.* London: Lawrence & Wishart, 1963.

Newton, Kenneth. *The Sociology of British Communism.* London: Penguin, 1969.

"On Leaving the Communist Party." Anon. article. *Twentieth Century* CLV, no. 923 (February 1954): 130-44.

Pelling, Henry. *The British Communist Party: A Historical Profile.* London: Adam and Charles Black, 1958.

Rees, David. "The Old and the New Left." *Interplay* III, no. 5 (December 1969-January 1970): 26-29.

Strange, Arnold. "The CP's Retreat from Moscow." *New Statesman* LXXVIII, no. 2019 (21 November 1969): 717-18.

Wood, Neal. *Communism and British Intellectuals.* London: Gollancz, 1959.

————. "The Empirical Proletariat: A Note on British Communism." *Political Science Quarterly* LXXIV, no. 2 (June 1959): 256-77.

Young, James D. "The British New Left." *Survey,* no. 62 (January 1967): 84-89.

H. Greece

Carey, Jane P.C., and Andrew G. Carey. *The Web of Modern Greek Politics.* New York: Columbia University Press, 1968.

Kitsikis, Dimitri. "Greek Communists and the Karamanlis Government." *Problems of Communism* XXVI, no. 1 (January-February 1977): 42-56.

Kousoulas, D. George. *Modern Greece.* New York: Charles Scribner's, 1974.

————. *Revolution and Defeat: The Story of the Greek Communist Party.* London: Oxford University Press, 1965.

Legg, Keith R. *Politics in Modern Greece.* Stanford: Stanford University Press, 1969.

Papageorgiou, Efthimios. "Communism in Greece." *Problems of Communism* X, no. 3 (May-June 1961): 38-44.

Yannakakis, Ilios. "The Greek Communist Party." *New Left Review,* no. 54 (March-April 1969).

I. Iceland

Cornell, Richard. "The Communist Parties of Scandinavia." *Survey* XXI, no. 4 (Autumn 1975): 107-20.

Gilberg, Trond. "Patterns of Nordic Communism." *Problems of Communism* XXIV, no. 3 (May-June 1975): 20-35.

Olmstead, Mary S. "Communism in Iceland." *Foreign Affairs* XXXVI, no. 2 (January 1958): 340-47.

J. Ireland

O'Riordan, Michael. "Inspiring Changes." *World Marxist Review* XVII, no. 5 (May 1974): 48-49.

Wheeler, Marcus. "Soviet Interest in Ireland." *Survey* XXI, no. 3 (Summer 1975): 81-93.

K. Italy

Adams, Gordon M. " 'On the Pavement Thinking 'bout the Government:' Notes on Il Manifesto." *Politics and Society* I (August 1971): 449-62.

Agnoletti, E.E. "Forces et faiblesses du communisme italien." *Esprit* XXIII, nos. 230-31 (September-October 1955): 1551-62.

Allum, P.A. *The Italian Communist Party Since 1945: Grandeurs and Servitudes of a European Socialist Strategy.* Occasional Publication no. 2 of the University of Reading Graduate School of Contemporary European Studies. Reading, England: University of Reading, 1970.

————. *Italy—Republic Without Government?* New York: Norton, 1973.

Andreucci, Franco, and Malcolm Silvers. "The Italian Communists Write Their History." *Science & Society* XL, no. 1 (Spring 1976): 28-56.

Are, Giuseppe. "Italy's Communists: Foreign and Defense Policies." *Atlantic Community Quarterly* XIV, no. 4 (Winter 1976-77): 508-18.

Ball, George W. "Communism in Italy." *Atlantic Community Quarterly* XIV, no. 2 (Summer 1976): 178-87.

Barnett, V.M. "Competitive Coexistence and the Communist Challenge in Italy." *Political Science Quarterly* LXX, no. 2 (June 1955): 230-57.

Bartoli, Edgardo. "The Road to Power: The Italian Communist Party and the Church." *Survey* XXI, no. 4 (Autumn 1975): 90-106.

Bates, Thomas R. "Antonio Gramsci and the Bolshevization of the PCI." *Journal of Contemporary History* XI, nos. 2 and 3 (July 1976): 115-31.

Birnbaum, Norman. "A New Version of the Socialist Tradition?" *Politics and Society* I, no. 4 (August 1971): 441-47.

Blackmer, Donald L.M. "The International Strategy of the Italian Communist Party." In *The International Role of the Communist Parties of Italy and France,* edited by Blackmer and Kriegal, pp. 1-33. Harvard Studies in International Affairs, 33 (1975).

————. "Italian Communist Strategy for the 1970's." *Problems of Communism* XXI, no. 3 (May-June 1972): 41-56.

————. *Unity in Diversity: Italian Communism and the World.* Cambridge: MIT Press, 1968.

————, and Sidney Tarrow, eds. *Communism in Italy and France.* Princeton: Princeton University Press, 1975.

Boato, M. "Irapporti fra Partito Comunista Italiano e movimento studentesco." *Critica sociologica* XVII (1971): 86-135.

Braga, Giorgio. *Il communismo fra gli italiani: saggio di sociologia.* Milan: Edizioni di comunità, 1956.

Broadhead, H.S. "Togliatti and the Church, 1921-1948." *Australian Journal of Political History* XVIII, no. 1 (April 1972): 76-91.

Cammett, John. *Antonio Gramsci and the Origins of Italian Communism.* Stanford: Stanford University Press, 1967.

Cantril, Hadley. *The Politics of Despair.* New Haven: Basic Books, 1958.

Clark, Martin, and R.E.M. Irving. "The Italian Political Crisis and the General Elections of May 1972." *Parliamentary Affairs* XXV, no. 3 (Summer 1972): 198-223.

Cozzola, Franco. "Consenso e opposizione nel parlamento italiano: Il ruolo del PCI dalla I alla IV legislatura." *Revista italiana di scienza politica* II (April 1972): 84.

Davidson, A.B. "Tendencies Toward 'Reformism' in the Italian Communist Party, 1921-1963." *Australian Journal of Politics and History* XI, no. 3 (December 1965): 335-49.

———. "The Varying Seasons of Gramscian Studies." *Political Studies* XX, no. 4 (December 1972): 448-61.

Denitch, Bogdan. "The Rebirth of Spontaneity: *Il Manifesto* and West European Communism." *Politics and Society* I, no. 4 (August 1971): 463-77.

Devlin, Kevin. "Moscow and the Italian CP." *Problems of Communism* XIV, no. 5 (September-October 1965): 1-10.

Ducoli, John. "The New Face of Italian Communism." *Problems of Communism* XII, no. 3 (March-April 1964): 82-90.

Edelman, Murray. "Causes of Fluctuation in Popular Support for the Italian Communist Party Since 1946." *Journal of Politics* XX, no. 2 (May 1958): 535-52.

Evans, Robert H. *Coexistence: Communism and Its Practice in Bologna, 1945-1965.* Notre Dame: Notre Dame University Press, 1967.

Favre, Pierre, "Le modèle léniniste d'articulation parti-syndicats-masses, le parti communiste italien et l'unité syndicale." *Revue française de science politique* XXV, no. 3 (June 1975): 433-72.

Fiori, Giuseppe. *Antonio Gramsci: Life of a Revolutionary.* New York: Dutton, 1971.

Fried, Robert C. "Communism, Urban Budgets, and the Two Italies: A Case Study in Comparative Urban Governments." *Journal of Politics* XXXIII, no. 4 (November 1971): 1008-51.

Galli, Giorgio. *Il bipartismo imperfetto: comunisti de democristiani in Italia.* Bologna, 1966.

———. *Storia del partito comunista italiano.* Milan: Schwarz, 1958.

———, and A. Prandi. *Patterns of Political Participation in Italy.* New Haven: Yale University Press, 1970.

Garosci, Aldo. "Palmiro Togliatti." *Survey* IX, no. 53 (October 1964): 140-47.

Germino, Dante L., and Stefano Passigli. *The Government and Politics of Contemporary Italy.* New York: Harper, 1968.

Gozzini, Mario, ed. *Il dialogo alla prova: Cattolici e comunisti italiani.* Florence: Vallecchi editore, 1964.

Greene, Thomas H. "The Communist Parties of Italy and France: A Study in Comparative Communism." *World Politics* XXI, no. 1 (October 1968): 1-38.

Hamrin, Harald. *Between Bolshevism and Revisionism: The Italian Communist Party 1944-1947.* Stockholm: Scandinavian University Books, 1975.

Hellman, Stephen. "Generational Differences in the Bureaucratic Elite of Italian Communist Party Provincial Federations." *Canadian Journal of Political Science* VIII, no. 1 (March 1975): 82-106.

Hughes, H. Stuart. *The United States and Italy.* Rev. ed. Cambridge: Harvard University Press, 1965.

Kogan, Norman. "Impact of the New Italian Regional Government on the Structure of Power with the Parties." *Comparative Politics* VII, no. 3 (April 1975): 383-406.

———. "Italian Communism, the Working Class, and Organized Catholicism." *Journal of Politics* XXVIII, no. 3 (August 1966): 531-55.

———. "National Communism versus the National Way to Communism: An Italian Interpretation." *Western Political Quarterly* II, no. 3 (September 1958): 660-72.

Lange, Peter. "What Is to Be Done—About Italian Communism?" *Foreign Policy,* no. 21 (Winter 1975-76): 224-40.

Leich, John Foster. "The Italian Communists and the European Parliament." *Journal of Common Market Studies* IX, no. 4 (June 1971): 271-81.

Leoni, F. "El movimiento comunista en Italia." *Revista de estudios politicos,* nos. 171-72 (May-August 1970): 141-49.

Levi, Arrigo. "Berlinguer's Communism." *Survey* XVIII, no. 3 (Summer 1972): 1-15.

——. "Euro-Communism and East-West Relations." *Survey* XXII, nos. 3 & 4 (Summer-Autumn 1976): 91-94.

——. "Italian Communists: The Commedia of Unity." *Interplay* II, no. 7 (February 1969): 8-11.

——. "Italy's 'New' Communism." *Foreign Policy,* no. 26 (Spring 1977): 28-42.

Macchi, A. "Il 'compromesso storico.' " *Aggiornamenti sociali* XXV, no. 12 (April 1974): 233-46.

Mancini, Federico, and Giorgio Galli, "Gramsci's Presence." *Government and Opposition* III, no. 3 (Summer 1968): 325-38.

Pasquino, Gianfranco. "Before and After the Italian National Election of 1976." *Government and Opposition* XII, no. 1 (Winter 1977): 60-87.

Passigli, Stefano. "Italy," In *Comparative Studies in Political Finance,* edited by Richard Rose and Arnold J. Heidenheimer, pp. 718-36. *Journal of Politics* XXV, special issue (November 1963).

Paulson, Belden H. *The Searchers: Conflict and Communism in an Italian Town.* Chicago: Quadrangle, 1966.

Rovan, J. "La crise du parti communiste italien en 1956." *Revue française de science politique* VIII, no. 3 (September 1958): 603-20.

Sani, Giacomo, "Mass Constraints on Political Realignments: Perceptions of Anti-System Parties in Italy." *British Journal of Political Science* VI, no. 1 (January 1976): 1-32.

——. "The PCI on the Threshold." *Problems of Communism* XXV, no. 6 (November-December 1976): 27-51.

Sartori, Giovanni, "European Political Parties: The Case of Polarized Pluralism." In *Political Parties and Political Development,* edited by Joseph LaPalombara and Myron Weiner, pp. 137-76. Princeton: Princeton University Press, 1969.

Sassoon, Donald. "The Italian Communist Party's European Strategy." *Political Quarterly* XLVII, no. 3 (July-September 1976): 253-75.

Segre, Sergio. "The 'Communist Question' in Italy." *Foreign Affairs* LIV, no. 4 (July 1976): 691-707.

Serfaty, Simon. "An International Anomaly: The United States and the Communist Parties in France and Italy 1945-1947." *Studies in Comparative Communism* VIII, nos. 1 and 2 (Spring-Summer 1975): 123-46.

Spriano, Paolo. *Storia del partito comunista Italiano.* Vols. I-IV. Turin: 1967, 1969, 1970, 1973.

Sprigge, S. "De-Stalinization in the Italian Communist Party." *World Today* XVIII, no. 1 (January 1962): 23-29.

Stern, A.J. "The Italian CP at the Grass Roots." *Problems of Communism* XXIII, no. 2 (March-April 1974): 42-54.

Tarrow, Sidney J. "The Italian Party System Between Crisis and Transition." *American Journal of Political Science* XXI, no. 2 (May 1977): 193-224.

————. *Peasant Communism in Southern Italy.* New Haven: Yale University Press, 1967.

————. "The Political Economy of Stagnation: Communism in Southern Italy, 1960-1970." *Journal of Politics* XXXIV, no. 1 (February 1972): 93-123.

Timmermann, Heinz. "National Strategy and International Autonomy: The Italian and French Communist Parties." *Studies in Comparative Communism* V, no. 2 (Summer 1972): 258-76.

Urban, George. "Dante, the Italians, and the PCI." *Survey* XXII, no. 2 (Spring 1976): 118-39.

Urban, J.B. "Italian Communism and the 'Opportunism of Conciliation,' 1927-1929." *Studies in Comparative Communism* VI, no. 4 (Winter 1973): 362-96.

————. "Socialist Pluralism in Soviet and Italian Communist Perspective: The Chilean Catalyst." *Orbis* XVIII, no. 2 (Summer 1974): 482-509.

Vaccarini, I. "L'esperienza culturale del partito communista Italiano." *Aggiornamenti sociali* XXIII, no. 12 (November 1972): 645-62, 739-60.

Vree, Dale. "Coalition Politics on the Left in France and Italy." *Review of Politics* XXXVII, no. 3 (July 1975): 340-56.

Werner, J. Feld. "The French and Italian Communists and the Common Market: The Requests for Representation in the Community Institutions." *Journal of Common Market Studies* VI, no. 3 (March 1968): 250-56.

White, Stephen. "Gramsci and the Italian Communist Party." *Government and Opposition* VII, no. 2 (Spring 1972): 186-205.

Willis, F. Roy. *Italy Chooses Europe.* New York: Oxford University Press, 1971.

L. *Luxembourg*

Verkade, Willem. *Democratic Parties in the Low Countries and Germany.* Amsterdam: Universitaire pers Leiden, 1965.

Weil, Gordon L. *The Benelux Nations: The Politics of Small Country Democracies.* New York: Holt, Rinehart, and Winston, 1970.

M. Netherlands

Kool, Frits. "Communism in Holland: A Study in Futility." *Problems of Communism* IX, no. 5 (September-October 1960): 17-24.

Stapel, Jean, and W.J. de Jonge. "Why Vote Communist?" *Public Opinion Quarterly* XII, no. 3 (Fall 1948): 390-98.

Verkade, Willem. *Democratic Parties in the Low Countries and Germany,* Amsterdam: Universitaire pers Leiden, 1965.

Weil, Gordon L. *The Benelux Nations: The Politics of Small Country Democracies.* New York: Holt, Rinehart, and Winston, 1970.

N. Norway

Cornell, Richard. "The Communist Parties of Scandinavia." *Survey* XXI, no. 4 (Autumn 1975): 107-20.

Gilberg, Trond. "Patterns of Nordic Communism." *Problems of Communism* XXIV, no. 3 (May-June 1975): 20-35.

———. *The Soviet Communist Party and Scandinavian Communism: The Norwegian Case.* Oslo: Universitetsforlaget, 1973.

Hegge, Per Egil. " 'Disunited' Front in Norway." *Problems of Communism* XXV, no. 3 (May-June 1976): 49-58.

O. Portugal

Bruneau, T.C. "Portugal: The Search for a New Political Regime." *World Today* XXXI, no. 12 (December 1975): 478-87.

Clark, Joseph. "Portugal—Between Hammer and Anvil?" *Dissent* XXIII, no. 2 (Spring 1976): 130-31.

———. "For Portugal: 'Democracy, Period.' " *Dissent* XXII, no. 3 (Summer 1975): 225-26.

Grayson, George W. "Portugal and the Armed Forces Movement." *Orbis* XIX, no. 2 (Summer 1975): 335-78.

Hottinger, A. "Rise of Portugal's Communists." *Problems of Communism* XXIV, no. 4 (July-August 1975): 1-17.

Maxwell, Kenneth. "The Thorns of the Portuguese Revolution." *Foreign Affairs* LIV, no. 1 (January 1976): 250-70.

Mujal-Leon, Eusebio M. "The PCP and the Portuguese Revolution." *Problems of Communism* XXVI, no. 1 (January-February 1977): 21-41.

Plastrik, Stanley. "Portugal's Dangling Revolution." *Dissent* XXII, no. 4 (Fall 1975): 331-35.

Story, Jonathan. "Portugal's Revolution of Carnations: Patterns of Change and Continuity." *International Affairs* LII, no. 3 (July 1976): 417-33.

P. *Spain*

Broué, Pierre, and Emile Témime. *The Revolution and the Civil War in Spain.* Cambridge: MIT Press, 1972.

Cattell, David T. *Communism and the Spanish Civil War.* Berkeley: University of California Press, 1955.

Hermet, Guy. *The Communists in Spain.* Lexington, Mass.: Heath, 1974.

Meaker, Gerald H. *The Revolutionary Left in Spain, 1914-1923.* Stanford: Stanford University Press, 1974.

Mujal-Leon, E.M. "Spanish Communism in the 1970s." *Problems of Communism* XXIV, no. 2 (March-April 1975): 43-55.

Payne, Stanley G. " 'Eurocommunism' and the PCE." *Problems of Communism* XXVII, no. 1 (January-February 1978): 77-80.

Preston, Paul. "The Dilemma of Credibility: The Spanish Communist Party, the Franco Regime and After." *Government and Opposition* XI, no. 1 (Winter 1976): 65-83.

Story, Jonathan. "Spanish Political Parties: Before and After the Election." *Government and Opposition* XII, no. 4 (Autumn 1972): 474-95.

Q. *Sweden*

Davidson, Phillips. "A Review of Sven Rydenfelt's *Communism in Sweden.*" *Public Opinion Quarterly* XVIII, no. 4 (Winter 1954-55): 375-88.

Cornell, Richard. "The Communist Parties of Scandinavia." *Survey* XXI, no. 4 (Autumn 1975): 107-20.

Hagberg, Hilding. "The Experience and Tasks of the Communist Party of Sweden." *World Marxist Review* VI, no. 9 (October 1963): 18.

Josen. "Former Swedish Communist Party Chairman Publishes Book." *Dagens Nyheter,* 22 July 1966. Translated by the Joint Publications Research Service.

Tarschys, Daniel. "The Unique Role of the Swedish CP." *Problems of Communism* XXIII, no. 3 (May-June 1974): 36-44.

R. West Germany

Dyson, K.H.F. "Left-Wing Political Extremism and the Problem of Tolerance in Western Germany." *Government and Opposition* X, no. 3 (Summer 1975): 306-31.

Fisher, S.L. *The Minor Parties of the Federal Republic of Germany.* The Hague: Martinus Nijhoff, 1974.

Loss, Richard. "The Communist Party of Germany (KPD), 1956-1966." *Survey* XIX, no. 4 (August 1973): 66-85.

McWhinney, E. "The German Federal Constitutional Court and the Communist Party Decision." *Indiana Law Journal* XXXII (Spring 1952): 295-312.

Mies, Herbert. "The October Revolution and Our Time." *World Marxist Review* XVIII, no. 11 (November 1975): 3-13.

Von Schmertzing, Wolfgang P., ed. *Outlawing the Communist Party.* New York: Bookmailer, 1957.

INDEX

About the Author

R. Neal Tannahill is a political scientist from Houston, Texas. He has contributed articles to such journals as *Commonweal,* the *Journal of Political and Military Sociology, World Affairs,* and *Studies in Comparative Communism.*